BORDERS OF BELIEF

BORDERS OF BELIEF

Religious Nationalism and the Formation of Identity in Ireland and Turkey

GREGORY J. GOALWIN

RUTGERS UNIVERSITY PRESS

New Brunswick, Camden, and Newark, New Jersey, and London

Library of Congress Cataloging-in-Publication Data
Names: Goalwin, Gregory J., author.
Title: Borders of belief : religious nationalism and the formation of identity
    in Ireland and Turkey / Gregory J. Goalwin.
Description: New Brunswick, New Jersey : Rutgers University Press, 2022. |
    Includes bibliographical references and index.
Identifiers: LCCN 2021045901 | ISBN 9781978826489 (paperback) |
    ISBN 9781978826496 (hardback) | ISBN 9781978826502 (epub) |
    ISBN 9781978826519 (mobi) | ISBN 9781978826526 (pdf)
Subjects: LCSH: Nationalism—Ireland—Religious aspects. |
    Nationalism—Turkey—Religious aspects. | Nationalism—
    Religious aspects—Catholic Church. | Nationalism—Religious
    aspects—Islam. | Church and state—Ireland. | Islam and state—Turkey.
Classification: LCC BL65.N3 G63 2022 | DDC 201/.72—dc23/eng/20211123
LC record available at https://lccn.loc.gov/2021045901

A British Cataloging-in-Publication record for this book is available from the British
Library.

References to internet websites (URLs) were accurate at the time of writing. Neither
the author nor Rutgers University Press is responsible for URLs that may have expired
or changed since the manuscript was prepared.

♾ The paper used in this publication meets the requirements of the American National
Standard for Information Sciences—Permanence of Paper for Printed Library
Materials, ANSI Z39.48-1992.

www.rutgersuniversitypress.org

Manufactured in the United States of America

For my family, especially Avery, who make everything possible.

CONTENTS

BORDERS OF BELIEF

1 · BORDERS AND BOUNDARIES OF THE NATION

Constructing a Theory of Religious Nationalism

In June of 1913, Irish schoolteacher, poet, and political activist Patrick Pearse gave an address at the grave of famed Irish nationalist hero Wolfe Tone. He and his audience had gathered, he argued, "to express once more our full acceptance of the gospel of Irish Nationalism." He described the experience of coming into contact with Tone's pure soul as coming into "a new baptism, unto a new regeneration and cleansing." Though Tone was himself a "heretic" (a Protestant), Pearse argued he "put virility into the Catholic movement" and recognized "that in Ireland there must be, not two nations or three nations, but one nation"; Protestants must be brought into amity with the Catholic majority to achieve freedom for all.[1] Elsewhere, Pearse continued to describe the new nation he and his colleagues sought to build in religious terms, repeatedly drawing upon Catholic themes of martyrdom, equating the national community's suffering with that of Christ, and predicting a similar triumphant resurrection in power and glory.[2]

For Pearse and many of his colleagues, religion played a powerful role in the ways they conceptualized, defined, and policed the boundaries of the national community. Indeed, Pearse's Catholic nationalism was the culmination of a tradition of merging religion with nationality that nineteenth-century Irish Dominican preacher Tom Burke summarized by arguing, "Take an average Irishman—I don't care where you find him—and you will find that the very first principle in his mind is, 'I am not an Englishman, because I am a Catholic!'"[3] By the time the majority of Ireland achieved independence in 1922, Catholicism had become the foundation of Irish national identity. When the first constitution of the Republic of Ireland was passed in 1937, it contained an article that granted a special status for Catholicism in the national government, proclaiming that "The State recognizes the special position of the Holy Catholic Apostolic and Roman Church as the guardian of the Faith professed by the great majority of the citizens."[4]

At the same time as nationalists in Ireland were describing their quest for independence in religious terms, nationalists a continent away, in the territory of the collapsing Ottoman Empire, were also constructing religiously oriented definitions of national identity. In an influential pamphlet laying out the theoretical groundwork for a new Turkish nationalist movement, writer and politician Yusuf Akçura summarized the relationship between religion and nationalism in the Muslim world and in his own native Ottoman Empire by explaining, "One of the fundamental tenets of Islam is expressed in the saying 'Religion and Nation are One.'"[5] His fellow nationalist theorist Ziya Gökalp took this perspective even further, arguing in his 1923 treatise on Turkish nationalism that "Religion is the most important factor in the creation of national consciousness as it unites men through common sentiments and beliefs. It is because of this that genuinely religious men are those who have national fervor, and that genuine nationalists are those who believe in the eternity of faith."[6] Such religious passion is important, he argues elsewhere in the work, for after all, "In truth a man desires more to live with those who share his language and religion than with those who share his blood, for the human personality does not dwell in the physical body, but in the soul."[7]

At first glance, such pronouncements seem odd coming from the two intellectual fathers of Turkish nationalism, a movement that has self-consciously portrayed itself as secular and modernist, rather than religious in orientation. Yet such was the power of this view of Turkish nationalism, a vision that equated religious faith with belief in the nation, Muslim identity with Turkish identity, that it soon came to overpower the secularist ideals that spawned the movement. When the new Republic of Turkey was proclaimed in 1923, its constitution included an article explicitly providing that "The religion of the Turkish state is Islam, its official language is Turkish, and its capital is Ankara."[8] Even the noted secularist and leader of the Turkish revolution, Mustafa Kemal Atatürk, in his famous 1927 *Nutuk*, a six-day, thirty-six hour speech recounting, and in many ways defining, the official history of the nationalist movement's victory, could not help but describe the movement's struggle in religious terms, arguing that during the early years of the nationalist movement, "Christian elements were also at work all over the country, either openly or in secret, hoping to realize their own particular ambitions and thereby hasten the breakdown of the State."[9] Kemal's juxtaposition of loyal Muslim Turks seeking to stave off the actions of "foreign" infiltrating Christians and form a new national community would serve to reify preexisting paradigms of communal interaction, confirming Islam as a crucial dimension of Turkish national identity, and helping to exclude from the nation those who did not conform to the majority religion.

As these two brief examples reveal, religion and nationalist politics have a long history of interaction, playing an important role in countries around the world.

For centuries, successive waves of nationalist movements have shaped and reshaped the global political and cultural landscape. Such movements, powerful enough in their own right, are made even more potent when fused with religious ideologies. Under these circumstances, religious identity becomes a key determinant of ethnic and national belonging, a process that has become increasingly prevalent in the modern world as nationalist movements seek to define themselves, in defiance of classical modernization and secularization theories, in religious terms. This use of religion to define membership in the nation raises several significant questions about the relationship between religion and nationalism: if, as traditional sociological theories indicate, the world is becoming increasingly secular, why have nationalists such as those in Ireland and even Turkey turned to religion as a key component of national identity? Why did religious identification become politically meaningful, and how did nationalists go about the process of group identity formation, constructing national communities around religious identities? Put differently, why do some nations fail to develop into the sort of secular, civic type of states that secularization and modernization theories predict, but instead utilize religious identity as a key signifier of national identity? This book approaches these questions through a comparative-historical analysis of two key religiously oriented nationalist movements, using the cases of Ireland and Turkey to develop a more sophisticated theory of religious nationalism.

While religious nationalism is a powerful phenomenon that has dominated international headlines and attracted significant notice from academic researchers, there remain important gaps in the scholarly literature. Most studies examining religious nationalism tend to confine their analysis to a single case, providing in-depth examples of the ways religion has functioned in a particular social and historical context. There are surprisingly few rigorously comparative studies of religious nationalism that examine such complicated phenomena across geographical and cultural boundaries. Those comparative studies that do exist often focus exclusively on Christian versions of religious nationalism in Europe,[10] the United States,[11] or in very recent rejections of secular varieties of nationalism.[12] Furthermore, scholars of religious nationalism have tended to focus on the motivations and actions of religiously oriented nationalist movements, rather than on the ways in which such movements develop, how religion and nationalism first become intertwined as key facets of identity.[13] In contrast, this study examines patterns of religious nationalism that extend beyond Europe, examining the processes by which religion and nationalism became intertwined in two distinct major religious traditions within and beyond the boundaries of Europe. Likewise, this project examines such interactions in greater historical perspective, arguing that religious nationalism is not merely a rejection of modern secular nationalism rising out of the end of the Cold War, but has long been an alternate pattern of nation formation that has been prevalent throughout much of modern history. Most importantly, this project seeks to understand the genesis of religious nationalism, how religion

first becomes politicized, and how it serves as a marker and key defining characteristic of national identity.

In this regard, I develop a boundary-oriented model to argue that in diverse
regions religion serves as a powerful means of identity formation, a way of differentiating members of the nation from those outside it. This model builds
on the group formation theories of scholars such as Fredrik Barth,[14] Rogers
Brubaker,[15] and Andreas Wimmer.[16] Rather than take nations or ethnic groups
as reified and bounded social groups, these theories emphasize that ethnic,
national, and religious identities are relational, processual, and dynamic constructs. Such groups are, in fact, social, cultural, and political projects rather than
unified actors. This is no less true of religiously oriented nationalist movements,
which seek to define national identity in relation to religious identity. In essence,
religious identification becomes a symbolic boundary, creating distinct in-groups
and out-groups that help define national belonging and crystallize collective identity. Understanding that religiously oriented nations are the end result of a political
process where religious identity has come to serve as the organizing characteristic
around which national identity has formed and solidified raises significant questions about how this process occurs. The continued existence of such processes is
particularly interesting in the modern context, given that scholarly study of these
issues throughout most of the twentieth century was dominated by modernist
secularization theorists who argued that the changing structural conditions
imposed by the transition to the modern world would make religion less politically, culturally, and socially relevant.[17] Instead, religious identifications have
remained powerful characteristics around which boundaries of national identity
form, often with divisive and violent results.

The rise of new national communities is often a difficult process, driven by
existential threats to cultural identity that accompany the collapse of empires,
and, almost by definition, entailing rapid social and political change as previous
forms of social organization break down and are replaced. I argue that nationalists turn to religion in the face of such chaotic and threatening change because it
provides a powerful sense of collective identity and an alternate cultural tradition
to fall back on when political bonds face serious and disruptive challenges. In the
tempestuous beginnings of nation formation, nationalists are forced to forge new
national identities, determining who will, and who will not, be members of the
nascent national community. I argue, against some recent interpretations,[18] that
this is particularly true in areas with significant populations of religious minorities,
or that have been threatened by foreign powers of a different religion. Under
these circumstances religious identity becomes a key cultural difference on which
nationalists can seize, providing a powerful reservoir of cultural myths and symbols, a long collective history, and an authoritative tradition on which nationalists
can rely as they struggle to create new political, cultural, and social boundaries that
forge a new and independent national identity.

RELIGION AND NATIONALISM

The study of nationalism and that of religion have complicated and intertwined histories in academia. At its core, nationalism is a political doctrine that argues that the borders of a political community should correspond with the boundaries of a particular ethnic or cultural group, the "nation." This correspondence of different boundaries thus ensures self-determination and political autonomy, as each nation is theoretically able to control its own destiny. The academic literature on nationalism is profuse, and sociologists, historians, and political scientists alike have studied the rise of nationalism and the transition away from a world of empires and toward a world of nation-states.[19] The serious sociological study of religion, rather than the study of its decline and absence, however, took longer to develop. Much as the sociological study of culture achieved little purchase until the "cultural turn" of the 1970s and on, scholars paid little attention to religion until the 1990s, when researchers began to recognize the continued power of religious identities and focus more purposively on the role they played in international and domestic politics. From the 1979 Islamic Revolution in Iran to the religious civil war that consumed Lebanon throughout the 1980s, from the Troubles in Northern Ireland to the bloody religious violence that accompanied the collapse of Yugoslavia, to struggles between Israel and Palestine, violence between Hindus and Muslims in India, abortion clinic bombings in the United States, the influence of Al-Qaeda and the attacks of September 11, 2001, and the rise of the Islamic State, religion was driving politics, identification, and violence everywhere that scholars looked. This global salience of religion and religious politics caused scholars of religion and politics to reconsider assumptions about the relationship between religion and society.

Religion's continued salience well into the national period has forced scholars to consider the ways in which religion and the national community can intersect. In his work on the subject, Rogers Brubaker has identified four distinct ways the relationship between religion and nationalism can be fruitfully studied.[20] The first is to view religion and nationalism as analogous phenomena. Theorists who took this approach argued that the national community was merely a desacralized version of the religious community, a new form of social organization for a new era. In this formulation, the decline of religious belief that is purported to have begun in Europe during the seventeenth century and continued into the modern period is causally linked to the rise of nationalism and the dominance of nation-states as the primary social organization of modern times. Religion, ethnicity, and nationalism can all serve as axes around which social segmentation occurs in heterogeneous societies. The second approach to religion and nationalism, according to Brubaker, is to view religion as a central cause of or explanation for nationalization, providing a justification to explain nationalism's power, endurance, or strength. Such was the tactic taken by Anthony D. Smith, among others, who saw in religion the beginnings of an ethnic core, a central reservoir of structuring myths and symbols on which national cohesion and solidarity can be built.[21] The third approach is to view religion and nationalism as inextricably intertwined: religion provides a set of boundaries around which national borders can form. Religion can thus play an important role in determining who is, and even more importantly who is not, included in the national community. Finally, religious nationalism can be seen as a distinct type of nationalism, a movement concerned with crafting a nation solely of and for a community of religious members, an earthly reflection of the community of believers that transcends the secular.

Scholars who have focused on religious nationalism tend to fall within one of the four approaches that Brubaker identifies. Mark Juergensmeyer, for example, long recognized as one of the pioneers in the study of religious politics, identifies religious nationalism as a repudiation of and backlash against the imposition of secular nation-states.[22] In Juergensmeyer's formulation, religious nationalism reflects a failure of secular forms of nationalism to penetrate into the communities of religious belief that structure the lives of many people around the world. In response to increasing levels of globalization, the spread of secularized American and European culture, and the threat to traditional values, religious nationalists have turned inward, renewing their focus on traditional forms of religious practice and belief, and seeking to shape societies that reflect centuries of religious orientation. Roger Friedland has taken a similar approach, identifying in religious nationalism a deep concern for the politics of gender, sexuality, and family life, and a concomitant rejection of the godless sexual mores of contemporary society in favor of societies that place stricter controls on female sexuality in masculine-dominated societies of religious faith.[23] Other scholars have placed more of an emphasis on borders and boundaries of the nation. John Armstrong argued that religion could play a powerful role as border guard of national identity.[24] Anthony Marx contends that religious forms of nationalism are a reflection of modern states' push for centralization, building cohesion at the expense of internal collective "others,"[25] while N. Jay Demerath presents a model wherein religion can take on aspects of a distinctive culture, a process he refers to as "cultural religion," in the modern world.[26] Steve Bruce has taken a related approach, arguing that "modernity undermines religion except when it finds some major social role to play other than mediating the natural and supernatural worlds."[27] In Bruce's formulation, this most often occurs under conditions of cultural threat, when religion serves as a means of cultural defense, and cultural transition, helping people cope with a shift in life circumstances by providing a psychological and sociological anchor. Philip Barker, meanwhile, has built on Bruce's work and that of John Coakley[28] to argue for the importance of religious frontiers, places in which two religions meet on the edges of civilizations, for the creation of religiously oriented national identities.[29]

More recent literature has sought to distinguish religious nationalism from related phenomena such as civil religion and secular nationalism. Philip Gorski examined the relationship between these varieties of religious and political interaction in the case of the United States, concluding that religious nationalism entails an effort to create "maximum fusion" between religious and political spheres.[30] J. Christopher Soper and Joel Fetzer have built on this perspective to argue that religious nationalism only flourishes in religiously homogeneous societies. To these scholars, religion only functions as a center of social and political organization when it provides a clear central identity unifying most of the populace. Because of this, it is the country's religious demographics, the relative support religious groups provide its national frame, and the linkages between religion and the state in the country's founding documents that determine the relationship between religion and nationalism. Such relationships develop or change, as Geneviève Zubrzycki has recognized,[31] but can also be remarkably stable over time.[32]

These approaches provide an excellent place to start, but do not adequately theorize the interrelationship between religion and nationalism on a global scale. Despite the advances that have been made in recent years, the study of religious nationalism still suffers from many of the problems that its two parent literatures, research on nationalism and studies of religion and secularism, hold in common. Many of the most important theoretical works on religious nationalism emphasize the experiences of religions and societies in Europe. This is the approach Philip Barker takes, for example, in centering his work explicitly in the experience of Europe's three most religious states.[33] Anthony D. Smith, too, emphasized the experiences of "chosen peoples" but does so explicitly in the context of European societies.[34] Even Juergensmeyer, who draws on cases from around the world, still frames his exploration of religious nationalism in a way that casts religious forms of politics as a reaction, a backlash, against European notions of secularism and secular nationalism.[35] Similarly, the overt concentration on Europe and the United States has led to an overemphasis on Christianity, as even scholars doing comparative work center their research on the experiences of Christians in European societies such as Ireland, Poland, and Greece.[36] Where scholars have approached such issues outside of Europe and European Christianity, they tend to take a single-case approach, examining only the ways in which a single religion plays a role in a single national context.[37]

In contrast, this book takes a different approach, providing an analysis that explicitly compares the familiar ground of Christian nationalism in Europe with the experiences of an important non-Christian, non-European case. In this, I seek to answer the challenges proposed by Courtney Bender and her colleagues in their exhortation to study "religion on the edge."[38] Decentering the study of religious nationalism allows us to "provincialize Europe," in Dipesh Chakrabarty's terms,[39] viewing the European experience of religious nationalism, here represented by the frequently studied case of Catholicism in the Republic of Ireland, as merely one path among many in the search for collective identification and self-governance. In this comparative method, I also seek to address the dearth of comprehensive and qualified research into the global experiences of secularization and religious politics identified by Gorski and Altinordu.[40] While detailed, fine-grained studies of individual religious nationalist movements are certainly important, a comparative approach that incorporates non-Christian, non-Western cases into the growing body of literature on religion and nationalism can reveal patterns of political action and boundary formation, belief and identification, that can improve our understanding of the ways religion and nationalism combine, and the powerful effects they can have on the societies involved. In what follows I explore three theoretical innovations that provide the foundation for a more comprehensive understanding of religious nationalism. I then turn to my own theory, outlining a set of conditions under which religious nationalist movements can form and succeed in forging national states. I explain why Ireland and Turkey make such excellent cases for testing this theory before outlining the structure and approach the rest of the book takes as I present and draw conclusions from these studies. Ultimately these case studies challenge many of the traditional understandings of how such processes work, pointing instead to the primacy of boundary mechanisms and the importance of social closure in the development of religious nationalism. At the same time, they reveal the ways religious nationalism intersects with other arguments for nation formation and the power religious definitions of national identity can have even for otherwise secular movements.

GROUP BOUNDARIES, CHAINS OF MEMORY, AND THE COMPLEXITY OF SOCIAL IDENTITY

The studies of religion and nationalism alike are not without their challenges. The power and importance national and religious traditions have in people's lives can make them difficult to conceptualize. Both phenomena are often seen as natural, ubiquitous, and taken for granted as ordering characteristics that define who we are. Yet such formations are not, in fact, "natural" and primordial entities fixed outside of time and place. They are not ideal constructs that only serve to lend identity and a sense of belonging to their individual members. Rather, nations and religions, like any social groups, are socially constructed, the products of social processes of aggregation, exclusion, invention, and imagination. As Rogers Brubaker has concisely argued about ethnicity, such constructions "are not things *in* the world, but perspectives *on* the world."[41]

Nationalist and religious rhetoric that sees such formations as eternal does not acknowledge the fluidity, contingent nature, and constant political and social maneuvering required to solidify and rally support—key elements of all constructed groups. Abandoning theories that view membership in social groups as innate and embracing those that view ethnicity, nationality, and religion as socially constructed is an important first step. Nevertheless, the continued emphasis on groups and collective group behavior remains a problem in social thought. Indeed, "the tendency to partition the world into putatively deeply constituted quasi-natural intrinsic forms is a key part of what we want to explain, not what we want to explain things with; it belongs to our empirical data, not to our analytical toolkit."[42] Categories do not equal groups, they merely serve as a potential base for "groupness." Instead, the processes that result in group formation—mobilization of members of a *category* into a politically or socially organized *group*, willing to take action—are often the result of deliberate actions on the part of individuals and organizations. This is not to say that religion, ethnicity, nationality, and so on are not important; indeed, "social life is powerfully, though unevenly, structured along ethnic lines; and ethnic and national categories are part of the taken-for-granted framework of social and political experience."[43] Rather, scholars seeking to understand groups under the rubric of ethnicities or religions must focus on the political processes, organizations, and individual actors that have worked to construct groups out of categories, mobilizing support for political ends. As Brubaker has explained, "*That* ethnicity and nationhood are constructed is commonplace; *how* they are constructed is seldom specified in detail."[44]

Here I examine the processes by which nation formation takes place. Where do nations get their character? Their borders and sense of membership? I build on theoretical approaches that emphasize group boundaries as key to this definitional process—dividing a distinct in-group from a well-defined out-group. Such approaches have been fruitfully deployed to examine the foundational elements of national communities and the mechanisms by which nations coalesce into the structures we see today. In this section I go further, however, extending the boundary-making approach to examine specifically religious forms of nationalism, a phenomenon that social science's secular focus has left particularly undertheorized. I argue that mechanisms of group closure can most effectively explain the relationship between religion and nationalism, how religious definitions of the nation come to dominate conceptions of what the national community should be.

The focus on processes and relations rather than substantialist groups is a key innovation in the study of nations. Analyzing the processes by which ethnic and national groups form entails a focus on the context of group formation, revealing that ethnicity and nationhood are often contextual, mattering far more in certain circumstances than others.[45] Such an approach thus requires an analysis that looks not just at the strategic decisions of political and ethnic entrepreneurs as they seek to rally support for their causes, but beyond them as well, to focus on the everyday life of the citizens subject to their calls for ethnic and national solidarity and mobilization. These analyses should focus on the reception of political calls for ethnicization and nationalization and the conditions under which individuals accept and buy into them. Even more importantly, it should emphasize those in which they do not, but instead continue about their daily business, paying little attention to ethnic and national distinctions. Often such quotidian understandings of identity forced elite nationalist entrepreneurs to adjust and build nations around facets of identity that would not have been their first choice. As Eric Hobsbawm convincingly argued, nations are in fact "dual phenomena, constructed essentially from above, but which cannot be understood unless also analysed from below, that is in terms of the assumptions, hopes, needs, longings and interests of ordinary people, which are not necessarily national and still less nationalist."[46] Only an approach that attends carefully to these assumptions, hopes, needs, and longings, tracing the very specific circumstances and times when and where they become national and nationalist, can hope to understand the formation of ethnic and national groups and the ways in which they manage to attain political and social power.

It should be added, however, that much of the theorizing in this vein has focused on constructions such as nations and ethnic groups, neglecting religions as socially constructed products of group formation processes. Much like nations and ethnic groups, religions are often seen as monolithic "groups" or unitary social actors whose members all believe and respond in similar ways. This perspective reifies religious groups as singular actors, rather than recognizing them as assemblages of people with often widely varying viewpoints and identifications, and does not take into account the myriad debates, maneuvers, and processes that are part and parcel of the construction of any sort of group. Moreover, such a perspective does not take into account that, as with ethnicity and nationalism, religion is not always the central motivating factor in even very religious people's lives. Rather, religious identity and ideology become salient at particular times and particular places, relying heavily on social, political, and religious contexts. People who identify as Muslims, for example, as with those who identify with any religion or social group, do not identify *only* or *always* as Muslims, and they may not identify *primarily* as Muslims, depending on circumstances that vary on an everyday basis.[47]

The critical importance of such an acknowledgment is nowhere more evident than in situations of conflict and violence in which actors who are also religious take part. Though religion can certainly provide motivation for violence, exclusion, and acts of hate, religion is not always foremost in the minds of perpetrators,[48] and indeed, despite knee-jerk efforts to tar all coreligionists with the same brush, not all those who share a religion necessarily share political opinions, let alone inclinations toward violence.[49] Scholars are slowly beginning to emphasize the role of religious actors rather than groups, and examining the ways in which context affects the practice and performance of religious identities.[50] However, religious groups continue to be treated uncritically, viewed as monolithic and unchanging, irrational cultures, and there is little focus on how such groups are formed.[51]

Rather than accepting that "religions" or "religious groups" do things and act of their own volition, then, we need to recognize the processes and interactions that underlie religious identification. In this, the sociology of religion has often focused too much on issues of identity and belief, following research on Protestantism in America that emphasizes these characteristics of religion over others.[52] Here I follow new trends in decentering the study of religion from American and European Protestantism, moving beyond the focus on belief and arguing for the importance of religious practice and social organization.[53] It is as important to understand the ways in which religious traditions are "invented" and religious communities "imagined" as it is their national and ethnic counterparts. Indeed, just as it is reductive and obscuring to say that "Greeks" or "Turks" do this or that, it is equally problematic to say that "Catholics," "Protestants," "Christians," or "Muslims" act as unitary social actors. Scholars interested in religion's impact on social and political life need to focus on how and why groups coalesce around religious beliefs. As Brubaker has argued for ethnicity, one way to approach this problem is to emphasize religious "identification" rather than religious "identity,"[54] the processes that underlie group formation, underlining the dynamic nature of groups of all sorts and emphasizing "everyday religion," as one recent influential volume has termed it.[55]

The tendency of scholars of ethnicity and nationhood to subsume communities defined by religious categories under the general label "ethnic" further complicates efforts to understand this relationship.[56] Joseph Ruane and Jennifer Todd have identified three specific flaws in this approach, arguing that it indiscriminately focuses on group boundaries rather than their meaning and organization, fails to recognize the distinctive character each brings to symbolic distinction and social division, and fails to explain the variation of ethnic outcomes: why in some circumstances "ethnicity" leads to particularly persistent or intense forms of intergroup conflict while in others it does not.[57] In contrast, an approach that manages to tease out the interactions between ethnicity and religion, the circumstances under which they run in parallel or crosscut each other, and the decisions actors make in emphasizing one, the other, or both, can provide powerful insights into patterns of group formation. Similarly, recognition that all such groups, be they religious, ethnic, or national, vary significantly in salience over time, sometimes proving politically and motivationally relevant, other times not, can add significant nuance to our understanding of how and why individuals and social actors make the processual decisions they do in mobilizing for religion, ethnicity, nationhood, or some combination thereof. In this regard, ethnicities, nations, and religious groups can and should be understood as similar phenomena, analogous forms of social organization that differ largely in their emphasis, rather than their function, but that are all powerful motivating forces and whose interaction can have profound effects on political and social life.

The effort to focus on how social groups are constructed is thus particularly important in cases such as religious nationalism, in which multiple socially constructed identities and groups interact and affect political and social life. A theory of religious nationalism seeking to understand the ways in which religious identification and ideology serve as fundamental organizing characteristics around which national group identities can crystalize needs to look at the ways in which both national *and* religious groups are constructed and mobilized. The study of nationalism, and especially religious nationalism, is best pursued as a study of practice, of the performative nature of group formation, and of the myriad interactions, performances, and conflicts that make up everyday identity. It emphasizes that both "religion" and "nation" are processual and performative categories whose members can be mobilized into groups, not unitary social actors in their own rights. As Pierre Bourdieu has argued, one needs to treat groupness as a variable, seeking to understand the dynamics of group making as a social, cultural, and political project that works to transform categories into groups and increase levels of groupness among members of the category.[58] The question is: How is such an approach to be realized? Is it possible to analyze the construction of ethnic, national, and religious groups in a way that fruitfully adds to the understanding of how religion, ethnicity, and nationalism operate in society yet is still sensitive to the constructed nature of such phenomena, analyzing not just the constructed nature of communal identities but how and why they are created? A boundary-oriented approach, focusing on social closure and the markers of difference that groups establish around themselves is one useful way of approaching this effort, and it is to such a perspective that we will now turn.

GROUP BOUNDARIES

Much of the work on social boundary making owes its origins to the pioneering work of Norwegian anthropologist Fredrik Barth. In a seminal introduction to his 1968 edited volume *Ethnic Groups and Boundaries*, Barth sought to understand why ethnic groups persisted over time, despite significant population turnover and the frequent flow of personnel across ethnic boundary lines.[59] Key to Barth's work is his argument that ethnic groups are "culture-bearing units," although not necessarily defined by cultural content. In essence, Barth argues that ethnic cultures are an effect, not a cause, of group-making processes: ethnic boundaries make the group, not the "cultural stuff" it encloses. As he explains in a later work, "a boundary is a particular conceptual construct that people sometimes impress on the world. . . . [W]e can use boundaries as a metaphor for how abstract categories, natural classes and kinds, are separated and marked off from each other."[60]

Barth's emphasis on boundaries draws our attention away from static conceptions of ethnicity, nation, and religion as discrete, natural, and unchanging social units and recognizes them as ascriptive and exclusive—defined through negotiation and entailing a conception of difference between those enclosed within the group boundary and those who fall outside it. The way those boundaries are defined and what they center around or emphasize as central concepts of identity and so on matters less than that the boundaries exist and that members of the group recognize them and their differentiating power. In this sense, ethnic, national, and religious identity is often formed in specific reference to and contrast against those who fall outside the group, a "significant other" that serves as a mirror against which one's own sense of self can be defined.[61] As Barth argues, "people's own experience of a cultural contrast to members of other groups is schematized by drawing an ethnic boundary, imposing a false conceptual order on a field of much more broadly distributed cultural variation."[62] Collective identity is thus constituted by dialectic interplay of processes of internal and external definition. "Self" is constructed against the "Other" and "Other" against the "Self." Barth's work has sparked a series of theoretical innovations examining such processes in contexts ranging from the American colonial Southwest, to the ancient Mediterranean world, and forward into modern processes of globalization and resistance.[63]

A similar approach has been taken by sociologist Andreas Wimmer, who has built on Barth's boundary metaphor to emphasize the process of boundary making that forges ethnic and national groups. In his work, Wimmer develops a model that both outlines and systematizes the boundary-oriented approach to the study of ethnic groups, but also seeks to transcend it, developing a comparative analytic focused on understanding how and why ethnicity matters in certain societies and contexts but not others. For Wimmer, "ethnic categorizations—defining who is what—are an intrinsic part of the struggle over power and prestige that lies at the heart of the process of social closure."[64] In this type of struggle, individual and collective actors work strategically in a variety of social and political fora to maximize their own access to power and opportunity. Wimmer's primary goal, then, has been to develop a comparative analytic capable of explaining all of the various ways in which such struggles over power and prestige have been translated into group boundary formations, surveying and mapping the various strategies individual and collective actors use to redefine the boundaries of their respective groups and obtain political and social advantage.

Wimmer's close analysis reveals a finite array of modes of boundary formation, shared mechanisms that govern ethnic boundary making across a wide variety of social and historical contexts. Such mechanisms include: (1) those that expand the number of people included; (2) those that contract boundaries and thus reduce the number of people they enclose; (3) those that seek to change the meaning of existing boundaries by challenging ethnic hierarchies; (4) those that attempt to cross boundaries by changing one's one categorical positioning; and (5) those that aim to overcome ethnic boundaries by emphasizing other crosscutting levels of identity through strategies of "boundary blurring."[65] But how are such boundaries determined in the first place? What makes ethnic boundaries salient in some contexts and not others? Answers to such questions are critical to understanding how group boundaries operate in society, and how and why groups select specific characteristics around which to organize their collective identities. Wimmer identifies three distinct factors that influence the political and social salience of particular conceptions of identification and the boundaries that are drawn around them. First, Wimmer argues that the institutional setup of society provides incentives to emphasize certain characteristics over others, and thus set up particular types of boundaries around social groups. Since, for Wimmer, the formation of ethnic groups is largely the product of classification struggles over power in a particular social field, it comes as no surprise that he identifies the distribution of power within the social field as a second critical element in efforts to construct group boundaries. Finally, the reach of established social networks, with their ability to transmit ideas and values, power and privilege, can help determine exactly where ethnic boundaries are drawn.[66] These three conditions provide the context under which decisions about ethnic identification and the construction of ethnic boundary making are made.

The institutional structure of the modern state provides one of the most important impetuses for ethnic formation. The historical context of modern state systems is a significant incentive for ethnic formation as states seek to determine who should, and who should not, be a member of the political community. The modern state, which divides the social and political world into distinct and bounded political formations, encourages states to "make" national populations that owe allegiance to the state and to their fellow citizens. States are driven to create distinctive national ethnic groups and differentiate them from ethnic and other groups that are not to be considered members of the new national state community. An individual's position within the hierarchy of the social field plays a powerful role in determining which characteristics they will emphasize and around which level of ethnic differentiation they will choose to construct social boundaries. Individuals will choose the level of ethnic categorization that is perceived to provide the most benefit to themselves individually, seeking to maximize the potential gain both within the ethnic group and vis-à-vis those outside the group. Finally, the extent of social networks helps determine where and when specific ethnic boundaries will be formed. Networks of political alliances can help determine where the boundaries between "us" and "them" are drawn. Under conditions with significant lines of political networks that transcend ethnic groups, ethnicity as such is less likely to be emphasized as a salient characteristic for group identity, while situations with distinct lacks of political linkages across ethnic lines are more prone to ethnic differentiation and to emphasizing ethnicity as a key facet of political and social life.

According to this perspective, institutions, power, and networks play an important role in boundary-making processes. Institutions and networks, in particular, determine when and where ethnic boundaries matter, as well as determining who they will encompass and who they will exclude. The distribution of power within a social field also helps to determine the particular properties of the boundaries, their political salience, cultural significance, social closedness, and historical stability.[67] Two key characteristics of the power distribution in a social field—the degree of power inequality and the reach of consensus—are critical in determining the characteristics of boundary formation. The reach of consensus, whether the groups and individual actors involved agree on the salience of the ethnic categorization and boundary for social life, determines the extent to which boundaries are politically salient and long lasting. Power inequality directly impacts the degree of social closure and the strength of ethnic and group boundaries. Where degrees of power differential are high, degrees of social closure are also high as politically powerful actors seek to inscribe strong boundaries differentiating themselves from the powerless. This is important because high degrees of social closure, and the stronger boundaries they entail, lead, as Pierre Bourdieu[68] and Max Weber[69] have previously argued, to stronger levels of cultural differentiation as groups set themselves apart through strategies of symbolic boundary making. The stronger the degree of social closure, defined and reinforced through inequality and consensus, the more politically salient boundaries become. The more politically salient, historically stable, and psychologically relevant these boundaries are, the more entrenched they become in the fabric of society. Power distribution and the ways ethnic actors negotiate and come to grips with the power differentials within the political field, in sum, strongly impact the degree to which ethnic boundaries become politically salient and deeply entrenched. In essence, ethnic and group boundaries matter when power differentials make them matter, and ethnic and political actors maneuver and manipulate such boundaries to ensure better access to political and social power for themselves and their coethnics. Work by scholars such as Brubaker, Barth, and Wimmer provide convincing accounts of the salience of boundary-formation processes to the study of ethnic groups and offer a useful approach to the ways in which social actors form and maintain collective groups and conceptions of identity. Yet these perspectives, important as they are, only partially explain the particular form of group-making process that is our focus here. Religious nationalism is a project that relies upon markers of religious difference to define the boundaries of the ethno-national community. The general practice among social scientists of viewing religious identification as a mere subcategory of broader conceptions of ethnicity rears its head again here. While Brubaker, Barth, and Wimmer do occasionally discuss religion, they only rarely touch upon the specific characteristics of religious identification or seek to understand how specifically religious definitions of identity might affect processes of group making.[70] To paraphrase Brubaker himself,[71] "categories of practice," vernacular understandings of religion serving as a coterminous stand-in for ethnicity, are too often being confused with "categories of analysis," sophisticated understandings of how different facets of social identity, be they religious, ethnic, or national, function as the key foci of group-making processes. When examining religious nationalism, it is still necessary to disentangle the complex weave of social identity, examining the ways in which conceptions of religion can serve as the building blocks of ethnic consciousness, and religious and ethnic consciousness as the foundation of conceptions of national identity.

One possible avenue for understanding the specific role that religion can play in the construction of ethnic and national identity is to focus on the role such formations play as guardians and exponents of public and collective memory.[72] Memories and historical narratives of peoplehood and identity are of critical importance to the national project because the rise of nationalism entails a rapid reconfiguration of identification and forces people to wrestle with where and how new national boundaries should be established. The rapid transition from traditional and prenational communities to new conceptions of nationalism entails a rapid reconfiguration of social and collective identity and, crucially, a concomitant destruction of traditional methods of social organization. Nationalizing communities are often forced to ask questions such as: Who are we? What sorts of elements make us a distinct people? And who is a member of the nation and who should fall outside its boundaries? These questions strike to the very heart of identification and social organization.

The destruction of traditional social organization and the subsequent necessity to reconfigure and redefine notions of individual and collective identity and belonging is a characteristic of much of modern life. Scholars of modernity have heavily focused on the rapid and radical changes that accompany the rise of modernity in societies around the globe.[73] The development of the modern world has brought with it ever-increasing amounts of social change, rapid and radical social transformations that have destroyed the traditional social and cultural bonds that hold society together. Such social transformations have been visible in the decline of traditional community, increases in urbanization and social mobility, and, most importantly for our purposes, the rise of secularization and the disintegration of traditional structures of belief. This transformation has had a powerful effect on social life. The chaotic nature of rapid change, however, has had devastating effects not merely on traditional forms of social and communal organization, but also for the new modern societies it generates. As French sociologist of religion Danièle Hervieu-Léger has argued, one of the most important of the constructions destroyed in the transition from traditional community to modern society is the maintenance and reproduction of social and collective memory."[74] Indeed, social, cultural, and psychological forms of continuity are eroded through the effect of social change as individuals lose touch with the traditional values and orientations of their communities, swept up on the winds of progress and modernity and left adrift in a new form of society. The effects of social change have been so powerful that "one of the chief characteristics of modern societies is that they are no longer societies of memory, and as such ordered with a view of reproducing what is inherited."[75] The disintegration of collective memory, so powerfully necessary for the construction of distinct social groups and conceptions of national and ethnic identity, is a crucial consequence of the disintegration of many of the traditional social bonds that held together premodern societies.

Yet, as Hervieu-Léger explains, the disintegrating effects of modernity and its accompanying change provides an opportunity for the resurgence and continued salience of the religious beliefs for which it was once thought to spell the end. The transition under modernity from societies of memory to societies of change, breaking the collective bonds of belief and community that once held social organizations together, has created a vacuum as individuals and societies seek a sense of community and collective identity around which to orient. Hervieu-Léger argues that, contrary to the predictions of secularization theorists and others who see religion as disappearing, religion can serve as a powerful means of filling this vacuum, providing the type of collective memory and identity so desperately craved by people and societies in modernity. Indeed, religion and religious organizations were one means of creating such bonds before the advent of modernity.[76] Hervieu-Léger argues that religion continues to fulfill this role in many modern societies. This does not mean that religion is confined to nostalgia or fond remembrance of past traditions. Instead, religion serves as a legitimizing force in modern lives. "What defines tradition . . . is that it confers transcendent authority on the past,"[77] giving an ancient and authoritative history and sense of meaning for modern audiences. In essence, religion functions as a *chain of memory*, in Hervieu-Léger's formulation, legitimizing, consolidating, and giving importance to modern social formations by tying them to traditional forms of social organization and collective life.

It is this connection between modern and traditional society that is of key importance for those seeking to understand the continued salience of religion in modern life. More than that, the connection provides powerful insights into the relationship between religion and nationalism, and why nationalist actors so often draw upon conceptions of religion and religious identification as a means of constructing group and national boundaries around their newly forming communities. As many scholars have argued, the sense of tradition and the variety of representations, images, and attitudes that religion can engender, is precisely what nationalists of all stripes seek to invent, imagine, or appropriate in their quest to form new nations.[78] This sense of tradition is far more important than a mere abstract or academic desire to know about history, or even the effort to gain a conception of a nation's origins. Rather, traditions and the collective memories and attitudes they bear are constitutive of the very fabric of nations themselves.[79] Tradition manages to serve so powerful a role in society because of the peculiar social formation of nations themselves. Often new constructions, nations need to provide a powerful justification for why their citizens and inhabitants should profess loyalty to the new community.[80] Much of the scholarly research on nationalism has sought to identify exactly how such justifications are created, examining characteristics such as a common emphasis on a historic golden age,[81] ethnic inclusion and exclusion,[82] shared vernacular languages,[83] or high economic cultures.[84] Nationalists and national communities routinely seize upon religion's reservoir of signs and symbols, beliefs and attitudes, to serve as a "chain of memory" and foster support for the new national community. In this they explicitly tie the traditional forms of social life and collective organization transmitted by religion's emphasis on memory to the political and social structure of newly forming national states.

THE COMPLEXITY OF SOCIAL IDENTITY

But how is this connection between religion and the nation formed? What are the processes by which the myths, symbols, and other "cultural stuff" that religion preserves become associated with collective memory and national identity? How do such cultural forms come to serve as fundamental axes of boundary formation and group differentiation? In this regard, social identity complexity theory, a recent approach pioneered by social psychologists, can provide important answers. Social identity complexity is a theoretical construct designed to reflect the relationship between the crosscutting layers of identity that make up an individual's overall conception of self. In essence, a person's degree of social identity complexity refers to the "degree of overlap perceived to exist between groups of which [that] person is simultaneously a member."[85]

As Roccas and Brewer explain, scholars are most interested "[w]hen ingroups defined by different dimensions of categorization overlap only partially. . . . In this case some of those who are fellow ingroup members on one dimension are simultaneously outgroup members on the other."[86] Under such circumstances individuals construct their own subjective sense of social identity as they seek to reconcile their relationship to multiple nonconvergent in-group memberships. Social identity complexity reflects how this reconciliation has been accomplished, the product of a cognitive process by which individuals recognize and interpret information about their own in-groups. "*Low complexity* means that multiple identities are subjectively embedded in a single ingroup representation, whereas *high complexity* involves acknowledgement of differentiation and difference between ingroup categories."[87] Ultimately, it is the individual's own perception of the relationship between his or her in-groups that is of critical importance. "In sum, the more a person perceives the groups to which he or she belongs as sharing the same members, the less complex is his or her social identity."[88] Individuals with high social identity complexity often conceptualize their social identity in such a way that others who share *any* salient dimension of identity are considered part of the social in-group. Conversely, individuals with low social identity complexity often conceptualize their own sense of identity such that others must share *all* relevant characteristics of identity in order to be considered members of the social in-group, conflating multiple levels of identity into a single overarching concept of group belonging.

Ultimately, it is the relationship between self and other that lies at the center of these identity processes. Research has shown that the ways in which people conceive of their own in-groups—whether they develop a high or low level of social identity complexity—is affected by a variety of factors. Experience with groups outside of one's own social categories, tolerance for uncertainty and ambiguity and openness to change, for example, have been correlated with a higher degree of social identity complexity and thus a more open concept of group membership. Conversely, little experience of diversity, stress, a need for closure, and in-group threat have all been found to have a negative effect on social identity complexity as individuals harden the boundaries of their social in-groups.[89] Roccas and Brewer suggest that threat to one's social in-group represents one of the most powerful influences on perceptions of social identity complexity. Indeed, "When there is a perception of threat, individuals perceive their ingroup as more homogeneous and perceive the self as more similar to the ingroup and more different from the outgroup."[90] These reactions to situational context thus have an important impact, not just on the ways individuals present their own self-identity but also on how they view people who are thought to fall outside the membership of their own in-group. Studies have shown that individuals with a high degree of social identity complexity are far more likely to be tolerant of differences and members of out-groups, recognizing that membership in their in-groups relies upon multiple levels of identification, rather than excluding outsiders out of hand.[91] Individuals with a low degree of social identity complexity, however, are more likely to be intolerant of differences, their multiple layers of identity all reduced to a single expression of the in-group, outside of which all others are considered different.

Social identity complexity theory is a fruitful way to approach religious nationalism because it specifically focuses on the way that different facets of identification, such as religion, ethnicity, and nationalism, are combined into a single overarching in-group, providing a theoretical mechanism to explain the ways that religion and nationalism can be combined to precipitate a specific form of boundary formation and maintenance. Nationalizing groups seek to create new national formations and to impose distinctive boundaries that enclose the new national community and differentiate it from "others." Religion's potency as a link to an authoritative traditional past makes it a powerful tool for the development of collective identity such as that sought by nationalists. Religion's "chain of memory" valorizes and sanctifies the new national community in a way few other characteristics of identity could. Religion thus does not survive merely by taking on "non-religious roles," as in Steve Bruce's formulation.[92] Rather, religion always serves to fulfill many functions in social life, including as a guardian of memory and a force for collectivization and community development. As scholars such as Grace Davie have shown,[93] it is even possible to "belong without believing" in the modern world, maintaining a connection to and faith in the continuity of the group and its boundaries "for which the signs preserved from the traditional religion now serve as emblems."[94]

This helps further explain the phenomenon of religious nationalism even in a secularizing modern world, because it is not the "cultural stuff" in Barth's formulation, the religious content of the group, that necessarily matters, but simply the boundary between ethno-religious or religio-national groups. Ethnic and national formations can thus continue to rely on religion as a powerful reservoir of constitutive symbols and memories, even in a time when fewer people are practicing religion or professing religious faith, because religious boundaries continue to have salience, even when the "religious stuff" does not. The core of myths, symbols, and memories transmitted and passed down by religious forms help structure these boundaries, providing a scaffolding around which conceptions of difference can form, even during times when religious practice and personal belief have become less and less important in social life.

A NEW THEORY OF RELIGIOUS NATIONALISM

Here I draw insights from these theories to present my own theoretical approach to understanding religious nationalism. I argue that it is these processes of social boundary formation, collective legitimization, and conflation of social identities that provide the foundation for movements that integrate religion and nationalism. But under what conditions do such processes take place? How do religious visions of the nation prevail over alternative formulations of what national identity should look like? It is important to note that religious nationalism is never the only option for nationalist entrepreneurs seeking to create distinctive national communities. In both of my cases, political, ethnic, and cultural visions of the nation all circulated at the same time as national sentiment was coalescing around religious difference. How did religious versions of nationalism win out over competing claims that at times appeared as viable as those that ended up succeeding, or even more so?

I argue that a particular set of social and historical circumstances underlie religious nation formation. The first of these is a need for group formation. Nationalism often arises during moments of social change, when previously existing political and social structures have begun to break down. In many cases nationalism emerges out of the collapse of empires as the withdrawal of imperial power provides opportunities for, and even requires, new social formations.

These radically shifting environments provoke two innovations in those who would seek to create new political structures to replace imperial rule. The first of these is the construction of a national community, the idea that there is, or should be, some set of people who represent a distinct community around which a new state should form. The second is a need to legitimize the choices made to determine who should be part of that community, the boundaries that define in- and out-groups. This often involves a search for authenticity, for justification, and for a foundation on which the community can be built. As Hervieu-Léger has argued, religion can provide a particularly meaningful foundation for those looking to justify national boundaries. Religion brings with it a reservoir of symbolic matériel that lends historical depth and cosmic meaning to newly formed boundaries. Under the tumultuous conditions of imperial collapse and the reformulation of social boundaries, such characteristics provided ready-made content to "fill up" and add meaning to newly formed communities challenged by the rapid changes inherent in the modern world.

A second prerequisite for religious nationalism is a belief that one's national community, though often amorphous and ill defined, is facing pressure from some sort of "other." What this threat looks like can be widely variable. At times it involves external assault from a colonizing power. Other times it reflects a response to internal danger, a backlash against breakaway populations challenging the status quo. Even natural disasters, if experienced in socially unequal ways, can call into question a population's social structures. Such threats to the perceived equilibrium of a society's hierarchies of power often encourage political entrepreneurs to act, envisioning new social relationships that might advantage their perceived in-group. In this regard, exogenous shocks or social ruptures can often serve as the impetus for national movement formation. Though some social threats are long-lasting and continuous, moments of distinct crises often call social identities into question, making them suddenly matter in ways they had not previously. These sorts of crises often encourage people to draw their spheres of social relations more tightly, enclosing only those who they feel are like them in some particular way. By constructing group boundaries that separate an in-group from a perceived out-group, social actors create new social formulations that argue for the primacy of a new homogenous community: a distinctive nation or group constructed in opposition to external threat.

This process explains the growth of nationalism and the formation of national identities, but more is required for nationalists to turn to religion as a unifying characteristic. I argue that nationalists are particularly prone to turn to religion as a key signifier of identity in situations of religious diversity. This argument challenges earlier findings such as those of Rieffer and of Soper and Fetzer, who argue religious nationalism is more likely in situations of homogeneity.[95] In contrast, a deeper examination reveals that it is only under diverse conditions that religion matters as a distinguishing characteristic, drawing clear dividing lines between the "us" and the "them." In such conditions, nationalists are able to draw upon and make relevant religious distinctions even when they had not previously been politically relevant. This creates the circumstances for the forging of religious and political identities in a way that creates new communities, national but defined along religious lines. Such efforts have been particularly important in states that fall along boundary regions between religious populations. States in these religious borderland regions are often religiously complex, and their populations regularly come into contact with religious diversity. It is only through opposition, through the need for differentiation, that individuals and social groups turn to new facets of identify for organizational purposes. Religiously homogenous populations and ones that face no need to grapple with the complexities of religious difference rarely turn to religion as a marker of identification, one that effectively creates social distinctions between in- and out-groups.

Finally, I argue that religious nationalism provides but one pathway to national organization. Scholars interested in religious nationalism have often viewed it in sharp contrast to secular nationalism or civil religion, movements that favor very different relationships between religion and the state. I argue that rather than an either/or relationship, religious nationalism can develop at the same time as other ideas of the national state. Nationalists of all stripes often coexist within nationalist movements. I again contrast this finding with that of Soper and Fetzer, who argue that the growth of religious nationalism is a result of the support or opposition religious communities hold for the nation-building process and the role of foundational documents in codifying the state's relationship to religion. I argue instead that both religious groups and national communities are relational and formational structures, adaptive and responsive to the changing arguments made by nationalist entrepreneurs. In both of the cases I study, secular nationalists who pioneered the movement were forced to give way before the groundswell of religious sentiment and the efforts of those who viewed religion as the key dividing line between the national community and those outside of it. In this regard, elite representations of the national community, such as founding documents and secular arguments about civic and civil distinctiveness, often prove more aspirational than accurate. Rather, in deeply religious societies religion can provide the core around which most people viewed their own identify, an organizing mindset that helped make sense of the world. When secular nationalists called for revolution and independence, religious populations were often more than willing to go along, but did so in a way that constructed national belonging around the facet of identity that really mattered to them, that of religion.

These then are the conditions under which religious nationalist movements form: moments of structural social change, communal threat, religious diversity, position in religious borderlands, and a high level of religiosity. Under such conditions religious populations can be adept at incorporating secular ideas of nationalism into the frameworks of identity that guide their day-to-day life. In what follows I test this theory through two extended case studies. In both I examine the rise of secular nationalists and the growing importance of national independence and distinction. I contrast these often elite understandings of how nationalism should work with the real ways common people understood their identities on the ground. I find that far from being mutually exclusive, religion and nationalism fused in a way that created new national identities, ones with religion at their core, that created strong boundary lines between the national community and those who might threaten it.

ABOVE AND BELOW: MAPPING A METHODOLOGICAL APPROACH TO THE STUDY OF RELIGIOUS NATIONALISM

This book analyzes two carefully selected cases, Ireland and Turkey, to trace the ways in which religion and nationalism intersect. Ireland and Turkey are by no means the only cases that could illustrate the idea of religious nationalism. Other scholars have pointed to, among many others, the experiences of India,[96] Israel,[97] and the United States[98] as paradigmatic of the interaction between religion and politics. The experiences of these, and many others, provide equally valid approaches, yet Ireland and Turkey hold several unique advantages. Ireland and Turkey went through nationalization processes at roughly the same time, crafting new national identities out of complicated imperial pasts as they struggled to come to grips with histories of colonialism and debates over self-determination. Yet it is the differences between the two cases that are perhaps most instructive. Comparing a case of Christian nationalism in Europe to a Muslim variety of religious nationalism outside of Europe provides an opportunity to draw upon, yet break free from, the traditional theories of religious nationalism, which have privileged Christian and European experiences over those of other religions and geographical areas. Examining a well-studied case such as Ireland, which fits most definitions of religious nationalism and has even served as the foundation of much nationalist theorizing, allows us to examine traditional theories of religious nationalism "on their own turf" as it were. Yet incorporating the case of Turkey, one which has received much less focus from scholars of religious politics, indeed often serving as a counterexample of secular triumph over religious identities, allows us to test such theories in an entirely different context.

Ireland is often considered a prototypical case of religious nationalism, as Irish nationalists drew upon notions of Catholic identity in an effort to gain popular support for independence from Protestant Britain. Yet some scholars have argued that the true impetus for Irish nationalism was not religion, but political, ethnic, class, or even "tribal" differences.[99] If this is so, how and why did Irish nationalism come to be expressed in religious terms? Rather than taking "Catholics" and "Protestants" as bounded politically acting groups in Ireland, we should instead ask how these religious identities became symbols and signifiers of more complicated political positions. How did national identity crystallize in Ireland, and why did Catholicism come to serve as the facet of identity around which the most successful definitions of Irish national identity would focus? Why did the nation develop the way it did? Such questions can only be answered through a thorough historical analysis of political processes in Ireland that took centuries to mature, and a national movement that has long been conflicted, contradictory, and contentious.

While Ireland is a more obvious example of religious nationalism, Turkey is a rather unorthodox case to include as an example of this process. Turkey has long considered itself a secular state, and the nationalist movement that founded the country relied upon a rhetoric that defined the nation in explicitly civic and secular terms. Much of the modern scholarship about Turkish nationalism and the construction of the Turkish nation has accepted this paradigm and has emphasized similar characteristics. Yet the relationship between Islam, secularism, and politics in Turkey is much more complicated than this simplistic picture and has been so from the moment of Turkey's founding. Indeed, despite the secular rhetoric of Turkey's nationalist movement, the maneuvering that led to the creation of the Turkish nation involved a significant religious dimension, as the Turkish government pursued policies that discriminated against, expelled, and exchanged populations of religious minorities in an effort to religiously homogenize the population of the newly formed nation. This reliance on religious characteristics to define the boundaries of national identity makes Turkey an apt case for a study of religious nationalism. Juxtaposing the Turkish experience with the more classically religious nationalist movement in Ireland reveals the ways that religious nationalism functions as a practice and the processes by which religious identities become the salient characteristic for defining national identity.

This project utilizes historical methods to analyze the importance of religion in the construction and maintenance of national identity. Believing with Erik Hobsbawm that nationalism can only truly be understood when approached simultaneously from above and below,[100] I take a multilevel approach, studying both the official rhetoric and religious policies of both states, as well as the everyday experience of religious and political identities in the lives of everyday citizens. An analysis of official rhetoric and state policies in areas such as immigration, the relationship between religious organizations and the state, and treatment of religious minorities provides a top-down approach to the study of religious nationalism. This analysis reveals the extent to which nationalist and government leaders sought to use religion to strengthen national boundaries, consolidating national identity through religious homogenization and exclusion. In contrast, examination of the everyday lived experience of common citizens provides a bottom-up approach that reveals the ways people really thought about their religious and national identities on the ground. Most importantly, as Rogers Brubaker has shown elsewhere, such an approach reveals the times and circumstances in which such identities are, or are not, politically relevant. This type of analysis thus helps us understand the conditions under and process by which religious identities become politicized in the minds of the populace.

This chapter has drawn together an array of social scientific theories about the construction of group identities to examine the ways that religion and nationalism can combine to craft a uniquely powerful vision of social integration. Scholars of ethnic and national boundary making have argued that it is the constructed and ever-fluid dividing lines between social groups that play a much more influential role in identity formation than the "cultural stuff" that they enclose. In this regard, ethnic and national boundaries provide a form of social closure differentiating the "us" from the "them" in a way that promotes group cohesion and solidarity. Yet how those boundaries are formed, why they acquire such significance and draw on particular elements of identity to form the foundation of identity, is less well understood. Here I draw on theories from the sociology of religion to explain why in some cases religion provides these elements, providing a common core of cultural elements but also a key method of differentiation between those who share memory and history and those who don't. In many cases this leads to the conflation of different facets of identity as people develop senses of self that require membership in all levels of the community—religious, political, and ethnic—in order to truly belong to the in-group and be considered fellow members of the nation. At its core, religious nationalism is an effort to define these in-groups in a way that most clearly constructs a community that can share a new form of identity, crafting a sense of difference and collective identity in a powerful effort to construct new in-groups.

From here, I move on to the two cases. Chapters 2 and 3 examine the relationship between religion and nationalism in Ireland. Chapter 2 takes a top-down approach to study elite and official definitions of the nation. This chapter traces the development of nationalism in Ireland from its earliest beginnings in the twelfth century, through the development of mass politics in the nineteenth century, the Gaelic Revival in the late nineteenth and beginning of the twentieth centuries, and the establishment of an independent Ireland in 1922. This survey of Irish nationalist history highlights the development of several distinct definitions of national identity in Ireland, products of complicated debates and conflicts between different populations and policy makers in nineteenth-century Ireland. Ultimately this analysis reveals the dynamic and relational process by which national identity crystallized in Ireland, as political and ethnic entrepreneurs drew on religious and cultural forms to define what it meant to be a member of the national community. Chapter 3 then takes a different approach, examining the everyday religious experience of the common people in Ireland and the ways in which religion eventually became mobilized as a defining characteristic of what it meant to be Irish. This chapter analyzes the intersection of religion and politics in the Great Irish Famine in the middle of the nineteenth century, before discussing the ways in which the cultural politics of the Gaelic Revival took on an increasingly religious dimension following the 1916 Easter Rising and the execution of a series of Catholic heroes, before concluding with a discussion of the ways in which religion has served as a fundamental boundary line between communities in Northern Ireland in the last half of the twentieth century. Combined, these two chapters take a multifaceted approach, examining not just the ways in which religion can become politicized, but also the ways in which the religious dimension of identity can shape nationalizing processes and the cultural content of national identity.

Chapters 4 and 5 then move on to the Turkish case, taking a similar approach to analyze the role that Islam has played in constructing and conceptualizing Turkish national identity. Chapter 4 once again takes a top-down approach, analyzing official documents and policies to understand the ways in which Turkish politicians and policy makers sought to craft a particular way of thinking about what it meant to be a Turk. Seeking to create a new national state out of the collapse of the Ottoman Empire, nationalists in the Republic of Turkey worked to create a radical shift in social and political organization. Yet a close look at the processes of nation building that Turkish nationalists unleashed reveals a complicated process of negotiation and compromise as newfound ideas of secularization and modernization comingled with traditional forms of religious and culturally based social organization. Despite an official rhetoric that described the nation in secular terms, in immigration policy, treatment of religious minorities, and policies designed to benefit Muslim Turks, Turkish policy makers consistently used religion as a key marker of national identity. Chapter 5 examines everyday experiences of religion in the late Ottoman Empire and the early Republic of Turkey, focusing on the ways in which intercommunal relationships between Muslims and Christians helped drive political processes. In areas such as the Armenian Genocide in 1915, the Greco-Turkish population exchange in 1923, anti-Christian pogroms in Istanbul in 1955, and electoral politics throughout the twentieth century, Turkish citizens have routinely demonstrated the ways in which religion continued to shape commonplace ideas of national and social identity. To be a Turk automatically meant being a Muslim in the eyes of many, and a historical approach centered on the experiences and beliefs of the common people reveals the extent to which such ideas continued to permeate the nation even in a supposedly secular state.

It is important to note that though in both cases above I describe these chapters in opposition, privileging top-down narratives in the first chapter of each dyad before turning to bottom-up approaches, this strict delineation is in many ways artificial. Every nationalist movement contains elite and populist elements, and it is the interaction and negotiation between multiple conceptions of nationalisms that determine each movement's particular character. Because of this, certain people, events, and movements appear in both chapters of each case study.

Though each chapter from each case maintains its focus on elite or popular representations of the nation respectively, this overlap reflects the complex nature of nationalist movements in general. Elite nationalist entrepreneurs must always gain popular support for their ideals, while populist conceptions of identity are often strong enough to force even the most zealous of elite ideologues to compromise in the name of mass appeal. This complexity and the interplay of elements within a national movement in many ways form the core of this book, and these different conceptions of national identity weave their way in and out of both chapters in each case, much as they do in nationalist movements themselves.

Finally, a concluding chapter draws these cases together, tracing how religion and nationalism continue to play a powerful role in shaping political and social events in Ireland and Turkey today. In the recent debate over the United Kingdom's "Brexit" from the European Union, Northern Ireland has found itself torn between those who seek to remain in the EU and those who seek to remain in the UK. The challenges brought about by the Brexit vote have thus resurrected nationalist impulses that had been dormant since the Good Friday Agreement ended conflict in Northern Ireland in 1998. What had long been thought buried is once again an issue of key concern, as nationalist political parties such as Sinn Féin have once again called for Northern Ireland to be reunited with the Republic of Ireland to the south, an echo of nationalist politics based on religious concerns that have been swirling in Ireland for centuries. Similarly, Turkey too has seen issues of religion and nationalism rise once again to the fore, as the current government under the controversial figure of Recep Tayyip Erdoğan has sought to move the country in a direction that privileges religion over Turkey's traditional secularist rhetoric. The result has been a complicated political situation in which secularists and religiously oriented actors have clashed time and again, in arenas such as 2013's Gezi Park protests, and the 2016 aborted coup attempt that sought to drive Erdoğan from power. Most recently, a series of purges of hundreds of thousands of Erdoğan's political opponents in politics, the judiciary, the military, and academia, and the April 2017 passing of a referendum to reform Turkey's political system in a way that has granted Erdoğan significant amounts of power as president, reveal the extent to which such concerns continue to serve as a focus for Turkish national politics. This chapter examines these recent events in the context of the boundary-oriented approach to religious nationalism developed here, providing a final word on the ways that religiously oriented ethnic and national boundary making continues to shape political processes in Ireland and Turkey today, an important testament to the power such formulations hold in the national imaginaries of both states.

2 · THE GOSPEL OF IRISH NATIONALISM

Religion and Official Discourses of the Nation in Ireland

The modern Irish nation-state was founded rather explicitly on religious beliefs, with both the original 1922 constitution of the Irish Free State and the current 1937 constitution of the Republic of Ireland providing a privileged position for Catholicism.[1] For most of its history, Catholic teaching dictated laws covering important social issues such as contraception (legalized with strong restrictions in 1980), divorce (illegal until 1996), and abortion (legalized only for cases of risk to the mother in 2013).[2] Despite a recent decline in measures of religiosity and religious attendance, the population of the Republic of Ireland continues to register as one of the most strongly religious in all of Europe, and indeed the world.[3] And that population has been, since the creation of the independent Irish state in 1922, almost exclusively Catholic. The partition of Ireland carved off the largest segment of the Protestant population of Ireland and established it, along with a significant number of Catholics, in the newly created country of Northern Ireland. The departure of British officials and their families and the exodus of Protestants who feared to live under Catholic hegemony further decimated what had been an active and politically powerful Protestant minority in the republic. Clearly, it seems, Irish identity at some point became intimately intertwined with Catholic identity: to be Irish is to be Catholic, and Catholicism continues to play a powerful role in shaping Irish politics, culture, and society.

Yet the easy characterization of Irish national identity with Catholicism is not as simple as it might appear. While religion has come to define what it means to be Irish, that was not always the case. In reality, the history of Irish nationalism is far more complex than these simplistic narratives would suggest. To take just a few examples, even the notion of an ancient unified Irish "nation" is questionable in the extreme. A closer look at Irish history reveals that there was no real conception of a unified Irish nationality until relatively modern times.[4] Likewise, in contrast to the facile characterization of Irish nationalism as a struggle between Catholics and Protestants, many of the earliest ideas of Irish nationalist thought were developed by Protestants, and Protestant leaders continued to have an important role in the Irish nationalist movement up until independence.[5] Indeed, the Irish nation that finally gained its independence in 1922 bore little resemblance to many of the conceptions of the nation that drove earlier efforts at national independence.[6] Rather than the uncomplicated narrative that has come to dominate popular conceptions of Ireland, the true history of Irish nationalism is, in fact, a long story of contestation and compromise, of multiple nations, identities, and types of nationalism competing for political and social dominance.

This transition from a multiplicity of identities to a nation that emphasized a singular religious and national character, and indeed conflated those two dimensions of identity as one and the same, raises important questions for scholars of religious nationalism. How did the conception of Ireland as a Catholic nation form? Why did religious identification become politically meaningful and how did nationalists go about the process of group identity formation, constructing national communities around religious identities? Given the multiple definitions of Irish nationalism, many of them pioneered by Protestant leaders, how did the religious definition of a Catholic Ireland win out and become the dominant conception around which the nation-state would form? When early nationalist efforts led by Protestants gave way to Catholic-led efforts in the nineteenth century, there was no guarantee that religion would be the unifying characteristic around which the nation would form. Some Protestant efforts had centered around the quest for political freedoms, and later both Protestant- and Catholic-led movements alike focused on Gaelic culture as the distinctive national characteristic. Understanding the nature of modern religious nationalism in Ireland thus requires us to trace how the relationship between religion and nationalism developed.

Such a diachronic approach raises the question of where to begin, a question that has long vexed scholars of Irish nationalism.[7] There are good arguments for beginning the study of nationalism in Ireland with the twelfth-century Norman invasions, seeing in the scattered resistance to incursions by Strongbow and Henry II the first seeds of what would become a unified Irish national identity and independence movement. This is the narrative that the Irish nationalist movement in Ireland has long supported, seeking to establish legitimacy for the modern struggle by claiming a deep-seated primordial past. Many scholars, too, have taken this approach.[8] Given that the issue of Irish nationalism is inextricable from Ireland's relationship with England, the imperial power against which the movement has long fought, such deep historical events certainly have relevance for the study of modern ideas of Irish nationality.

And yet, to speak of Irish nationalism in the twelfth century is perhaps a mis-
nomer. Despite modern mythologizing efforts to invent an ancient historical tradition, many of the earliest expressions of resistance to English incursion placed
little emphasis on the idea of Ireland as a unified nation or national community.
Even if we are willing to grant the title of nationalism to the scattered efforts of
various Irish kings and tribal groups, it is certainly clear that this resistance was
not religious in character. The lack of a religious divide between Ireland and then
Catholic England meant religion was not a useful category around which differentiated groups could form.[9] Even after the Reformation, when England became
a Protestant state, lack of political and economic power among the Catholic population in Ireland meant that efforts to create an Irish nation and independent
Irish state would be led by the Protestant landlords who dominated the political
and economic system of Ireland for much of its history. These efforts naturally
did not emphasize religion, but instead viewed Irish Protestants as the true
nation of Ireland, and held little regard for the Catholic majority, who were
mostly peasants and excluded from political and social power. What Catholic
social movements did arise in the seventeenth and eighteenth centuries focused
far more on achieving equal political rights for Catholics than they did on any
sort of independence.[10] Yet it is to those early days of political conflict that Irish
nationalists themselves have turned in their quest for legitimation, and so a brief
discussion of the early period of English control of Ireland will set the stage for
the analysis of the later nationalist movement to come.

MEDIEVAL AND EARLY MODERN PRECURSORS
OF THE IRISH NATION

The Mythic Past: Early Conceptions of the Irish Nation

The version of Irish nationalism that eventually won out in Ireland tends to
view the modern nation as the most recent manifestation of a primordial Irish
nation, one that can trace its roots all the way back to the Gaelic Irish who inhabited the island before the twelfth-century Norman invasions.[11] The Irish nation,
this perspective argues, is autochthonous and eternal, existing before the colonizing presence of the British and thus far more legitimate than those social and
political formations forced on the island by the British conquerors who dominated the island for most of the last eight hundred years. Yet there is a significant
mythological component to this version of Irish history, an invented tradition
that presents an ontological narrative supporting the nationalist movement's
political claims. The reality, as with most things, is far more complex. While the
Gaelic Irish certainly predated the coming of the British, their claim to be the
original indigenous inhabitants of Ireland is questionable. In fact, the Gaels were
no less conquerors than later waves of invaders, arriving in Ireland between 500 and
300 B.C.E. and establishing themselves at the expense of the island's earlier inhabit-

ants, before acculturating and forming a new hybrid society and culture.[12] More importantly, for much of ancient Irish history, the political and social life of the island remained fragmented, a patchwork system of various clanships and kingdoms with little sense of a common national identity.[13] While there is evidence for there being high kings, some historical, others mythological, holding suzerainty over part or all of Ireland from the seventh century on, such kings never ruled the island as a unified political state. In actual fact, the position of high king served more as an overlord for a collection of independent kingdoms, and significant political fragmentation and conflict remained.[14]

In this regard, it is difficult to say, as many nationalists have, that the Irish response to the Norman invasions of the twelfth century represents a sort of primitive nationalism, a resistance by the Irish nation against the foreign domination by invading colonizers. In fact, the first Norman invasion has been described as "more in the nature of a response to an invitation,"[15] beginning in 1169 when Dermot MacMurrough, king of Leinster, invited Norman knights led by Richard FitzGilbert to the island to help subdue his rebellious subjects. This first "invasion" was followed closely by Henry II, who arrived to establish an English royal presence in Ireland in 1171, reasserting control over the Norman forces, capturing Dublin, and expanding the English presence. This effort culminated in the establishment of the Lordship of Ireland, political dominion over the island that theoretically encompassed the whole of Ireland but in reality only ever expanded to parts of it, increasing and decreasing with the fluctuating power of both the English and indigenous Irish rulers. There was indeed Irish resistance to these efforts, with various Irish kings and lords pushing back against the Norman encroachment. Yet just as frequent was accommodation and compromise, as several petty kings made politically advantageous deals, or swore fealty to Henry. In fact, Henry was often greeted warmly by the indigenous Irish kings, who saw in his control the opportunity to curb the advances of the Norman knights, who had been expanding their territory unchecked. In essence the Norman invasions in the twelfth century were "not the beginning of a process of 'Irish' resistance to the English which lasted unbroken from 1171 to 1921: there never were two 'sides' in Ireland whose struggle can be reduced to such simple proportions."[16]

Rather than a strict differentiation between colonizing English and brutalized Irish, in fact, significant cultural contact and intercourse between the two populations led to increasing levels of hybridity and a certain "Hybernicization" of the "English by blood" populace living in Ireland, resulting in the creation of a new Anglo-Irish identity. As the Statutes of Kilkenny in 1366 lamented, "now many English of the said land [Ireland], forsaking the English language, fashion, mode of riding, laws, and usages, live and govern themselves according to the manners, fashion and language of the Irish enemies, and also have made divers marriages and alliances between themselves and the Irish enemies aforesaid."[17] Many of the earliest efforts to curtail the rights of the native Irish population, put into place by the Irish Parliament, an institution established by the English kings that exclusively represented the new Anglo-Irish rather than the native Irish, sought to curb any intermingling of the two communities. Focused on areas such as fashions of hair and dress (1297), entrance into religious orders (1310), and intermarriage (1366),[18] these restrictive statutes were efforts to maintain social and cultural boundaries between the two communities, products "not of English domination, but of English fear that the tide of their power was ebbing, and of the recognition that the division based on descent was in danger of obliteration."[19]

What emerges is a complex interweaving of accommodation, compromise, and scattered cultural struggle. The resistance to the Norman invasion and the early English colonization of Ireland was thus not a nationalistic movement in the true sense, with an Irish populace fighting for independence from a foreign and destructive other. The complex interplay of cultural and political identities, and the growing strength of Anglo-Irish identity among the "English by blood" population living in Ireland reveals a far more complicated picture of national identity and nationhood in medieval Ireland, one that would have important repercussions for Irish nationalism in early modern and modern times.

Precursors of Nationalism: Rebellion, Plantation, and the Irish Penal Laws

The English Reformation in the sixteenth century dramatically impacted the history and identity of Ireland as well. In its transition from Catholicism to Prot-estantism, England transformed Ireland from a borderland region in which a variety of political, social, and cultural categories served as salient characteristics of identity to one in which stark religious divisions played an increasingly impor-tant role in national identification. Though the English held nominal control of the entirety of Ireland from the late twelfth century on, true English power extended little beyond the fortified east of the island, known as the Pale. The regions beyond the Pale were largely controlled by independent Anglo-Irish and Gaelic lords, and Irish language and culture dominated. A series of rebellions by important Irish lords further weakened English power in Ireland, but even then, lack of political unity or a common goal, social, political, or religious, makes it impossible to speak of such efforts as truly nationalist in character.

Irish rebellions instead remained isolated and fragmented affairs, never involving the whole of Ireland, and were strictly waged for the advancement of various lords. Irish rebellions spurred Tudor rulers such as Mary I and Elizabeth I to impose an escalating series of policies designed to pacify the island. Efforts such as occupation by English troops, "Surrender and Regrant," in which Irish lords would be granted royal charter in exchange for fealty, and direct seizure of Irish land, culminated in the Plantation of Ulster. Thousands of Protestant English and Scottish settlers were transplanted to Ireland in an effort to both assert control and spread English language and culture.[20] Such efforts proved successful at bringing most of the island under English law and custom; however, they alienated not just the indigenous Gaelic Irish, but many of the Anglo-Irish, polarizing Irish society and setting the stage for further conflict.

The mass seizure of Irish land and its redistribution to English settlers caused significant resentment among the Irish. Conflicts over orthodoxy and the debate between Catholicism and Protestantism roiled politics throughout the British Isles. That these settlers were Protestants, deliberately transplanted into Ireland to serve as a new ruling class that would be more loyal to Protestant James, caused consternation among both indigenous Gaelic Irish and the Anglo-Irish descendants of the original Norman invaders, who would soon come to be known as "Old English."[21] Both groups had retained their Catholic faith, and England's conversion to Protestantism and increasing distrust of even the Old English Catholics in Ireland served to create a distinct religious frontier in which religious orientation became a signifier of allegiance to the crown. The plantation was coupled with increasing religious discrimination by the Protestant English as they sought to crack down on the Catholic population of Ireland to ensure their continued control of the island. Policies based on religious affiliation in this way had the unlikely effect of forging a common bond between the two Catholic populations in Ireland, Gaelic Irish and Old English alike. Though the two populations had little in common to this point, the imposition of a significant Protestant population in Ireland redrew many of the traditional social and cultural identities that had prevailed in Ireland. Many English officials began to view all Catholics in Ireland under the same rubric, subsuming political and ethnic identities underneath an overarching religious category, a theoretical fusion that, though overly simplistic, was to have profound consequences for the development of views of the nation and national identity in Ireland.

Protestant English distrust for Catholics of all sorts caused even more problems in Ireland during the lead up to the English Civil War during the seventeenth century. Spurred on by fears of rising Parliamentarian power and an expected invasion by the anti-Catholic opponents of Charles I, Irish Catholics launched a rebellion in 1641 that seized control over much of the island. Though this rebellion reveals a significant alliance between the elites of the Gaelic Irish and Old English ethnic groups, one predicated significantly on religious identity, it is still difficult to speak of such efforts as having truly nationalist motivations. The rebellions took place in support of the English monarch Charles I, and the Old English, at least, continued to consider themselves Englishmen and loyal subjects of the English crown, even though they wanted more immediate political control of governmental policies in Ireland.[22] This uneasy alliance between Old English and Gaelic Irish along religious lines, despite significant political, social, economic, and cultural differences in other facets of identity, was further sealed by the Cromwellian invasion of Ireland in 1649. After a Parliamentarian victory in the English Civil War, Oliver Cromwell led the victorious forces into

Ireland to both reassert political control over the region and extract revenge for Irish support of the Royalists. Cromwell viewed his campaign as being as much a religious crusade as an effort to assert political control, and his brutal tactics have made him one of the most hated men in all of Irish history.[23]

English politics again intruded on Irish history during the Glorious Revolution of 1688–1689 when, after an earlier restoration of the monarchy under his brother Charles II, King James II was overthrown. Angered by James's policies of religious tolerance and Protestant fears of a resurgent Catholic dynasty, the English Parliament invited the Protestant William of Orange to take the throne. After gaining some support from France, James fled to Ireland, where he remained very popular, in an effort to further gather Catholic Irish support for his cause. James was pursued in short order by William, and clashes between the two culminated in the breaking of the siege of Derry and the Battle of the Boyne, events that have taken on powerful roles in the mythology of Protestant unionists in modern Northern Ireland.[24] In Derry, one of the few Williamite strongholds in Ireland, William's naval forces broke James's siege and rescued the beleaguered Protestant population of the city in 1689. William's army then decisively defeated James at the Battle of the Boyne in 1690, setting the stage for the end of the war a year later and ensuring the victory and rise of a Protestant ascendancy in Ireland that would have a devastating effect on Irish Catholics.

As a result of Irish support for the defeated James, English rulers instituted a series of religiously oriented Penal Laws, designed to ensure the continued dominance of Protestants in Ireland by restricting the religious, political, and economic activities of Irish Catholics.[25] Such laws encompassed a broad spectrum of social and political life, banning Catholics from serving in most public offices or as members of Parliament, banning intermarriage with Protestants, excluding them from voting, teaching school, or buying land on long leases, and requiring that Catholic land inheritances would be equally divided among descendants in an effort to limit individual Catholics' control of large landed estates, among many others.[26] These laws furthered the division of Ireland along religious lines, fostering resentment among Irish Catholics, and continued the amalgamation of the Old English and Gaelic Irish populations as more and more elements of Irish social and political life were driven by differences in religion rather than ethnic or class differences, as had been the norm for most of the island's history.

The Development of Nations and Nationalism

This brief historical sketch thus reveals how identity processes functioned in early Irish history. Throughout most of this period it is impossible to define the various political and military conflicts as being between unified and distinct "English" and "Irish" nations. Political affiliation was a shifting and tenuous thing from the twelfth-century Norman invasions through the seventeenth-century Wars of Religion in England and Ireland, with political gain often outweighing religious, ethnic, and cultural distinctions. It is also still difficult to speak of the various Irish rebellions and political actions during much of this time period as being nationalistic in origin. Such actions were products instead of fragmentary and amorphous political allegiances, rarely focused on independence for the island and never involving the whole of Ireland or extending to more than various segments of the elite upper class. What we do see, however, are the very beginnings of processes that would lead to the development of distinctly Irish forms of nationalism. This development is most evident in two trends that had an important effect on the formation of true Irish nationalism in the nineteenth and twentieth centuries.

The first trend was an increasing sense of an Irish identity—that being Irish meant something significantly different from being English and that there should be some sort of Irish nation that would reflect this self-identification. What that Irish identity was, and what the Irish nation should encompass, however, were subjects of debate. Various populations in Ireland defined "Irishness" in different ways, and Gaelic Irish, Old English, and "New" English all had different conceptions of Irish identity. The differences in these conceptions of Irish identity were so profound that there were essentially three separate Irish nations operating in Ireland. The differences between these would drive much of Irish politics in the nineteenth century as all three competed for political power and influence in Ireland and England alike. Ultimately the political and social conflict and compromise between these three Irish nations, and the constituencies they represented, would shape the development of the unified Irish nation, hammering out a new definition of Irish national identity and forging a new national community that would eventually gain independence from Britain in 1922.

The second trend was an increasing reliance on religion to shape social and political boundaries in Ireland. Whereas earlier conceptions of identity in Ireland had emphasized ethnic, class, and cultural characteristics, the English Reformation and the rise of Protestantism created a new axis along which group formation could take place. Before this time, commonalities of religion between England and Ireland meant that there was no religious differentiation between the two regions, and so religion was not a politically useful category of identity. The increasingly sharp differentiation between Catholic and Protestant identities, however, made religion a far more powerful force in Irish society. From a fluid region in which various other dimensions of identity became most politically salient at different times, Ireland became a more strictly defined borderland between Catholic and Protestant cultures. Protestantism became associated with support for the British and, after the Irish Penal Laws were imposed, increasingly became the religion of the politically, socially, and economically powerful.[27] In contrast, Catholicism was associated with rebellion and poverty, as increasingly strong restrictions limited the political and economic power of Catholics of all ethnic backgrounds in Ireland. This growing social dichotomy significantly altered how people living in Ireland thought about their own identities. Increasingly religion became the salient category around which political and social movements oriented themselves.

These two crucial trends in Irish history did not always intersect, however. The three competing nations in Irish society each had their own definitions of Irishness and did not always orient themselves around religious conceptions of identity. The New English, in particular, were largely Protestant in nature and so pursued explicitly secular varieties of nationalism in an effort to maintain their standing and power in Irish society. Even the Catholic Old English and Gaelic Irish nations frequently turned to other characteristics in their respective quests for political recognition. Thus, though it became increasingly obvious that religion was an important characteristic in Ireland, and it did play an increasing role in Irish politics, not all of the myriad strands of Irish nationalist thought utilized it for group-forming and political purposes. It is only in modern mythologizing of the Irish nationalist movement that such varied groups, movements, and processes have all come to be seen as a single unified eight hundred–year quest for Irish national independence. The remainder of this chapter will consider each of these distinct national communities in turn, examining their specific and varied conceptions of what it meant to be Irish and what the Irish nation should mean. The chapter will then turn to the three distinct types of nationalist politics that the various groups in Ireland pursued throughout the nineteenth and twentieth centuries, before examining how an explicitly religious conception of the nation prevailed and subsumed political and cultural forms of nationalism within an overarching framework that viewed the quest for an Irish nation as a conflict between Catholicism and Protestantism.

MULTIPLE NATIONS, FLUID IDENTITIES

Each of the three Irish nations had a distinct way of imagining the Irish national community, and each had its own traditions, history, and definition of precisely what it meant to be Irish. These three distinct Irish nations laid the foundation for what would eventually become a unified version of Irish national identity and history. The state-building nationalism that would eventually succeed in attaining independence from the United Kingdom drew upon each of these earlier forms of national identity in different ways and to different extents, weaving together a hybrid nation and fashioning a unique cultural and national identity. These earlier versions of the Irish nation, fragmentary, conflicting, and discontinuous as they may have been, played a powerful role in shaping the discourse and ideology on which the modern nation rests.

The Gaelic Nation
The Gaelic nation arose among the descendants of some of the earliest recorded populations in Ireland, and so in that sense did have some claim to antiquity. Yet

in reality, the idea of an ancient Gaelic national identity that had existed through-out most of Irish history was a historical anachronism.[28] It was only after the arrival of a distinct "other," the ethnically distinct Normans and later the reli-giously distinct Protestant settlers, that Irish populations began to place a signifi-cant emphasis on their Gaelic roots, reaching back into antiquity for a defining characteristic around which they could differentiate themselves from invading populations and strive to craft a more unified identity and political response.

For most of its history, the Gaelic Irish nation was easy to ignore, however. Following the arrival of the various waves of English colonists, the Gaelic Irish were pushed into the poorer western regions of the island, sent "to Hell or Con-naught"[29] by the encroaching English, and politically and economically marginal-ized. Though it had a distinct cultural identity, Gaelic Ireland had little political power and little influence on the governing of the island. The formation of two distinct Irelands, one Protestant and powerful, the other Catholic and excluded from the public sphere, was reflected in the government and in class divisions in Ireland. Nevertheless, the Gaelic Irish nation has had a powerful impact on the development of modern Ireland. It is from this version of the Irish nation that modern Irish nationalism has drawn its cultural content. Modern Irish national-ism continues to view the Gaels as the ethnic core from which the modern nation has sprung.[30] Much of this is the result of a Gaelic Revival movement during the nineteenth century that sought to use Gaelic identity as a means for promoting national group solidarity and spurring popular support for the national cause.

The Old English Nation

The Old English nationality in Ireland represented a hybrid identity, combining elements of Englishness inherited from their Norman ancestors with native Irish cultural and social practices. For much of their history, the Old English consid-ered themselves Englishmen who simply happened to live in Ireland.[31] The hybrid nature of the Old English identity has led to a variety of different names for the population, including English by blood, Anglo-Irish, Old English, and simply English. Early in their history in Ireland the Old English possessed a cul-tural and ethnic background distinct from the Gaelic Irish who surrounded them, based largely on their English inheritance. By the dawn of the nineteenth century, however, these distinctions had largely faded, with the Old English picking up what had previously been thought of as Gaelic traits through pro-cesses of acculturation, compromise, and cultural fusion. This process continued to such an extent that by the nineteenth century the Old English had even become known as "more Irish than the Irish."[32] The liminal positionality of the Old English, balanced between the native Irish on one hand and the English in England on the other, led to their developing a distinctive set of cultural charac-teristics and a distinct form of national identity, religiously Catholic and thus distinct from Protestant England.

The political and economic marginalization of the Gaelic Irish made them easy to ignore for the Old English, and the Old English soon came to think of themselves as the "true" nation in Ireland. The Old English were politically powerful and played an important role in both Irish politics and those of England. Moreover, the Old English, with their political and economic dominance of most of Ireland, became accustomed to rule, and most of their political positions throughout the sixteenth and seventeenth centuries were driven by their desire to stay in control of Ireland and remain politically relevant. These efforts to stay in power were made more complicated by the English Reformation and the growing sentiment of the English crown that the Old English's Catholicism made them politically untrustworthy. The idea that *cuius regio eius religio*—the religion of the monarch should be the religion of the people—led the English in England to favor the Protestant "New English" who had been transplanted into Ireland, polarizing Irish society along religious lines and beginning the process by which the Catholic Old English and Catholic Gaelic Irish would merge in the seventeenth century, putting aside the last vestiges of ethnic and national divisions in favor of religious unity.

The Old English joined the Gaelic Irish in the rebellion of 1641, causing Rory O'More, a Gaelic Irish rebel, to argue upon meeting them, "we are of the same religion, and the same nation; our interests and sufferings are the same."[33] The oath of association between the two communities further asserted their unity, arguing "there shall be no difference between the ancient and mere Irish and the successors of English, moderne or ancient" so long as "they be professors of the holy church and maintainers of the country's liberties."[34] The tendency of the English to view all Catholics as different, most manifest in the brutality of Oliver Cromwell's forces toward both populations, further cemented this once seemingly impossible bond. This merging of nations, however, brought to Irish nationalism the political strength and belief in their right to rule that had been so characteristic of the Old English community. This belief in political independence and self-governance provided the foundation for much of the political organization and action that led to the eventual creation of the modern Irish state.

The New English

The third and final nation operating in Ireland during the early modern period was the "New English," those settlers brought over from England and Scotland and transplanted, largely into the north of Ireland, during the seventeenth century. These settlers were the ancestors of the modern unionist population in Northern Ireland that continues to claim allegiance to and solidarity with the United Kingdom. Exclusively Protestant, these settlers were brought in to serve as a new ruling class in Ireland following the Irish rebellions of the seventeenth century. The New English were settled on land that had been seized from rebellious Catholic populations, and the imposition of this new religiously other population created an immediate religious divide between the new settlers and the Gaelic and Old English populations who had previously been resident on the land. The New English received a variety of advantages from the English government and gradually took over the preeminent role in Irish society that had been occupied by the Catholic Old English.[35]

Eventually, as the Old English had before them, the New English developed a distinctly Irish sense of identity. A sense of exclusion from centers of power in England led the New English to feel marginalized, and so despite their religious similarity, Protestants in Ireland began to reinterpret their space on the edges of Englishness, crafting a new identify for themselves. The success of the Penal Laws imposed during the seventeenth century had made the Catholic populations of Ireland far less politically relevant, excluding them from the centers of power and influence.[36] Such restrictions on Catholicism caused many Protestants to believe that the Catholics themselves were ceasing to exist, dwindling into nothingness and soon to be entirely replaced by the Protestant New English. William Molyneux, for example, explained that the vast majority of the inhabitants of Ireland were descended from the British and there was "remaining but a mere handful of the ancient Irish at this day . . . not one in a thousand."[37]

If, then, Ireland was an ancient kingdom, joined to England in a political union and home of a distinctive nation, as the Old English had long argued, the "disappearance" of the Catholics in Ireland clearly meant that the Protestant community that had taken over political control of Ireland must also be heir to the nation itself. This sentiment was compounded by the spread of Enlightenment ideals of self-government and national independence that spread through Europe following the French Revolution. The combination of political power and the development of a consolidated Protestant identity in opposition to the Catholic populations led some Protestants to question Ireland's continued association with the United Kingdom. It was from the Protestant community, then, now entrenched as the political, social, and economic elites in Ireland, that the nationalist movement that eventually succeeded in attaining independence drew much of its ideology and early support. In fact, many of the earliest true nationalist leaders in Ireland were Protestants, a reality that complicates the modern Irish nationalist movement's claim to an unbroken Gaelic Catholic nation.[38]

VARIETIES OF NATIONALISM IN MODERN IRELAND

The division of Ireland into three distinctive demographic groups was reflected in the politics of nationalism that dominated the political discourse of the nineteenth and twentieth centuries. Rather than the monolithic movement that modern Republicans so proudly refer to, nationalist politics, like national identity itself in Ireland, was far more complicated and contentious. While all three varieties of nationalism had as their goal the independence of Ireland from England, they varied in the different elements of the national community on which they focused and the different conceptions of national identity that they championed. The nationalist movement that eventually succeeded in gaining independence for most of the island drew upon these competing strands of political, cultural, and religious nationalist thought, combining them into a movement that took religious identity as its salient characteristic and had broad-based appeal across the spectrum of Irish social cultural identities. Even then, this process was not a smooth one, as the Irish Civil War of 1922–1923, and even the eventual outbreak of the Troubles in Northern Ireland in 1968, all too bloodily proved. Nevertheless, the process by which these varied strands of national politics were woven together into a cohesive movement, and indeed a singular nation, that could eventually achieve its goal of nationalist self-government reveals a great deal about the process of nation formation.

Political Nationalism

Political nationalism in Ireland had its roots in the complicated relationship between England and Ireland in the late eighteenth century. While Ireland had had its own Parliament from 1297 on, it had a very limited amount of political power, a reality that frustrated the largely Anglican aristocratic class of Ireland. Statutes such as Poyning's Law, imposed by Henry VII of Britain in 1494 to ensure that the Irish Parliament could not meet until its proposed legislation had already been approved by the English monarch,[39] significantly curtailed the amount of political power the Irish were able to exercise. This arrangement was acceptable to many of the Irish aristocracy during the tumultuous sixteenth and seventeenth centuries, but the victory of the Protestant ascendancy began a transformation of political relationships in Ireland. The defeat of Catholic forces and the imposition of the Penal Laws made Old English and Gaelic Irish populations alike seem less threatening to the Protestant landowners in Ireland.[40] This newfound security was coupled with the sense among the aristocracy that Ireland was increasingly being viewed by the English as a colony, a status that was intolerable to a population that still considered themselves English, even if a distinctly Irish strand of Englishmen.[41] Unlike a colony, they argued, Ireland had its own Parliament and courts and, in the words of Anglican Member of Parliament Henry Grattan, Ireland "had . . . all the weight and dignity of a respectable and free nation, long before its connection with England."[42] Thus believing their positions to finally be secure, protected from the dangers of Catholic rebellion, Protestants in Ireland began to chafe at the political restrictions and colonial attitudes inherent in the relationship between England and Ireland, which threatened their security from an entirely different angle. Nevertheless, the Protestants in Ireland were very clear about their political goals. While they desired legislative independence for the Irish nation, by which they meant exclusively Anglican Protestant landlords, they sought to achieve it within constitutional means, gaining self-legislation but remaining subjects of, and eminently loyal to, the English crown.[43]

Notable Protestants such as Jonathan Swift, Henry Flood, and William Molyneux had spoken out earlier against the political system that subordinated Ireland to the whims of England,[44] but it was under Grattan that the Irish Patriot movement, as it came to be called, achieved its greatest success. The departure of British troops for America during the American War for Independence, and the consequential threat of invasion by the French, led to the formation of a powerful militia in Ireland. Originally intended to protect the island, these Irish Volunteers, as they were known, soon took on a second purpose. With the absence of a regular garrison of English troops, the Irish Volunteers had a significant amount of power, and Grattan and other political nationalists from the Irish Patriot party used them as a bargaining tool to pressure the English into relinquishing some political power to the Irish Parliament. Such efforts resulted in the Constitution of 1782, a series of legal changes that gave the Irish Parliament much more control of the island and led Grattan to declare the independence of the Irish Parliament and the establishment of a free Irish nation.[45]

Grattan's independent Parliament was to be short lived, however, as the actions of another segment of Irish political nationalists led the English to impose far stricter control over Ireland. Despite the concessions by the English government in 1782, political power in Ireland was still restricted to a relatively small segment of the landed aristocracy. Catholics were still largely excluded from the political process, as were smaller dissident Protestant groups such as Presbyterians and Methodists in the north of Ireland. Inspired by French revolutionary ideology, a group of Anglican liberals from the ruling aristocratic class gathered together with Catholics and members of smaller Protestant minorities to found the Society of United Irishmen in 1791.[46] To the United Irishmen, the Parliamentary reforms won by the Grattanites did not go nearly far enough, and they advocated reformation of property-based political laws that restricted voting rights to a small clique of the wealthiest landowners, and for true independence for Ireland from British interference.

The Society of United Irishmen was conceived of as being explicitly antisectarian, incorporating members from all religious and social orientations, placing significant emphasis on overcoming the traditional schisms in Irish society and uniting to achieve separation from English control. Indeed, this independence was the movement's chief concern, for as they argued, "We have no national government; we are ruled by Englishmen, and thus servants of Englishmen, whose object is the interest of another country, whose instrument is corruption; whose strength is the weakness of Ireland."[47] A short-lived rebellion managed to galvanize popular support for the cause, but to negative effect for nationalists. After bloodily crushing the rebellion, the English government passed the Acts of

Union in 1800, dissolving the Irish Parliament and officially unifying the two separate kingdoms into the United Kingdom of Great Britain and Ireland.[48]

The union between Britain and Ireland served as the focus for political nationalism throughout the nineteenth century. Successive waves of repeal movements, with varying levels of support from Protestants and Catholics alike, sought to dissolve the union and reacquire the short-lived gains made under Grattan's Parliament.[49] Though there were various attempts to achieve independence throughout the early nineteenth century, the Home Rule movement reached its most powerful state during the 1870s and 1880s under the leadership of Charles Stewart Parnell. A Protestant landlord from the wealthy aristocratic class, Parnell nevertheless forged an alliance between the poor agrarian-focused Irish National Land League and the more upper-class and constitutionally focused Home Rule League, forming a new Irish Parliamentary Party that was largely Catholic in membership. This party dominated Irish politics from 1880 on, succeeding in getting several Home Rule bills introduced in the British Parliament. The key issue for Home Rule, as always in Irish political nationalism, was how to bring together the disparate populations that remained divided along religious, social, and economic lines.

It was largely Parnell's own charisma and strength of will that molded these disparate elements into a cohesive political movement during this period. Parnell was able to accomplish this by speaking to the agrarian Catholics and landholding Protestants alike, laying out a political program that placed allegiance to the nationalist cause over the sectarian differences that had long plagued Irish society. This was helped along by the rise of a Catholic middle class in Ireland and a subsequent decline in class tensions between Catholics and Protestants. The solution to fully forging these disparate populations into a focused movement, however, was found, as ever in Irish politics, in antipathy to England. Though the various populations operating in Ireland could often not always agree on who or what the Irish nation should be, political nationalism combined "that hearty contempt for the English establishment that any well-connected Irish Protestant worth his salt was capable of harbouring,"[50] a legacy of marginalization and exclusion from the power centers of England, with the sense of "this great racial conflict, which has been going on so long, which began in blood and suffering 700 years ago, and has continued through seven centuries of oppression and misery"[51] harbored by Catholic populations.

Efforts at political nationalism, then, sought to place Enlightenment ideals of liberalism and self-governance at the forefront of Irish political thought. As John Hutchinson has argued, the goal of political nationalists was not about distinctiveness or creating a unique cultural identity, but was instead about achieving equality with the British and gaining citizenship rights within the United Kingdom.[52] Such efforts were often explicitly antisectarian, calling on all members of the Irish nation to unite in service of the nationalist cause. As we have previously seen, however, definitions of the Irish nation differed widely among the various populations present in nineteenth-century Ireland. Many of the earliest efforts at political nationalism were sponsored by members of the Protestant elite in Ireland, and the reforms they sought applied only to the rights of the Protestant upper class.[53] To members of the Anglican Church of Ireland, they were the true inheritors of the ancient and illustrious nation of Ireland, secure in their belief that the Catholic population of Ireland was both politically irrelevant and numerically disappearing. It was only with the rise of Parnell in the late nineteenth century that some of these divisions in Irish society began to break down. Product of declining social stratification in Ireland and a recognition that nationalism could only succeed with the participation of the growing Catholic middle class, this alliance was finally able to make substantial progress toward national independence.

Cultural Nationalism

The second type of nationalism operating in Ireland during the eighteenth and nineteenth centuries was culturally focused. While cultural nationalists in Ireland, like their political nationalist counterparts, did strive for Irish independence, they did so in a very different way. As John Hutchinson has argued, the key characteristic of cultural nationalism is that it is a romantic movement that places a heavy emphasis on the need for cultural regeneration of national moral character rather than liberal values of equality and self-governance.[54] Efforts such as these had their genesis in the upper classes of Irish society and rarely extended beyond the elites of society. Instead, cultural nationalists seized on key national symbols, "chosen specifically on pragmatic grounds to objectively affirm a specific vision of historical continuity and to differentiate the group from others."[55]

Cultural nationalists use symbolic markers of identity such as language, religion, dress, and visual imagery to draw connections between the modern nation and the halcyon days of a distant antique past when the nation was morally pure. As Hutchinson has argued, this preoccupation with the past does not necessarily make cultural nationalists regressive, as other scholars have argued.[56] Instead, he explains, "cultural nationalists act as *moral innovators*, establishing ideological movements at times of social crisis in order to transform the belief-systems of communities, and provide models of sociopolitical development that guide their modernizing strategies."[57] And indeed, a process of moral innovation was necessary for Irish Protestants who wished to achieve nationhood. The union of Britain and Ireland had a secondary effect of ending any claim that Protestants in Ireland had to having a nation of their own. Protestant nationalism had long been based on the assertion that Ireland was an ancient and independent kingdom, and thus its inhabitants should be allowed to govern themselves. The dissolution of that kingdom, and its absorption into the rest of the United Kingdom, meant that while Protestants could continue to be nationalists, they would have to base their claim to independence on something new, that Ireland represented a distinct *culture*, not just an ancient *kingdom*.

In Ireland, the development of a distinctively cultural form of nationalism took place in three phases. The first of these arose during the mid-eighteenth century and was primarily an elite movement among Protestant intellectuals. This movement placed a heavy emphasis on the revival of the Gaelic Irish language, and sought to return the island to what cultural nationalists saw as its primordial cultural roots as a holy island, inhabited by ancient heroes, scholars, and religious figures. Once again it was the English government's treatment of the various populations of Ireland that spurred the formation and consolidation of a distinct Irish identity, even among those in Ireland who still considered themselves politically and ethnically connected to England. Throughout the eighteenth century and into the nineteenth, the Protestant population of Ireland was an unsettled and insecure one, caught between the two poles of English and Irish cultural identities and not fully accepted by either of them. Considered Irish in England and English in Ireland, the Protestants had a very weak sense of ethnic identity, formed in opposition to the various other populations of the British Isles but not fully secure in their own ethnic and cultural heritage. The growing sense during the eighteenth century that Ireland was becoming little more than a colony, dominated by the economic and colonial interests of the English, and moreover that the Protestant population of Ireland was slowly losing its privileged position as true Englishmen and being lumped in with the "uncivilized" Catholics who comprised the rest of the Irish population, spurred a new sense of nationalism and identity formation among the Protestant elites. The rise of cultural nationalism among the Protestants of Ireland was thus an effort to reclaim a distinct, if ahistorical and constructed, sense of identity, drawing upon images of a golden age of the Irish past and the distinctiveness of Gaelic culture and language in their adopted country.

The second wave of cultural nationalism in Ireland took place during the 1830s, once again spurred on by elite Protestant intellectuals. This wave of cultural revivalism got its start among small scholarly societies that championed the historical, anthropological, and archaeological study of early Irish populations. The proponents of this scholarly study had more extensive motivations than simply creating an accurate scientific reconstruction of the Irish past. Rather, the cultural nationalists of the 1830s also felt "a deeper *moral* imperative to recover all aspects of the Irish experiences as a coherent identity in space and time, and to recreate it as a living reality in the present."[58] Instead of the ancient history of the pagan Gaelic past, however, this second wave of cultural nationalists, led by figures such as George Petrie and Samuel Ferguson, placed an emphasis on the early Middle Ages, when Ireland played a key role in the survival and growth of Christian values and classical learning.[59] This period predated the origins of the religious and political schism that dominated Ireland in the nineteenth century, and so was a shared cultural and religious legacy on which the various factions of Irish society could compromise and take national pride. Indeed, created as it was by Protestant intellectuals, the target of this wave of cultural nationalism was not the Catholic population of Ireland but the Protestant landlords and educated strata. "As the natural leaders of Irish society . . . Protestants, like previous settlers in Ireland, were to be persuaded to attach themselves to Irish sentiments and to assume their proper responsibilities for Ireland's social and economic development."[60]

This effort was bolstered by the actions of a group dubbed "Young Ireland," led primarily by Thomas Davis and John Blake Dillon. Fervent supporters of the effort to repeal the Acts of Union, the Young Irelanders founded their own newspaper, *The Nation*. The Young Irelanders also ought to bring together the Protestant minority and Catholic majority through focusing on the idea of Ireland as a distinct cultural and historical civilization. The Young Ireland movement remained primarily a small intellectual and elite one and placed an emphasis on propaganda and literature, as an unsigned editorial in *The Nation*, widely regarded as the movement's manifesto, argued "a legion of writers was more formidable than a thousand men all clad in steel."[61] Nevertheless, the Young Irelanders sparked a small, and ultimately unsuccessful, violent revolution of their own in 1848, drawing strength from the series of popular uprisings across Europe in 1848 and calling upon the Catholic peasantry to throw off the shackles of the Irish social structure.[62] The rebellion was doomed from the start and was quickly crushed, but the revolutionary ideology and the culturally focused rhetoric that the Young Irelanders managed to disseminate throughout Irish society would provide a powerful base for further nationalist efforts in Ireland.

The third and final wave of cultural nationalism in Ireland took place during the last few decades of the nineteenth century and the first few of the twentieth and has come to be known as the Gaelic Revival. The first two waves of cultural nationalism succeeded in drawing cultural and historical concerns to the attention of the elite in Ireland, and this new focus was evident in the profusion of culturally oriented societies that proliferated during the last half of the nineteenth century. The Society for the Preservation of the Irish Language (SPIL), founded in 1876, the Gaelic Athletic Association (GAA) in 1884, the Irish Literary and National Literary Societies in 1891 and 1892, the Gaelic League in 1893, and the Irish Literary Theatre in 1899 all played important roles in promoting different elements of traditional Irish culture. Such efforts were designed to highlight and develop a distinctly Irish cultural identity that would draw sharp boundaries between Irishness and Englishness, marking out a cultural sphere in which the Irish themselves could develop a national community. Though largely secular in origin, and still supported by members of the Protestant elite, cultural nationalism became more closely intertwined with, and eventually taken over by, issues of religion. It was religious nationalism, drawing upon the cultural

distinctiveness supplied by the Gaelic Revival and the political goals championed by political nationalists, that finally succeeded in achieving national independence for most of Ireland.

Religious Nationalism

As we have already seen, religious differences became an important political
concern in Ireland after the English Reformation, but did not truly become the
central organizing characteristic of group and nation formation in Ireland until
the Cromwellian invasion of Ireland in 1648 and the imposition of the Irish Penal
Laws restricting Catholic rights in the late seventeenth and early eighteenth centuries. Such actions polarized identity formation in Ireland, making religious
orientation an identifying characteristic for most of the Irish populace. Differentiating segments of society in this way also set the stage for the first stirrings of
Catholic organization as poor agrarian Catholics banded together in various
associations, societies, and peasant organizations that sought to defend Catholics against the depredations of the Protestant ascendancy. As Boyce has argued,
agrarian societies of this sort were not terribly political, and certainly not nationalist, but in the heightened atmosphere of sectarian and class tension that accompanied the polarization of Irish society, such groups provided the foundation for
revolutions in Irish society that were still to come.

It was around the issue of Catholic emancipation, not Irish separatism, that a
religiously oriented political movement in Ireland first achieved significant
power. In 1823 Catholic lawyer Daniel O'Connell established the Catholic Association, an organization dedicated to repealing many of the restrictions on
Catholic rights, especially those banning Catholics from serving in the British
Parliament. In a stroke of genius, the Catholic Association, which in its early
years drew its membership from the middle class and elite, opened its doors to
poor Catholics as well, charging membership fees of only a penny a month.[63]
This change in policy made the Catholic Association one of the first mass membership political organizations in European history, and significantly broadened
the emancipation movement's support base. Policies such as this sought to make
the Catholic Association a movement for every Catholic, not merely the wealthy
elite, and heightened the tendency to view both politics and group identity in
religious terms. Led by the tremendous personal charisma and political acumen
of O'Connell, the Catholic emancipation movement achieved great success, and
a series of laws passed in 1828 and 1829 walked back many of the most important
political restrictions on Catholics.[64]

The Home Rule movement too, though sparked by political nationalism and
led by a Protestant, took on an increasingly religious dimension. Under Charles
Stewart Parnell, for example, it was generally clear that though Parnell was himself a Protestant, he "represented, in fact if not in name, the Catholic nation."[65]
The repeal of the Penal Laws significantly improved the lives of Catholics in Ire-

land and the growth of a wealthy Catholic middle class during the second half of the nineteenth century as the region recovered from the devastating effects of the Great Irish Famine further empowered the Catholic population. This growing prosperity and the concomitant rise in education levels, literacy, and land-ownership among the rural populations of Ireland was significant enough to be termed a genuine social revolution[66] and transformed the face of Irish society and politics alike. This new economic base allowed Catholics to have much more of a say in Irish politics and significantly strengthened the Home Rule movement. Yet at the same time, the horrifying effects of the Irish famine contributed to a growing sense of discontent among poor and wealthy Catholics alike, who viewed the English as responsible for much suffering in Ireland.[67] This was compounded by the failure of repeated efforts to pass a Home Rule bill for Ireland in the British Parliament, and these two sources of antipathy combined to spark a radical version of nationalism that would combine political and cultural elements under the aegis of a mystical millenarian religious movement that would culminate in the violent Easter Rising of 1916.

The Easter Rising and the movement that led to it were explicitly religious. While earlier revolutions in Ireland had been largely the work of the Protestant minority, the Easter Rising of 1916 was essentially a revolution driven by, and for the benefit of, the Catholic nation. The Easter Rising was led by nationalists who were all Catholics, and many of them placed a higher emphasis on religion than had previous revolutionaries. Indeed, the rise of an entirely Catholic-led movement like the Easter Rising reveals the extent to which Catholic Ireland had developed. Though the movement incorporated earlier Protestant nationalist ideals, Catholics had gained enough political and social power to mobilize on their own; they no longer needed Protestant leaders to speak for them. The ideology that shaped it combined nationalism and mystical religiosity in an entirely new way. The Easter Rising is thus still seen as a watershed moment in Irish history. While the rebellion itself was largely unsuccessful, and in fact was quite small and was denounced by much of the Irish populace, it served as a catalyst for a much larger popular movement. The English crushed the Easter Rising and executed fifteen of its leaders shortly thereafter. These executions infuriated the Irish people, stirred up popular discontent against the English, and created new heroic martyrs for the Irish nationalist cause.[68]

Chief among the leaders and ideologues of the Easer Rising was Patrick Pearse, a teacher and political activist who drew upon the tradition of earlier nationalists in his arguments. Pearse's vision was one that combined the political focus of the United Irishmen with the cultural emphasis of the Young Irelanders, but subordinated both of these to a sort of sacralized version of Irish history, elevating nationalism and the quest for a Catholic Irish nation to a holy calling. At first glance, this seems an odd marriage of Catholicism with what had often been secular, or even anti-Catholic, political and cultural ideas. Indeed, the ideology that Pearse relied upon was largely Anglo-Protestant in origin.[69] To Pearse, however, such ideas were not contradictory to the religious faith that played an important role in his ideology. Rather, Pearse viewed the entire spectrum of nationalist agitating in Ireland as being in service to a single goal: the creation of a distinct Irish nation-state that would be politically independent, culturally Gaelic, and religiously Catholic.

In service of this goal, Pearse created a new form of mystical nationalism that fused religious belief with belief in the nation-state. Indeed, Pearse argued that devotion to the nation and devotion to religion are of the same order, for patriotism is "a faith which is of the same nature as religious faith."[70] In his writings Pearse fluidly combined these two ideas, effortlessly moving back and forth between religious and nationalist thought. In one pamphlet Pearse described the future that awaited Ireland after his rebellion, saying: "Let no man be mistaken as to who will be lord in Ireland when Ireland is free. The people will be lord and master. The people who wept in Gethsemane, who trod the sorrowful way, who died naked on a cross, who went down into hell, will rise again glorious and immortal, will sit on the right hand of God, who will come in the end to give judgment, a judge just and terrible."[71] Here, then, is a vision of the Irish nation that is explicitly religious in its rhetoric: oppressed Ireland, like the Christ she worshiped, would rise again in power. And it is the Irish people, the vast majority of whom were Catholic, that would hold power, not the Protestant elite.

Pearse and his colleagues timed their rebellion to coincide with Easter week, symbolically linking the revival of the Irish nation with the resurrection of Jesus.[72] The rebels succeeded in seizing key parts of Dublin and proclaimed the founding of an Irish Republic on April 24,[73] but were quickly overwhelmed by the superior numbers and armament of the British army and surrendered unconditionally six days later. Pearse and fourteen of the other leaders of the short-lived movement, including his brother Willie Pearse and famed Irish socialist James Connolly, were executed less than two weeks after surrendering. Yet in death, the leaders of the Easter Rising fulfilled another dimension of Pearse's eschatology. For much of his career Pearse had been obsessed with the heroic figures from earlier Irish nationalism, rebels such as Wolfe Tone, Robert Emmett, even the mythical ancient figure Cú Chulainn, who gave their lives for the cause of the Irish nation.[74] To Pearse the ghosts of these national martyrs called out for action, demanding that succeeding generations of Irish nationalists take up the cause. "There is only one way to appease a ghost," he argued; "you must do the thing it asks you. The ghosts of a nation sometimes ask very big things; and they must be appeased at whatever the cost."[75] Through their deaths in the Easter Rising, a rebellion they surely knew they could not survive, Pearse and his compatriots produced a new generation of ghosts, one far more immediate, memorable, and demanding than the revolutionaries of Ireland's past. And it was the presence and memory of these ghosts that drove the movement that would finally gain independence for much of Ireland and shaped the creation of the Irish nation-state.

The events of the Easter Rising and the sacrifice of Pearse and his comrades would have lasting repercussions in Ireland. The execution of the Easter Rising leaders caused a mass shift in public opinion that bolstered the nationalist cause and reinvigorated calls for Home Rule that had been put on hold following the outbreak of World War I.[76] People flocked in droves to a new nationalist party, Sinn Féin, and popular opinion shifted from support for a constitutional approach to nationalism to a physical force version of Irish republicanism that advocated violent revolution. In 1919 Sinn Féin won a landslide electoral victory and proclaimed a breakaway Irish Republic.[77] This result soon escalated into guerrilla warfare, as the newly formed Irish Republican Army struck out against British troops and members of the Royal Irish Constabulary in Ireland. This Irish War of Independence endured until 1921, when the British and Irish governments agreed to a treaty that would see the creation of the independent Irish Free State. This was not quite the victory that hard-liner Irish nationalists had in mind, however, for a provision of the Anglo-Irish treaty allowed Northern Ireland to break away from the Irish Free State and remain part of the United Kingdom.[78] While Protestants in Northern Ireland saw this as a victory, the Catholic response was split. Critically, the borders of Northern Ireland were established by a boundary commission that utilized religion as a key category of identification when partitioning the island. The boundary commission crafted the borders of Northern Ireland in such a way as to carve out the maximum amount of territory while still maintaining a Protestant majority, a critical concern for Protestants in Northern Ireland, who feared absorption into the Catholic-dominated Irish Free State.[79] The agreement let to a debate between the pro-treaty movement, which saw the independence of most of Ireland as worth sacrificing the north, and the anti-treaty movement, which refused to settle for anything less than an independent Ireland that encompassed the entire island. On this issue, the Catholic nationalist movement fractured, separating into competing factions based on political ideology.

While the Anglo-Irish treaty was officially nonsectarian, its provisions utilized religious orientation as a key ordering characteristic to determine membership in the two newly formed countries. The religious character of Ireland was further cemented by the leadership of the newly formed Irish Free State. Irish popular opinion was deeply divided by the provisions of the Anglo-Irish treaty that allowed Northern Ireland to secede, and acceptance of the treaty sparked a civil war between pro-treaty and anti-treaty forces in Ireland. The pro-treaty forces prevailed, and Michael Collins, a pro-treaty leader who had risen to prominence in the political vacuum that followed the execution of the Easter Rising's leaders, drew upon religion in an effort to heal the rifts between Catholic nationalists in the Irish Free State. Collins did this by turning the combatants' attention to the situation in the north, encouraging Catholic guerrilla resistance against the Protestant leadership in Northern Ireland, throwing Free State support behind the rebels and framing the conflict in religious terms. Such efforts aimed to reunite nationalist Catholics in the south "under the sign of a common and ancient hostility to the Ulster protestants"[80] and further highlighted the Irish Free State's Catholic identity, in opposition to Protestant Ulster, as a means of enhancing group cohesion, creating "the self" through conflict with "the other."

The identification of the Irish state with Catholicism was furthered under the leadership of Eamon de Valera, leader of the anti-treaty forces of the civil war and one of the most prominent survivors of the Easter Rising.[81] De Valera continued to denounce the partition of Ireland, and in a series of fiery speeches made a powerful appeal to Catholic nationalism, characterizing his opposition to the partition as an argument against alienating and giving away the sovereignty of the Catholics in Northern Ireland.[82] And indeed it was de Valera's version of Irish nationalism, rooted in the mystical religion of Pearse's millenarianism, that would play the most important role in shaping the Irish state. In 1937, as leader of the Irish government, de Valera oversaw the drafting and implementation of a new Irish constitution. This constitution, which established the modern Republic of Ireland, placed a heavy emphasis on the primacy of the Catholic religion and the importance of the Catholic Church for Irish national identity. The constitution explains that "The State recognises the special position of the Holy Catholic Apostolic and Roman Church as the guardian of the Faith professed by the great majority of the citizens."[83]

For much of its history, the Irish Republic's laws have continued to conform to Catholic teachings.[84] As one sociologist has put it, "Ireland may never have come close to being a theocratic state, but the Church's influence . . . meant that it came very close to being a theocratic society."[85] The population of the Irish state, too, became more Catholic following its independence. Those Protestants who were not part of the partitioned Northern Ireland often emigrated from the republic, fearing to live in a state that was overwhelmingly Catholic in nature. The result was that Protestants, who made up 12 percent of the Irish Free State when it came into being, have dropped to about 3 percent of the population today[86] and played far less of a role in independent Ireland than their predecessors had under the Union. Even today, though the republic has shown recent signs of growing secularism, Ireland remains one of the most religious nations in Western Europe.[87] The cultural reach of religion in Ireland is still such that to be "Irish" is to be seen as to be "Catholic," a melding of religious and national identification that owes its existence to centuries of development in Irish nationalism and concerted efforts among Irish nationalists to make Catholic identity the salient characteristic and central focus of Irish national identity.

CONCLUSIONS

This chapter has examined the evolution of nationalism in Ireland, tracing its development from the earliest stirrings of resistance in the twelfth century through the independence of most of the island in 1922 and into the social structure of the modern state that it founded. What this longue durée analysis reveals is a gradual crystallization of national identity in Ireland, a homogenization in which the panoply of different nations, movements, and types of nationalism that have been present at various times in Ireland's long history gradually were subsumed under the umbrella of religious nationalism. The nationalism that prevailed in Ireland drew upon a variety of elements on which earlier versions of nationalism had focused and incorporated them, subordinating them to a vision of the nation that equated national identity with Catholicism. This analysis adds nuance to the popular view of the relationship between religion, ethnicity, and nation in Ireland, revealing all of these phenomena as relational and processual, rather than static social forms. Rather than an easy conflation of Catholics as nationalists and Protestants as unionists, this analysis reveals that such constellations of identities are the product of focused boundary-making processes that draw upon various categories of collective identity in an effort to construct a singular and cohesive national identity.

In Ireland's case the process of national boundary formation took many forms among many populations over the centuries as various groups sought to achieve independence and self-governance. In every case, however, what it meant to be a member of the Irish nation was defined in contrast to Englishness. Even those settlers and descendants of settlers who came from England in waves, Old English Catholics and New English Protestants alike, quickly began to develop their own definitions of Irish national identity, conceiving of themselves as something distinctively different, even while maintaining nominal attachments to the rest of England. In later years, these differences began to sharpen, a product of growing discontent over centuries of British rule and misrule of Ireland. In this, the development of Irish nationalism fits well within the boundary-making approach to identity. Though ethnic and national boundaries were drawn and redrawn in Ireland to accommodate different populations at different times, focusing on a wide variety of political and cultural criteria to determine membership in the nation, that nation was always conceived in opposition to the cultural and political threat posed by the English nation.

By the nineteenth century a common sense of nationalism and national identity began to develop in Ireland. This identity drew inspiration from a variety of nationalist efforts and the categories of identity on which they focused, defining the Irish nation as politically independent, culturally Gaelic, and religiously Catholic. In this identity, the Irish nationalist movement placed the most powerful emphasis on religion, using the shared Catholic faith of the Irish population as a crucial characteristic to draw a firm boundary between Catholic Ireland and Protestant England. While nationalist efforts emphasizing political and cultural facets of Irish identity found minor levels of success, Irish nationalism became its most powerful as a mass movement only when rising standards of living afforded Catholics the political and economic power to get involved in the movement. When this finally occurred in the nineteenth century, Catholic Ireland began producing its own nationalist leaders, ones who would rally mass support to the nationalist cause by emphasizing the explicitly Catholic nature of Irish identity. It was this change to a version of Irish nationalism and national identity, which articulated class, ethnic, and national differences in explicitly religious terms and constructed a specifically religious view of the national community, that allowed nationalists in Ireland to rally mass support for their movement and finally achieve independence for most of the island.

This chapter has challenged some of the levels of "groupism" Brubaker identifies in the study of nationalism and ethnicity[88] by problematizing the facile connection between "Catholic" and "nationalist" in Ireland, revealing the fluid and processual nature of the nationalist movement as it developed over time, eventually taking on a religious character. Yet in many ways, this chapter continued to speak of social formations in the very same groupist terms I criticize, drawing sharp distinctions between types of nations and various ethnic, religious, and national groups operating in Ireland. Breaking down such assumed groups by examining how nationalism became religious in Ireland does only half the work of understanding religious nationalism as a social, cultural, and political project. Similarly, emphasizing elite efforts to rally support for various versions of nationalism and national identity omits the lived experience of the mass population that was the target of these efforts. It is to these two issues that the next chapter will turn. In this, the next chapter seeks to break such constructions down even further, examining what Catholicism and nationalism meant on a common quotidian basis, how such formulations operated in everyday life, and the conditions under which Catholicism and other forms of identity did, or did not, became politically salient at various times in the lives of the Irish population.

3 · RELIGION ON THE GROUND

Everyday Catholicism and National
Identity in Ireland

Elite efforts at nation formation are certainly important, but they do not always capture the nuanced nature of national and religious identification on the ground level. This chapter seeks to broaden the scope of analysis to examine how common people in Ireland, both south and north, conceived of the relationship between being Irish and being religious. This chapter thus takes a social historical approach, drawing on sources produced by common people who were forced to negotiate shifting political and social circumstances, to examine the social complexity of identity in Ireland and Northern Ireland. Such sources provide a wealth of insights into the relationship between different facets of identity, among them religion, ethnicity, and nationalism, and how people understood their own senses of self. Ultimately, it was the confluence and interaction of these distinct facets of identity that helped shape the development of national identity in Ireland. The relationship between religion, ethnicity, and nationalism, and the consequent negotiation of identity that their interaction entailed was most visible during periods of strife, situations in which people were forced to reexamine and reconceptualize their own identities and their membership in a variety of social groups. These periods of strife represent several distinct watershed time periods and events in which common conceptions of ethnic, national, and religious identity were put under significant strain. Periods such as this constitute what Isaac Ariail Reed has identified in different contexts as moments of structural breakdown, where social institutions and organizations are challenged, leading to a wholesale reconsideration of how people interpret the world around them.[1]

In the case of Ireland, the nineteenth century provided a whole series of such moments of structural breakdown. It was during this time period that conceptualizations of Irish national and religious identity began to cohere. The last chapter reveals a much more complicated relationship between Irish nationalism and

Catholicism than popular narratives have allowed. Rather, Irish nationalism has in many ways been a response to conceptions of religious difference and the desire for religious self-rule. Moreover, neither "Irishness" nor "Catholicism" was the sort of overarching and homogeneous category that is often assumed by analysts seeking to understand religion's role in nationalist movements. It wasn't until the transformative events of the nineteenth century, including political agitation, famine, revival, war, and revolution, that Irish nationalism truly took on the Catholic character that has come to define the movement.

This chapter will examine how common people's processes of identification and identify formation responded to several of the most important of these moments of structural breakdown, times in which the relationship between religion and social identity took on new or changing significance in the lives of Irish populations. This chapter thus represents what William Sewell Jr. has described as an "eventful sociology" that emphasizes historical context as motivation for social action.[2] It will start with the mass political movements for Catholic emancipation and repeal of the Acts of Union sponsored by Daniel O'Connell. We then turn to the catastrophic but transformative effects of the Great Famine, before examining the cultural focus of the Gaelic Revival and the 1916 Easter Rising that followed close behind. In this I take a more cultural approach, examining the types of writings, produced by common and elite writers alike, that spoke directly to the experiences of populations in Ireland who were working to construct new conceptualizations of Irish identity and to reconcile those conceptions with their Catholic and Protestant faiths. Finally, we turn to religion and nationalism after the Republic of Ireland's 1922 independence and the corresponding partition of Ireland, examining how decreased tension and threat eventually led to a slow decline in religion as a fundamental aspect of identity in the Republic of Ireland, while at the same time becoming an issue of life or death in Northern Ireland, where tensions between Catholics and Protestants living in close proximity have routinely erupted into intercommunal conflict and violence. At each rupture, it becomes clear that for the majority of the Irish people, conceptions of social and national identity have been explicitly mediated in religious terms. Yet this conflation of national identity with religion was not inevitable. Rather, this phenomenon was the result of specific historical circumstances, patterns of identification and organization structured by social and political contexts.

Though materials from early Irish history mostly attest to the experiences and concerns of the elite, the nineteenth century saw a significant growth in literacy rates as well as an expansion of national ideals and a sense of membership in the nation beyond the boundaries of the landowning elite.[3] Popular politics and the growth of both Catholic emancipation and economic reform movements among the lower classes brought political ideals to new audiences, and with them a profusion of new forms of political ephemera, speeches, and writings. This is especially true from the middle of the nineteenth century on, when radically changing social conditions brought about by the Great Famine and its aftermath transformed Irish society, culture, and politics. The trauma of the famine led to new notions of religion and society alike and sparked the production of oral histories and memoirs that shed important light on the ways that people conceptualized their national, religious, and social identities. Even where such evidence doesn't survive, reports on mass politics and statistics relating to religion and politics reveal a great deal about how people conceptualized the various facets of their identity. The Gaelic Revival in the late nineteenth century marked a further transformation of Irish society, one focused on cultural regeneration and recovery from both English imperialism and societal trauma alike. Irish writers produced a profusion of cultural works: literature, poetry, songs, and plays that spoke to mass audiences and reflected much of the reality of everyday life in Ireland.

It was during this nineteenth-century period of imperialism, decline, recovery, and regeneration that the most important conceptions of the relationship between Irish nationalism and the Catholic religion were forged. Such conceptions proved enormously influential in the Irish separatist movement that eventually succeeded in achieving independence for what would become the Republic of Ireland, with the formation of the Irish Free State in 1922. Similarly, understandings of identity forged during this time period would play an important role in the creation of Northern Ireland, which remained part of the United Kingdom after the partition of the island. Here, too, religious definitions of the nation would remain powerful, setting the stage for decades of internecine conflict between Catholics and Protestants seeking control of the Northern Irish state. In Northern Ireland, as in the Republic of Ireland, religious belief and debates over the meaning of ethnic, national, and religious identity served as inspiration for a wide variety of cultural and political works that speak to complicated efforts to forge groups, communities, and movements. In the Northern Ireland case, such efforts were intimately intertwined with similar efforts in the Republic of Ireland, as Northern Irish nationalists worked to create political and cultural narratives linking their own Catholic population to the greater movement for Irish independence and the Republic of Ireland's successful independence movement.

MASS POLITICS IN NINETEENTH-CENTURY IRELAND

While religion played a powerful role in the lives of the Irish population much earlier, it was not until the nineteenth century that the religious schisms that characterized Irish society gave birth to the type of mass consciousness and political action that are typically considered characteristic of a true nationalist movement. England's conversion to Protestantism in the sixteenth century and the seesaw battles among English monarchs that accompanied the transition made the debate over religion an issue of prominent concern in Ireland. As the last chapter discussed, these tensions were codified by the end of the seventeenth century, with the passing of the Irish Penal Laws, legislation designed to systematically advantage the small population of Protestants in Ireland over the interests of the majority Catholics. While this alienated both the indigenous Irish population and the wealthy Catholic Anglo-Irish landlords, little was done to advocate for their repeal for nearly a century. The harsh nature of the Penal Laws meant that religion served a structural role in Irish society, determining social position, life chances, and the ability to participate in a variety of economic, social, and political processes. Nevertheless, Catholicism did not seem to serve as an organizing element of social identity, failing to outweigh elements such as social class for most of the society. Wealthy Anglo-Irish landlords had little save religion in common with the impoverished agricultural laboring class that worked their fields, and ideals of Catholic solidarity or a nationalism based on religious similarity seem not to have penetrated much into Irish Catholic society. Indeed, for much of this time, ideas of nationalism, political independence, or even religious equality seem not to have penetrated into the mass of the Irish working poor at all, as low literacy rates and hardscrabble conditions meant that most Irish peasants had little access to, or time for, such lofty ideas.

This situation changed with the rise to power of Daniel O'Connell, an Irish Catholic lawyer whose religion disqualified him from rising high in the bar or attaining a judgeship. As early as law school, O'Connell had been involved in political agitation, and as a lawyer he made a name as a passionate defender of those accused of political crimes, including revolutionaries who sought equal rights for Catholics and Irish in the British political system. O'Connell segued from law to politics in the first several decades of the nineteenth century and founded a series of organizations, first the Catholic Board, then the Catholic Association, and finally the Repeal Association, designed to first appeal for rights for Catholics and then to agitate for repeal of the Acts of Union that had officially established Ireland's membership in the United Kingdom. It was in these organizations that O'Connell first brought about the advent of mass politics. O'Connell's decision to court the great, largely apolitical, mass of Catholic Irish capitalized on the slow growth of a fledgling Catholic middle class that was managing to prosper despite the effects of the Penal Laws.[4]

But O'Connell's ambitions reached even beyond them, seeking to mobilize the agrarian peasant class who constituted a majority of the population but had never had much say in political decisions of any kind. O'Connell's decision to charge membership dues of only a penny a month for entrance into the Catholic Association allowed even poor farmers the opportunity to be involved in what would become a significant movement.[5] With the money gathered from this "Catholic Rent" and proof of the vast support for Catholic emancipation in the number of people registered on its rolls, O'Connell's Catholic Association successfully agitated for increased rights for Catholic members of the population.

After years of political wrangling and maneuvering, the Catholic Association was able to achieve the repeal of most of the onerous requirements of the Penal Laws in 1829. Crucially, the Association's success in achieving equal rights for Catholics, including the opportunity for Catholics to sit in the British Parliament without swearing an oath of allegiance to the Church of England, served as proof positive of the power that mass political organizing could have. O'Connell, seizing the opportunity, capitalized on this support and his strong personal popularity to push for greater freedom for Ireland, to accompany the rights for Irish Catholics he had already achieved. It was in this effort, led by O'Connell's Loyal National Repeal Association, which agitated for devolution of power to Ireland without true independence, that popular politics and mass participation reached its greatest extent.

Efforts to involve the Catholic people in repeal efforts took two forms. The first tactic was the dissemination of political material in the form of newspapers and political tracts. Both O'Connell's organizations and other political groups such as the cultural nationalists in Young Ireland worked to improve popular education and spread political ideology to the masses. To this end, political campaigners published a profusion of newspapers, including *The Nation*, which would come to serve as a key mouthpiece of nationalist ideals. More importantly, however, the organizations established a significant number of reading rooms, sometimes even referred to as "*Nation* Reading Rooms,"[6] where those who did not have subscriptions to popular political media could come and read at their leisure. Critically, the reading rooms often contained areas not just for reading and contemplation, but rooms where illiterate members of the public could have the newspapers read to them, as well as places for political debate and discussion. An editorial in *The Nation* itself argued that "every institution of the kind should have two rooms, one for books and study, the other for newspapers and political business."[7] As Huston Gilmore has argued, the reading rooms, and *The Nation*, which was so often read there either individually or out loud, had a vast impact in efforts to reach the populace. "Thus while by the end of 1843, only a year after is foundation, the *Nation* was selling more than 10,000 copies a week, its readership numbered many thousands more."[8] Charles Gavan Duffy, who served as editor of the paper, estimated that at the peak of its popularity *The Nation* had a following of more than 250,000 and that the practice of public readings of the paper in reading rooms and public meetings meant that each copy "served from fifty to a hundred persons."[9] As Repeal Association Secretary Thomas Matthew Ray argued, reading rooms were designed such that "the industrious classes might . . . receive the exhortations of the Liberator [O'Connell] conveyed through the public prints, inspiring patriotism, and inculcating peace, order, and perseverance, in working out the regeneration of Ireland."[10]

In addition to the efforts of the Repeal Association itself, members of the Catholic clergy played an important role in transmitting political ideas to the masses. Catholic churchmen had often been apolitical themselves, tending to disapprove of some of the more violent efforts at revolution and fearing that allegiance to political groups, many of them led by Protestant aristocrats, might weaken the connection between the people and the faith. A Catholic-led movement for the emancipation of Catholics was something the clergy could back, however, and their support carried over to the efforts toward repeal of the Acts of Union. The institutional structure of the Catholic Church provided significant opportunities for the political efforts of the Repeal Association, and clergymen collected dues for the association and passed on political information to their congregations. As Gilmore has argued, "the importance of support from the Catholic priesthood as a means of transmitting political intelligence by oral communication, as the literate interpreters of O'Connell's mass following, cannot be overstated."[11] Reports of the Association's activities were common fodder for discussions at church services, and as the Association's historian explained, "on Sunday they were read aloud at the chapel door" with phenomenal success. Indeed, he continued, "It is quite incredible the anxiety for political information which this diffusion of the public prints generated."[12] As Benedict Anderson has famously argued, the development of a national vernacular print culture is essential to the construction of a sense of national community, an imagined solidarity in which people are able to conceptualize other members of the nation as being fundamentally like themselves.[13] In Ireland, rising levels of literacy, combined with concerted efforts at disseminating nationalist ideologies on the part of political activists, forged just such a print culture.

Moreover, the construction of reading rooms and oral performance practices both at reading rooms and in the context of church services and other gatherings allowed the common sense of nationality to expand far past the wealthier and literate segments of Irish and Catholic society. Thomas MacNevin, a member of Young Ireland, phrased this explicitly, arguing that a reading room should be "a place for training the mind, of culture for social feelings . . . to bring men of the different classes of the national party together. There are, and ever will be, differences in ranks—men are unequal. . . . We wish to get the men of the professions to mingle with the men of trade, and the richer shopkeeper with the poorer artisan."[14] The use of Catholic clergy as a network through which to distribute political ideas worked to cement the association between political agitation and religion that had already been forged by the Penal Laws and efforts to repeal them. The development of a popular form of politics that mixed religion with nationalistic ideas of equality and political rights created a powerful force that could reach, and interest, far more members of the population than any form of politics had before.

The scope of O'Connell's popular politics was evident in the size and makeup of the crowds that gathered to attend his "monster meetings," a series of political rallies that were held throughout Ireland. Reports put the numbers of attendees at upwards of 100,000 at a single meeting, a massive number that represented popular politics at an unheard-of scale in Ireland. Though numbers of this sort are hardly exact, and prone to significant levels of exaggeration or diminishment in support of ideological goals, even O'Connell's opponents recognized the power of his movement. As Lord Lieutenant of Ireland Earl de Grey argued, "Their numbers we have reason to know are grossly exaggerated; but they are large enough to paralyze the movements of society—and when O'Connell states in public that he has just been addressing 70,000, 80,000, 120,000 men, the world believes him, & the effect upon the bold or the timid mind is proportionate."[15] Much like the reading rooms, the monster meetings were designed to bring together "rich and poor, young and old, men and women, clergy and laity, town and country, magistrates and people, participants and spectators."[16] The monster meetings seem to have been successful in that regard. Their size alone testifies to the appeal such meetings had for people from all strata of the social spectrum. Numerous contemporary sources remarked, often disparagingly, on the diverse character of the crowd. One such newspaper article described the scene of a meeting at Ennis in June of 1843 by remarking, "Jaunting-cars and humbler vehicles lay scattered in countless numbers around, and thousands of respectable farmers . . . arrived on horseback, many of them having behind their 'better halves.' . . . So great was the demand for vehicles . . . that not even so much as a common car or a donkey could be had in Limerick, or thirty miles around."[17] The variety of vehicles and means of conveyance in attendance reflects the diversity of social classes represented at the meeting, and the paper's comment on the lack of available transportation reveals the extent to which such spectacles truly consumed the attention of the populace in the countryside for miles around

As Maura Cronin has argued, even the disparaging comments made by opponents of O'Connell's movement can reveal a great deal about the extent of the movement's popular appeal. Opponents argued that meetings such as one in Kilkenny in June 1843 were attended by "scarcely any individual with any pretension to respectability," while others described the meeting organizers as "street and hedge agents."[18] Yet this was precisely the population that O'Connell's movements sought to reach, and the reality that the massive size of his meetings had reached, and gained the support of, even the lowest classes of the people provided him with a rhetorical tool, as the repeal movement began to describe itself in truly nationalistic and popular terms. O'Connell himself described his support as coming from "The People, the true source of legitimate power" and argued that his supporters represented "the middle classes like himself—the bone, the nerve and sinew of the population."[19] As with efforts to distribute political newspapers, pamphlets, and other propaganda, O'Connell took pains to involve the Catholic clergy wherever possible, and supportive clergymen often "strongly exerted themselves" in promoting and urging attendance at the local meetings. Discussing the Church's support for the cause, O'Connell even urged some of his lieutenants to "do nothing without the cooperation of the clergy,"[20] recognizing the extent to which the organizational structure and moral standing of the Catholic priests could advance the movement's cause.

O'Connell's ability to spark political activism and attendance at his monster meetings reveals the extent to which nationalist ideas had managed to permeate even the lowest classes of Irish society. The coalition of nationalist activists and Catholic clergy expressed themselves through print media, in meetings that drew attendees from the countryside for miles around, and even at Mass on Sundays. Common people's enthusiasm for the political and their consumption of print media reveal the extent of their engagement with political causes. Moreover, the explicit ways this mass political organizing centered on religious concerns helped forge a system in which religious difference, already a key determiner of life and economic opportunities, became the lens through which political agitation was determined.

The Great Hunger

Though the movement for Catholic emancipation expanded political ideas to the mass public, it was the Great Famine in the middle of the nineteenth century that had the most powerful effect on the ways common people interacted with their government, society, and culture. The consequence, in large part, of the 1845 failure of the staple potato crop on which more than 40 percent of the population depended for survival, the Great Famine saw the Irish population fall by 20 to 25 percent, with more than a million perishing and a million more fleeing the island for better prospects in the United States and elsewhere.[21] Perhaps the most profoundly transformative event in Irish history, the Great Hunger sparked a radical reformulation of Irish society. The devastating effects of population loss through starvation, disease, and emigration upset institutions and severed cultural and societal bonds that had existed for centuries in a way that reverberated throughout all levels of Irish society. By the end of the famine in 1852, the demography of the island had been permanently changed, and with it Ireland's relationship with the British, who many held responsible for the lack of food and adequate relief efforts for the Irish poor. Perhaps most importantly, for the purposes of nationalism scholars, the famine entered folk memory, becoming a cultural touchstone and foundational element of a new sense of Irishness, one that now incorporated an emphasis on death and loss, and religious narratives of martyrdom, resurrection, and triumph in the face of incalculable odds. And yet it was the economic, social, and political changes that accompanied the loss of population and the restructuring of relationships within Ireland that drove many of these cultural and religious changes. The immense trauma and the changes it caused helped drive a new cultural and religious sense of what it meant to be an Irish nation distinct from, and in opposition to, Britishness and continued membership in the United Kingdom.

Demographic Changes

The most obvious and immediate effect of the Irish hunger was the massive demographic change that accompanied the death and departure of such a large percentage of the Irish population. A cheap nutritious crop that could be grown in large quantities even in poor soil, the potato had become the staple crop for poor farmers by the beginning of the eighteenth century. Moreover, encroaching need for pastures for beef production to be exported back to England limited the land available for native subsistence farming.[22] During this time, much of Irish agriculture functioned under a cottier system, wherein poor farmers would pay rent to and work for a large landowner in exchange for the use of a parcel of land on which to grow crops to support their own families. Most Irish agricultural land was thus organized into large farms owned by landlords in Britain and managed by middlemen who supported themselves by collecting rent for their absentee employers. Such an organization created a system ripe for exploitation, and tensions between landlords, middlemen, and tenants were a recurring problem. Middlemen furthered the problems inherent in the Irish agricultural system by refusing to grant long-term leases on parcels of land in an effort to maximize rent gained from them. Furthermore, the middlemen, who themselves leased large parcels of land from landlords on long leases at fixed and more reasonable rents, rapidly subdivided their holdings into smaller and smaller parcels, wringing the largest number of rents and income possible, which they would then keep. Their position protected many of the middlemen from the worst ravages of the famine, and some even managed to prosper. As one oral history account recalled, "Some local families were unaffected by the Famine or at least they managed to live. These mostly composed the agents of the landlords.... Not only did they manage to live but they got large tracts of land adjoining their own, when holdings were forsaken by those who emigrated."[23]

The rapid subdivision of land, combined with a massive expansion in the Irish population in the century preceding the famine, meant that by 1845, most Irish tenant farms were so small that only the potato would provide enough of a crop to support a family. It was these tenant farms that failed in large numbers when potato crops became untenable. Itinerant laborers, cottiers, and smallholders were thus the hardest hit when the famine came. With potato crops failing and no alternate sources of nutrition, the poorest classes of Irish society withered and died. The numbers were stark, and anecdotal accounts reveal the effect the devastation had on the countryside. As one source related, "There were 800 families in the parish of Kilglass before the Famine. There is not half that number now. In this townland of Ballykilcline, there were 80 families and most of them were evicted. There are only three houses in it now, and about a dozen people."[24] When tenant farmers could not pay the annual rents on their small parcels of land, middlemen and landlords took full advantage, expelling hundreds of thousands and further converting agricultural land to pasture for cows and sheep. This reapportioning of land led to the popular belief that "the landlord and the bullock drove the people off the land."[25] Moreover, the severity of the crisis and the heavy weight of the rents meant that what food was produced on Irish farms was often sold, with exports used to pay debts and keep the farmers on the land.[26]

That the famine disproportionately affected the poorer classes in Ireland meant that it had profound effects on Irish demography. During the mid-nineteenth century, fully 80 percent of Ireland's population of 8 million was Catholic, with only 20 percent of the population Protestant. Despite their numerical disadvantage, political and economic power continued to reside in the hands of the Protestant minority. Due to the historical circumstances recounted in the last chapter and their close ties to England, the Protestant population of Ireland tended to be wealthier, more powerful, and concentrated in largely urban areas in the east of Ireland. In contrast, much of the Catholic population, long politically, socially, and economically disadvantaged, was poor, rural, and agrarian. In consequence, mortality was much higher in rural Catholic regions than in urban Protestant areas, resulting in a rapid depopulation of the Catholic countryside and further strengthening Protestant control over the land. Mortality was worst in Connacht, where one in four died, but rural poor were vulnerable all across the island.[27] More than a million people emigrated from those same areas between 1846 and 1851, with the number reaching more than 5 million by 1910.[28] By the 1850s, the cottier class, which had been a feature of the Irish landscape for centuries, had almost completely disappeared.[29] Simultaneously, the famine had an impact on marriage and fertility rates across Ireland. Declining economic prospects forced Irish peasants to marry later or not at all, and those who did marry produced fewer children then pre-famine norms. In the decades after the famine, age of first marriage jumped from twenty-one for women and twenty-five for men, where it had been during the first decades of the nineteenth century, to twenty-nine for women and thirty-three for men. Whereas 10 percent of the population remained unmarried in pre-famine times, fully a third of Irish men and more than a quarter of Irish women never married after the famine.[30] Fertility rates declined apace, as the massive population boom that had characterized pre-famine Ireland reversed itself, with emigration and mortality far outweighing the number of children born yearly.

The famine also had powerful linguistic consequences. The poorer agrarian regions in the west of Ireland had long been centers of Irish language, resisting the spread of English in favor of traditional linguistic culture. The massive scale of death and emigration that accompanied the famine severely weakened the remaining community of Irish speakers, and the Irish language ceased to be the primary language for all but a small percentage of the population. Both the mortality suffered by the Catholic population and the loss of the Irish language would have profound consequences for the development of Irish nationalism. The decline of the Irish language would eventually provide a cause célèbre for the cultural nationalists of the Gaelic Revival who sought to return Ireland to its imagined ancient glory.[31] Similarly, the toll on Catholic communities served to heighten interreligious tensions between the upper-class Protestant population and the surviving Catholic population. Though Catholics had achieved emancipation in 1829, the poor condition of most of the Catholic peasantry kept any sort of nationalistic ideas far from most minds. Those Catholics who survived the Great Hunger, however, tended to be wealthier, and lingering tensions over the role of the British crown in first contributing to the causes of, and then not providing adequate relief for, the famine provided a powerful motivating factor for a new form of Irish Catholic political expression, one that would nationalize religion to an extent never before seen in Irish society.

Economic Changes

In its economic effects the Great Famine had two crucial consequences that would help forge a new alliance between Catholicism and nationalism in Ireland. The first of these was the destruction of the cottier system that so disadvantaged Irish agrarian peasants. The Irish population boom that occurred during the first half of the nineteenth century had led to a massive increase in the agricultural laboring class. By some estimates, roughly two-thirds of the Irish population consisted of cottiers, and even more served as itinerant agricultural laborers without a rented parcel of land of their own.[32] Following the famine, this population saw a drastic collapse. The number of cottiers and laborers dropped by 40 percent during the famine years between 1845 and 1851, and by another 40 percent in the sixty years that followed.[33] This decline represented a massive restructuring of Irish economic and social life. Contemporary sources recognize the toll the famine took on the aristocracy as well. As one respondent put it, "The local landlords were only like the tenants themselves. They had a few townlands under a head rent and when the tenants failed, they failed."[34] Interestingly, this seems to have only hastened a collapse that was already in progress, as many of the aristocratic estates that failed were poorly run operations owned by absentee landlords who were already under increasing levels of debt.[35] The tragedy of the famine made it clear that the increasing subdivision of land that had occurred under the landlords was utterly untenable. The massive decline in population caused by the famine, however, provided an opportunity for agrarian reform. As one scholar has argued, "the official view was that the price was worth paying. The assessment of the 1851 census commissioners was that we have every reason for thankfulness that years of suffering have been followed by years of prosperity."[36]

The collapse of both the agrarian labor force and many of the large aristocratic estates provided significant opportunities for the middle class of Irish society. The large drop in population brought with it a rise in average living standards for those who survived. Housing quality and access to land were both signifi-cantly improved. The cottier and itinerant laboring class was replaced by a new class of Irish farmers who became the largest and most important constituency in post-famine Ireland. Many of these new independent farmers, who controlled midsized farms far larger than the subsistence plots on which cottiers had resided, were the very middlemen who had been so hated by the agrarian working class they were replacing. Riding out the famine by collecting rents and evicting cottiers whose crops had failed, this middle class was best situated to capitalize on the reorganization of Irish land that followed the famine times. As later observers of this change recognized, "Many people who are today strong farmers in the district acquired their holdings at the time or perhaps later. Many of them were acquired because they acted as 'touts' or sycophants to the local landlord or his agent."[37]

Crucially, this population was not the absentee Protestant landlords who had controlled much of Irish land in the past. Rather, these farmers represented the rise of a new Catholic middle class. While the famine and the declining num-bers of agrarian poor shattered the coalition of supporters that had buoyed O'Connell's efforts for Catholic emancipation, a growing class of Catholic farm-ers and wealthy merchants brought religion to the forefront. During the 1850s, religious conflicts began to replace political battles as religious tensions that were fostered during the famine festered and Catholics became more and more hos-tile not just toward Protestant landlords but to the very connection between Britain and Ireland.[38] In this, the rapid growth of a Catholic middle class after the famine hastened a process that was already occurring during the first half of the nineteenth century. The success of O'Connell's repeal movement, slow and halting though it was, had opened new doors for Catholics throughout the island. Catholics had achieved some economic success during the eighteenth century, and the dismantling of the Irish Penal Laws meant that Catholics could more fully participate in politics, bringing their issues to the forefront of public debate. The growing economic strength of a Catholic middle class made those concerns impossible to ignore, setting the stage for the development of a true Irish nationalist movement, but one that would need to be expressed in Catholic terms.

Religious Changes

In addition to its important demographic and economic effects, the Great Fam-ine had a crucial impact on the organization and lived experience of religion in Ireland. Many Irish viewed the coming of the famine as a divinely inspired event. Interpreted through a religious lens, the famine was taken to be supernatural punishment for the sins of the Irish people. As one source recounted, "Most people think it was punishment from God for the careless manner in which they treated the crops the years previous when there was a very plentiful supply of potatoes."[39] Others recounted that the famine looked "like the hand of God" and described in almost biblical terms the profligate ways in which people drank milk and honey, where "every day was a holiday . . . and plenty of poteen drunk. They were too well off" before "[t]he Lord said that as time would go on milk and honey would decrease."[40] Indeed, the popular memory that coalesced about the famine in later years placed an emphasis on overpopulation, overabundance, and resultant "unrighteous" behavior that characterized the pre-famine years.

In fact, from the perspective of Catholics looking back on the tragedy, there was much to criticize about pre-famine Irish religious practice. In contrast to later years, when church attendance averaged upwards of 90 percent in much of Ireland,[41] pre-famine attendance was far less universal. While English-speaking and urban areas might have seen a weekly attendance at Mass of around 60 percent, poorer, rural, and Irish-speaking areas fell far short. Emmett Larkin, in a classic study of Irish Catholicism, pegged attendance at Catholic Mass as closer to 33 percent pre-famine.[42] David Miller, examining the impact of the Great Famine on Irish Catholicism, came up with a similar number, arguing for an attendance of between 25 and 30 percent.[43] In part, this low level of attendance reflected a lack of institutional infrastructure on the part of the Catholic Church. Larkin, again, analyzing the role of the Church infrastructure, places the number of priests as only 1 for every 3,000 people in Catholic Ireland.[44] Moreover, what clergy did exist in Ireland seem to have been lacking much in the way of moral authority. The lack of an institutional structure meant that religious practices were less formal than elsewhere, occurring in people's homes, schoolhouses, or village open spaces, and complaints abounded of priests who failed to live up to the dignity of their office, with widespread drunkenness, sexual impropriety, and heterodox practices among Irish clergy.[45] In large part these institutional failures can be traced back to the severe restrictions on the official practice of Catholicism imposed by the Irish Penal Laws. By the time the famine struck, less than twenty years after the repeal of the Penal Laws in 1829, the institutional infrastructure of the Catholic Church had improved only marginally, and the Church had not yet assumed the hegemonic status it would achieve in the post-famine years.

In its decimation of the agrarian peasant class and the near destruction of traditional Irish culture, the Great Famine had a tremendous effect on the role of Catholicism in Irish society. Church attendance rose rapidly, and Ireland has long held a place near the top of most measures of religiosity among European countries.[46] Simultaneously, the famine touched off a wave of institutionalization of orthodox Catholicism that spread throughout Ireland over the next quarter century. The reform-minded efforts of Bishop Paul Cullen, who arrived in Ireland in 1850, and a large investment of financial and human resources rapidly improved the institutional character of the Catholic Church. An influx of Catholic priests and the population decline caused by famine deaths and emigration dropped the ratio of priests to Catholics in Ireland from 1 in 3,000 to 1 in 900 by 1900.[47] These numbers led to what Larkin has famously called a "devotional revolution," a sea change in the ways in which the Irish people experienced Catholicism.

Yet how to explain this rapid growth in both religious infrastructure and, among the lay people, religious practice and belief? Some scholars have made a functionalist argument, following the likes of Durkheim, that the vast growth in attendance at Mass and the corresponding depth of religiosity and adherence to organized Catholicism that followed the famine represent a need to fill the void that the destruction of traditional Irish culture and popular religion during the famine had caused. "Whereas prefamine Irish peasant religion had functioned to help its participants deal with the old source of stress, the threat of starvation, its post-Famine counterpart functioned to help them deal with the new source of stress, the threat of rootlessness."[48] Such is the take Larkin advances as well, arguing that in the absence of traditional Irish culture, the new devotional revolution "provided the Irish with a substitute symbolic language and offered them a new cultural heritage with which they could identify and be identified and through which they could identify with one another."[49] In this sense, Larkin's argument is similar to the theory of religious continuity that Danièle Hervieu-Léger referred to in her description of religion as a "chain of memory."[50] Hervieu-Léger's analysis of modernizing societies argues that among the most important changes in modern society is the destruction of the traditional bonds of community, the sense of collective identity that prevailed in premodern times. Religion manages to survive, she argues, by filling many of the voids that are created by this loss of identity. In Ireland, the destruction of traditional folk culture and religion, and the population that participated in it, created a desperate need for a framework around which a new sense of identity could be constructed. In essence, the hierarchical structure of a resurgent Catholic Church provided a rationalization, in the Weberian sense, of Irish popular religion, creating an institutional core that tied social life to the organizational strength of the Catholic Church.

While this functionalist argument offers certain advantages, providing a causal explanation for the turn to orthodox Catholicism and its subsequent meteoric rise, it offers only partial answers to the complex questions of the role of Catholicism in Irish political life. Though the traditional Irish culture, represented by the Irish language and traditional popular religion, was weakened in the famine, it by no means disappeared. The fact that sources interviewed by Irish Folklore Commission oral historians nearly a century after the famine were able to recount a wide variety of fairy stories and supernatural occurrences testifies to the endurance of traditional religious forms.[51] Similarly, the devotional revolution Larkin identifies as being the result of a concerted increase in the number and morals of Catholic clergy occurred in the quarter century after the famine. The later arrival of this revolution presumably reflects a response to, rather than a cause of, increased demand for orthodox Catholicism among Irish populations. So why then did a more hierarchical and institutionalized form of Catholicism draw the attention of devastated populations seeking a new culture around which to form a central sense of identity?

One possible solution to this question can be found in the religious context within which the Great Famine took place. The trauma of the famine and the belief in British, and by extension Protestant, complicity in its extent led to increased tension between the Catholic and Protestant communities in Ireland. These tensions highlighted the religious, cultural, and class differences that fragmented Irish society and set the stage for increasing focus on religion in the nationalist struggle. The vast disparity in economic strength between the wealthy Protestant community in Ireland and the impoverished Catholic community that suffered the worst of the famine brought religious differences into sharp relief. Later accounts reveal the growing resentment of Catholic populations toward the Protestant community, which not only often had enough to eat but who also oversaw relief efforts for the poor. Stories flourished about Protestant landlords driving starving Catholics from their land and ordering the arrest of those who sought to collect leftover scraps from Protestant homes.[52] Others attributed to Protestants a general desire for genocide, and felt that Protestants took the opportunity of the famine to exterminate as many Catholics as possible. One story recounts how Protestants in Manch intentionally boiled relief soup in copper kettles that let off dangerous poisons, causing any number of deaths. As the respondent recalls, "One day the big fellows came to the man boiling and sharing out the stirabout. 'Well,' he says, 'how are things going on?' 'Ah good,' says the fellow in charge, 'there is so-many deaths reported again this morning.' 'That's right, that's right,' says the first fellow. 'Keep the copper boiler going.'"[53] Other Catholics resented the way some Protestants looked at the famine as an opportunity to spread their own religion. Many Protestant landlords and organizations set up soup kitchens that fed Catholics in exchange for conversion to Protestantism. Some sought to make it so that Catholics receiving aid would be forced to eat meat on Fridays, an act that was against Catholic practice.[54] Others promised food only if those receiving aid would attend a Protestant church service in exchange.[55] Results of these practices were mixed. While some starving Catholics took the relief aid offered, many were seen to attend Catholic Mass in addition to the Protestant church services. Others converted back to Catholicism immediately when their circumstances improved. Still others preferred to reject the relief efforts. One woman who was repeatedly offered plentiful food only to turn it down asked her dying son in anguish whether it was better to take the food or die. "In Irish he spoke 'Is fear an bás mathair,' . . . 'Tis better die, mother.'"[56]

The sense of resentment that developed in the wake of what many Catholics considered insufficient relief efforts, combined with what appeared to be

Protestants capitalizing on the tragedies of Catholics, made religion a central issue in the minds of many. With this in mind, it is not surprising that Catholicism became so centrally tied to Irish conceptions of self-identity. As many scholars of ethnicity and nationalism have noted, collective identity most often develops in opposition to an external and threatening "collective other."[57] Scholars studying the psychological underpinnings of social identity have similarly noted the role of stress, uncertainty, and in-group threat in the forging of social identity.[58] Such conditions often create a subjective sense of group identity that is lacking in complexity, creating in-groups that demand homogeneity across all facets of group identification.[59]

Such indeed seems to have been the case in Ireland, where the collective trauma forced a new conceptualization of collective identity and a subsequent emphasis on the Catholic faith as the core of the new Irish national state. In the case of Ireland, the Great Famine was a moment in which group identity suddenly mattered in everyday life. While religious affiliation had long structured the everyday reality for most people, determining educational and economic possibilities, as well as life changes and civil rights, it did so at a larger social structural level. In the Great Famine, religious affiliation suddenly became a matter of life and death in the most real and immediate way possible. Religion became a powerful facet of social identity, one that, as memory of the tragedy and resentment of Protestant indifference and maliciousness grew, would serve as the foundational core of a newly popular nationalist movement, one that would now demand not simply equality with, but independence from, a Protestant ruling class that had never governed with their interests in mind.

MEMORY, TRAUMA, AND THE GAELIC REVIVAL: THE (RE)BIRTH OF THE IRISH NATION

The nationalist movement that flourished in the wake of the Great Famine found itself in a new position. The mass politics of O'Connell's repeal movements and the vast resentment over the causes of and lack of relief for the famine had extended nationalistic ideas to segments of the population they had never before reached. Moreover, the winnowing of the population due to mortality and emigration left Ireland with a surviving Catholic population that was far wealthier than it had been before the tragedy. Yet it was also a population that was deeply scarred, victim of a trauma that had far-reaching and long-lasting repercussions. The destruction of traditional Irish culture, religion, and language further heightened the sense of loss and desolation felt by Catholics in the new Ireland. It was this sense of cultural loss, and a growing belief that the victims of the Great Famine had been martyred at the hands of British imperialism, that Irish nationalists drew on as they sought to craft a new independent nation. The decline of traditional Irish culture that had accompanied the Great Famine and the rapidly changing political and social situation during the nineteenth century represented a challenge for nationalists and common Irishmen alike. Nationalists, who were convinced that Ireland's distinctiveness merited independence, or at the very least a limited form of self-governance, were faced with a society that was quickly losing many of the distinct elements, in language, literature, culture, and historical memory, on which their claims for independence were founded. Even in religion, many contemporary observers lamented the "Protestantiza-tion" of Irish Catholicism as the growing Catholic middle class "rose to power within the existing socio-economic and political structures and through assimi-lating itself in all but religious denomination and politics to the culture of the Protestant elite."[60] Sensing Irish distinctiveness, and thus their justification for Irish separatism, slipping away, nationalists pursued a variety of strategies designed to kindle a reawakening of traditional Irish culture.

These cultural nationalists, who would give birth to a revolutionary Gaelic Revival, largely separated into two camps. One camp, composed largely of Cath-olics, sought to revive the Irish language, viewing language as the key foundation of a distinctive Irishness. The second, largely Protestant in origin, focused on literature, much of it produced in English but elaborating on traditional Irish mythology and culture, as the crucial means of crafting cultural differentiation. Both sides of the movement also relied on theater performances to get their messages across. Though they often clashed, together these two movements cre-ated a Gaelic renaissance that would infuse late nineteenth-century Irish society with a corpus of myths and symbols, inculcating a sense of a heroic past and a glorious future that could rally popular support for the political cause and craft a powerful sense of distinctiveness. In this regard, the Gaelic Revivalists crafted an ethnic and national boundary, one that differentiated the Irish people, who in their view deserved to be free and independent, from the insidious English cul-tural dominance that threatened to assimilate Ireland once and for all.

That the Gaelic Revival was led by cultural nationalists, however, does not mean that it was a movement entirely composed from the top down. As John Eglinton, a literary critic of the period, remarked, the cultural flourishing that accompanied the Revival succeeded only because it was successful in capturing and reflecting ideas that were prominent in society at large. He explained, "In short, we need to realise in Ireland that a national drama or literature must spring from a native interest in life and its problems and a strong capacity for life among the people. If these do not, or cannot exist, there cannot be a national drama or literature."[61] What nationalists of both stripes found, however, was that concep-tions of Irish culture and Catholicism had become so intertwined that it was impossible to call on one without mobilizing the other. Catholicism had come to define what it meant to be Irish in the minds of many, and religious conceptions of the nation would soon come to form the basis of what would be the Irish state that finally succeeded in achieving independence. It was for this reason that the Gaelic Revival, though led as much by Protestants as it was by Catholics, would result in the creation of an Irish national identity that was inseparable from Catholicism. Indeed, the Revival found its ultimate expression in the revolutionary religious zeal of Patrick Pearse, who combined ideas of cultural distinctiveness with Catholic apocalypticism to provide the ideological grounding of the revolution he, along with other leaders, would launch during the evocatively symbolic Easter week of 1916.

Linguistic Revival

The devastation of the famine significantly shrank the percentage of people who spoke Irish as their primary language. In decline throughout the first half of the nineteenth century, as English increasingly became the dominant language of public affairs, the famine provided the final blow, with the percentage of Irish speakers dropping from nearly 75 percent in 1851 to become a minority language by the late nineteenth century.[62] Those native Irish speakers who remained were confined to small isolated pockets, often in the rural west of Ireland, or in the exceedingly small number of academics and folklorists in Irish universities. The language had become, in the words of poet and literary critic Matthew Arnold, "the badge of a beaten race, the property of the vanquished."[63] This situation seemed intolerable for nationalists convinced of the enduring power and distinctiveness of Irish society. Irish linguist and politician Douglas Hyde summarized this argument in an 1892 lecture at the National Literary Society in which he argued for "The Necessity of de-Anglicising Ireland." Here Hyde calls attention to what he describes as the decline of the Irish race, arguing it was the result of "ceasing to be Irish without becoming English." Most importantly, he argues, "I wish to show you that in Anglicising ourselves wholesale we have thrown away with a light heart the best claim which we have upon the world's recognition of us as a separate nationality."[64] Hyde proceeds to illustrate an idyllic version of Ireland's heroic past, arguing that pre-nineteenth century Ireland was a land of cultural and literary genius, a society that fostered a distinct intellectual culture in which even relatively poor farmers regularly engaged with Irish antiquity, mythology, and poetry.[65] The extent to which Hyde's own Ireland had lost this ancient tradition, and indeed was losing its claim to distinct nationhood, spurred him to construct a new movement that would focus on reintroducing the fading language and culture of Ireland to late nineteenth-century society. To this end, Hyde and colleagues such as Eoin MacNeill founded the Gaelic League, an organization that would agitate for the spread of Irish language literature and the teaching of Irish in schools. Despite the emphasis on the revitalization of an ancient society and linguistic and literary culture, the focus of many Revivalists was firmly on their own present, designed to create a form of "critical traditionalism," one that would provide the foundation for a nationalist movement that would help achieve self-governance for the Irish people.[66]

In this regard, MacNeill believed that national and religious revival were inextricable, and he worked closely with Catholic intellectual and moral revival movements.[67] MacNeill forged a bond between the Irish language and Catholicism by appealing directly to Catholic clergy. More than that, however, the clergy's involvement in the language movement helped contribute to a growing sense that Irish culture, which was expressed through language, was itself inextricable from Catholicism. As D. P. Moran, who got his start working for Gaelic magazines before founding his own influential newspaper *The Leader*, was to argue, "when we look out on Ireland we see that those who believe . . . in Ireland a nation are, as a matter of fact, Catholics. . . . In the main non-Catholic Ireland looks upon itself as British and as Anglo-Irish," and those non-Catholics who sought to support the Irish nation "must recognize that the Irish nation is de facto Catholic."[68]

Though it grew slowly, Hyde and MacNeill's movement was in some ways successful. In 1878 the League succeeded in getting the Irish language added as an elective subject in the national primary education system, which had been founded by the English state in 1831 and had long been rigorously opposed to the teaching of Irish language and culture. Further success was achieved when the National University of Ireland, in 1908, established Irish language as a compulsory subject for graduation.[69] Yet the enduring legacy of the Gaelic League and linguistic revival movements was less the resurrection of the Irish language, which was difficult and remained inaccessible to many, but in the creation of an intellectual movement that reinforced the popular conception that Catholicism was an important characteristic of what it meant to be truly Irish, conflating different facets of social and individual identity into a single fused sense of identity.

The Irish Literary Revival

While Hyde, MacNeill, and their fellow linguistic nationalists focused on revitalizing the Irish language, another group of Revivalists turned to the issue of national culture in a different way, arguing that the Irish language, important as it may have been, had fallen too far from the consciousness of most people in Ireland. A true Irish national culture, they believed, needed to be expressed in English, the language that the vast majority of Irish people now spoke and that had become the language of state and public life. As Stanford A. Brooke argued, in a lecture titled "The Need and Use of Getting Irish Literature into the English Tongue,"

Irish literature is not to Ireland what English literature is to England. The mass of the Irish people know nothing of it, and care little about it. That they should know, and should care will do more for the cause of a true nationalism than all our political angers. Moreover, with the perishing of the Irish language as the tongue of the people—and its perishing with accelerating speed—the popular interest that once gathered round her past literature is vanishing away. . . . Translation, then, is our business. We wish to get the ancient Irish literature well and statelily afloat on the worldwide ocean of the English language, so that it may be known and loved wherever the English language goes.[70]

A variety of nationalistic authors hastened to answer Brooke's call. Writers and poets such as Standish O'Grady and Lady Gregory produced a variety of works translating and retelling traditional Irish folk stories. Linguistic nationalists often vehemently disapproved of this activity. In a letter to the editor of *An Claidheamh Soluis*, for example, Patrick Pearse argued that "Newspapers, politicians, literary societies are all but forms of one gigantic heresy that like a poison has paralysed the nation's energy and intellect. That heresy is the idea that there can be an Ireland, that there can be an Irish literature, an Irish social life, whilst the language of Ireland is English."[71] Nevertheless, the Irish Literary Revivalists had a powerful impact on the regeneration of Irish national culture. In their tales of mythical figures such as Cú Chulainn, Fionn Mac Cumhaill, and the Fianna, Revivalist authors created a corpus of nationalist heroes that would inspire a nationalist narrative and version of history that linked their contemporary struggle for Irish self-governance to an epic mythological past populated by rebels and warriors who could serve as examples of heroic defiance of imperial control. Nationalist authors found particular inspiration in the figure of Cú Chulainn, an Ulster warrior who single-handedly waged a guerrilla war against invaders led by Queen Madb, before ultimately succumbing to the invaders' superior numbers.[72] Even then, the mythology goes, Cú Chulainn tied himself upright to a rock, defiant even in death, and such was his martial prowess that Queen Madb's invaders hesitated to approach him, his heroic sacrifice and deathly vigilance providing enough time for Ulster to rally its warriors and repel the invasion. Indeed, the production of work focused on ancient Ireland played an important role in spreading nationalistic ideas of modern Ireland as defiant, distinctly different, and worthy of independence. As writer and literary critic Mary Colum argued, "It was surprising that the English government, which proclaimed [denounced] Land League meetings and threw the Irish Members of Parliament into gaol for some little political offense, took no notice, or only favourable notice, of this new ardour for native culture. One would think that even a child of ten would have realized that all this was bound to develop towards another and more determined fight to throw off the English yoke."[73] In its marrying of an image of an ancient Irish ideal civilization with ideas of independence, the Irish Literary Revival created a new Ireland as much as it resurrected an old, inventing a national tradition of fierce independence and providing a means by which common Irish people could imagine themselves a distinct community, one separate from the English imperialists that nationalists feared were quickly assimilating them.[74]

The Revival encompassed more than simply retranslation and retelling of ancient folklore, however, crucial though that was to their goal. The Revival also sparked the growth of a new, distinctly Irish form of literature, one that, though written in English, addressed themes of importance to everyday Irish people. Moreover, authors soon found that translation of Irish into English produced a language with a certain lyrical quality to it, a linguistic form that, when incorporated into literature that drew from Irish slang and language variations, created a new form of what Yeats somewhat sarcastically referred to as "Hiberno-English."[75] This distinct form of language combined with the Irish-oriented themes of Revivalist literature to produce an important form of literature, one that was recognizably distinct from the English literature of the time. Authors such as William Carleton and Charles Kickham produced novels that detailed life among the Irish peasantry, and the work of poets such as Yeats and Patrick Pearse, among many others, lent nationalism a certain poetic virtue.

While poetry and novels certainly were powerful forms of expression, it was in nationalist theater that the Irish Literary Revival truly hit its stride in appealing to the masses. As Máire Nic Shiubhlaigh, one of the Irish theater movement's most famous actresses, put it, "In a city [Dublin] where the greater part of the public turned to the stage for entertainment, where the Irish National Theatre Society and its various offshoots worked for the creation of national drama . . . it was hardly surprising that most of the younger folk were dabbling in the amateur theatre. Almost all the national clubs, literary, political or otherwise, were associated with theatrical groups in the young years of the dramatic movement."[76] The Irish theater movement reached its peak with the establishment, in 1904, of the National Theatre of Ireland, also known as the Abbey Theatre. Founded by a group including Yeats, Lady Gregory, and J. M. Synge, it sought to produce Irish plays addressing Irish themes written exclusively by Irish authors. The Abbey Theatre fostered many of the most famous playwrights of the day, and their subject matter addressed issues of popular concern for many Irish people. J. M. Synge, for example, "regarded his drama as a great collaboration between himself and the fiercely imaginative people he met in his travels all over Ireland."[77] Indeed, though superficially the Irish theater movement might be seen as a top-down expression of literary elites, it is clear that the subject matter of the most popular plays, many of them explicitly nationalist in tone, were a reflection of the tastes of the crowd and of the national community. The opening of Synge's *The Playboy of the Western World* in January of 1907, for example, was actually marred by riots, during and after the performance, by nationalist partisans who felt the play was not significantly nationalistic and impugned the moral character of Ireland. Crucially, the nationalistic response took the form of religious affront, as many felt that Synge's portrayal of native Ireland was a slur against both Irish womanhood and the religiosity of Irish Catholics.[78]

In contrast, plays such as *Cathleen ni Houlihan*, which was written by Yeats and Gregory and debuted in 1902, were explicitly and evocatively nationalist. Set amid the Irish uprising of 1798, the play starred Maud Gonne as the mythical title character, a mysterious old woman who appears at a peasant household to beg for help. A personification of Ireland herself, the old woman calls forth the household's son from his wedding day to join the rebellion. She demands from the young man a blood sacrifice, arguing that it was only through the blood of patriots that the nation could be redeemed. She acknowledges the pain that the sacrifice of Ireland's young men will cause, but she argues that it will not be in vain. Of the men who die in her cause, she says, "They shall be remembered forever, They shall be alive forever, They shall be speaking forever, The people shall hear them forever."[79] Yeats and Gregory make clear the gains that such sacrifices will make for the cause of Ireland. When the young man answers Cathleen's call and joins the rebellion, his parents rush to the door to call after them. But when they arrive they see not an old woman going down the path, as they expect, but "a young girl, and she had the walk of a queen."[80] In their evocative call to arms, Yeats and Gregory drew upon a symbolic imagery that explicitly equated the ancient mythological figure of Cathleen ni Houlihan with the cause of Irish freedom. Moreover, the use of a Hiberno-Irish dialect that drew heavily from the peasant English of rural Ireland, much of it contributed by Gregory, spoke to people in a familiar register, drawing together the political ideals of nationalism, sacrifice, and martyrdom with their routine and everyday existence. In contrast to Synge's *Playboy, Cathleen ni Houlihan* was met with immediate acclaim; each performance was greeted with "continuous applause" and "crowds being turned away" at the door.[81]

From Culture to Religion: Patrick Pearse and Religious Apocalypticism

Yet, for all their fervor in the nationalist cause, the Irish Literary Revivalists were largely Protestant in origin, concerned far more with cultural distinctiveness and political and cultural ideas than with religion. While many of the linguistic nationalists of the Gaelic Revival had relied heavily upon religion, their task was far more difficult. The complicated processes of language reform had far less popular appeal than did the mass attraction of entertainment products such as plays and literature. It was only in the joining of these two movements that Irish nationalism took on a significant multidimensional character, religiously Catholic, culturally Gaelic, and politically independent. This joining of facets of national identity reached its utmost extent in the person of Patrick Pearse, a Catholic author, schoolteacher, and political revolutionary who would serve as one of the leaders of the 1916 Easter Rising. Though Pearse began his career as a linguistic nationalist, arguing for the utmost importance of the Irish language and decrying efforts to promote Irish culture in the English language in the strongest of terms, he eventually mellowed, and his writings drew from both linguistic and Literary Revivalist traditions. The key to nationalism, in Pearse's mind, was the need for blood sacrifice, a sacrifice to appease the ghosts of ages past. Pearse couched his theory of nationalism in a language that explicitly integrated Irish cultural and Catholic religious traditions. In those volunteers and soldiers who lost their lives in the national struggle, Pearse saw analogues to both Jesus Christ and Cú Chulainn, twin emblems of the productive power of sacrifice. It was this vision of the nation, blood soaked and beholden to the martyrs of generations before, that would eventually prevail, crafting a crucial link between religion and national culture in the minds of many.

Pearse's mystical religion proved so successful precisely because Pearse himself was to provide yet another martyr to the nationalist cause. Scholarly opinion of the goals and the response to the Easter Rising has been mixed. Some have argued that the Rising was intended to be a true revolution, and that the rebels hoped the mass populace would rally to their side.[82] Others have suggested that the rebels would have known that the Rising had no true hope of being successful, and that it was instead designed to serve as the very sort of blood sacrifice that Pearse had obsessed about.[83] As one Irish Volunteer noted, when seeing a new Irish flag hoisted over the General Post Office, "It seemed almost impossible that this should really have happened. . . . This is worth being wiped out for."[84] That same volunteer quickly realized that being wiped out was indeed the fate awaiting the revolutionaries. Later, holed up in the GPO, he asked both Pearse and another leader, Tom Clarke, what their prospects were. "But in both cases I got no definite answer. Tom Clarke digressed immediately to say what a fight we should have put up [had circumstances been better]. But he did not by any means say that even in that case it would have been a victorious fight, or even a fight whose outcome could conceivably have been in our favour."[85] Similarly, while the populace did not rise up in support of the rebels, and immediate responses seemed to have been negative, some scholars have suggested that the lack of newspapers (the only one that succeeded in continuing printing was the unionist *Irish Times*) and English-founded rumors of German support for the Rising (a damning accusation, during the throes of World War I) was more to blame for the failure to rise than any lack of enthusiasm for the nationalist cause.[86]

Even so, propaganda and political ephemera made their way from the revolutionaries of the Easter Rising into the hands of the common people in Dublin and around the country, both during, and especially after, the Rising. Some pamphlets detailed casualty and deportation lists, as well as provided pictures of key people in the movement.[87] Others provided pictures of the aftermath of the revolution, or illustrated the revolt and its protagonists in pictures.[88] Another explicitly focused on the "Dead Fianna Heroes" of the revolution, telling their backstories and putting faces and histories to the names of those who died fighting for Ireland's freedom.[89] And die the leaders of the Easter Rising did. When the English crushed the rebellion, fifteen of the leaders of the revolution, among them Pearse and Connolly, were captured. They were executed shortly after, new blood spilled for Ireland, and new martyrs and ghosts to demand rebellion among those who remained.

The executions, including that of Connolly, who had been injured in the fighting and was executed tied upright to his chair, a modern echo of Cú Chulainn's famous mythological demise, were met with outrage and sparked a wide range of popular protest among the Irish people. The importance of the execution of the Easter Rising's leaders is visible in W. B. Yeats's famous poem "Easter, 1916," which, though written months after the rebellion, was not published until 1921. In it, Yeats evocatively emphasizes the importance of the individual men and women who fought for the cause. "I have met them at the close of day," he explains, detailing common everyday interactions with those he knew: "That woman" (Countess Markievic), who lived days of ignorant good will but who argued shrilly every night. "This man" (Pearse), who ran a school, "his helper and friend" (Thomas MacDonagh), who might have become famous had his life not been cut short. Even "This other man" (John MacBride), of whom Yeats had a poor opinion in normal life, but whom he now immortalized. All of them, individuals and average people who "have been changed in turn. Transformed utterly." Yeats questions what their sacrifice has meant: "Was it needless death after all?" No, he concludes. Their memory is like a stone that troubles the living stream, diverting it and shaping its course. Indeed, in their deaths, in their martyrdoms, they have not only been transformed themselves, but they have affected all of Ireland: "Now and in time to be / Wherever green is worn / are changed, changed utterly: / a terrible beauty is born."[90]

Pearse's Catholic revolutionism had helped cement the link between Catholicism and Irish separatism that had been growing for more than a century. While the Church had been lukewarm toward earlier revolutions, it backed Pearse's vision of a mystical Catholic Ireland wholeheartedly. Only seven of thirty-one bishops in Ireland condemned the Rising, while the *Catholic Bulletin* conveyed a significant amount of information about the struggle, including religiously oriented biographies of the revolutionaries.[91] The religious characteristic of the Easter Rising was visible to all. For the rebels, "the identification between Catholicism and Irish nationalism was absolute. . . . This is not to say that theirs was a clerical nationalism; far from it. . . . Rather theirs was . . . a confessional nationalism: Catholicism was the hallmark of Irish nationality, a badge to be worn proudly."[92] By this point the confluence of Catholicism and nationalism was complete in the minds of the common people as well. As Kevin Collins suggests, by the time of the Easter Rising many people had come to equate Anglicization and union with de-Catholicization, and viewed independence and nationalism as an essential means to maintain their faith and relationship with God.[93]

FROM 1916 TO THE PRESENT: RELIGION AND NATIONALISM IN THE REPUBLIC AND IN THE NORTH OF IRELAND

If Irish nationalism had largely been driven by Protestant thinkers in the nineteenth century, by the early twentieth it had become the domain almost exclu-

sively of Catholics. The Catholic population, still a significant majority, despite
all it had suffered, adopted nationalist ideas of self-determination and political
and religious independence and transformed them, reconceptualizing the idea
of an Irish nation such that its group boundaries coincided with those of Catholic identity. The mass politics of Catholic figures such as O'Connell and Pearse
combined with the intellectual and literary efforts to establish a distinct Irish
cultural community by Protestants such as Yeats. Such ideas permeated the
Catholic mass of the population to create a truly Catholic form of national identity. When the Irish Free State was established in 1922, following a three-year
guerrilla war between the Irish Republican Army (IRA) and the British army,
the key debate was not whether the new Ireland was to be a Catholic, Protestant,
or secular state, but instead centered on the question of how much of the island
the new Catholic state of Ireland should encompass. Indeed, the partition of Ireland into two countries, the independent Irish Free State (later the Republic of
Ireland) in the south and Northern Ireland, which remained part of the United
Kingdom, took place entirely upon religious criteria. The Irish Boundary Commission, which determined the borderlines between the two countries, worked
to establish a Northern Ireland that would encompass as much land as possible
while still maintaining a Protestant majority. The Irish Free State, in contrast,
became a country that was almost entirely Catholic in population. As the last
chapter showed, Irish politicians in the Free State explicitly pursued policies that
established Catholic social policies as the foundation of the Irish constitution
and the model of governmental policies.[94]

Catholicism has played a powerful role in shaping what it means to be Irish in
the modern Republic of Ireland. That the Protestant population, unwilling to
live under what they considered "Rome rule," or rule by Catholic principles,
emigrated en masse has only increased the extent to which Catholicism and Irish
identity have been intertwined.[95] Again, this association should not be seen
merely as a top-down process, however. Catholicism has long served as a powerful touchstone in the lives of most people in Ireland, and their individual religious practices and beliefs have helped construct a Catholic society. As John
Coakley has argued, in Ireland "the religious boundary is exceptionally clear-cut
at the individual level. The child is marked with the symbols of religious affiliation at an early stage, perhaps within days of birth."[96] This religious labeling,
structuring the marking of identity from birth, has led to a segmented society in
which religion shapes communities, determining which neighborhoods one
lives in, schools one attends, and jobs one works. Ireland's legislative politics and
voting patterns, too, have been heavily structured by religious affiliation. Social
policies on issues such as divorce, birth control, and abortion, all initially made
illegal by the constitution of Ireland in 1937, have repeatedly come up for refer-
enda in the Republic of Ireland. For most of its history, the Irish population has
routinely voted in alignment with Catholic policies. A referendum reaffirmed

abortion restrictions in 1983 by a margin of roughly two to one, and the right to life was subsequently enshrined in the Eighth Amendment to the Irish Constitution.[97] Divorce, too, was subject to referendum in 1986, and a movement to remove divorce restrictions from the constitution lost by the same margin. A referendum to allow divorce was eventually carried in 1995 by only the slimmest of margins, winning by less than 0.5 percent of the vote.[98] Laws permitting the sale and use of birth control were also regularly defeated, with contraception being legalized with significant restrictions only in 1980.[99] Catholicism, too, has often structured the daily life of Irish people. Attendance at church services in Ireland has long been among the highest in the world, with rates often exceeding 90 percent. Even in 2016, despite certain moves toward secularization, 78 percent of the Irish population identified themselves as Roman Catholic, while attendance rates at Mass, though slipping for most of the twentieth and twenty-first centuries, still remains stronger than in most similarly developed countries.[100]

Yet modern social statistics reveal other truths about religion in Ireland. Though Irish attendance at religious services and affiliation with the Roman Catholic Church remains relatively strong, there is no doubt that religiosity and religious identification have been declining in Ireland. What was once a nation that was 96 percent Catholic, with church attendance rates to match, has now fallen to roughly 78 percent and 40 percent, respectively. If it was once possible for Michael Carey to argue that "Faith and fatherland does . . . accurately describe Irish nationalism, that is, to be Irish is to be Catholic,"[101] or for Irish Dominican preacher Tom Burke to say, "Take an average Irishman—I don't care where you find him—and you will find that the very first principle in his mind is, 'I am not an Englishman, because I am a Catholic!,'"[102] this seems no longer the case. To be sure, Ireland remains Catholic in a cultural sense: most people still profess the Catholic faith, even if fewer than in the past, and many people still attend Catholic Mass, though less regularly than before. But Catholicism in Ireland today has lost some of its political and social impetus; it no longer serves as the driving force behind most forms of social organizing and activist activities. One explanation for this loss of motivating power can be found in Burke's quote above. Whereas in the past, Irish identity was always constructed as Catholic precisely because being Catholic meant that one was "not an Englishman," today, Ireland and the UK have buried many of their most pressing differences. Whereas Ireland was constructed to be a Catholic nation precisely in opposition to Protestant England, decades of peace and good relations have slowly eroded religion's role as a social boundary marker, a borderline between "English" and "Irish" communities that regularly came into close contact and competed over similar resources. Catholicism mattered to many Irish nationalists because it served as a firm and foundational characteristic around which to create national identity. From an ethnic and political perspective, Catholicism did its job, creating boundaries between competing groups and serving as a reservoir of symbols, myths, and cultural memories with which to "fill up" a new conception of Irish ethnicity and nationality. Once that Irish ethnic and national identity was estab-lished, however, and the British had largely withdrawn from the Republic of Ire-land, such conceptions were less important, and were slowly allowed to fade, and Catholicism ever so slowly became less important in the daily lives and political imaginaries of the Irish people. Though the Republic of Ireland has seen a great deal of stability and a concomitant decline in the importance of religion as an organizing element of society, this has not been the case in Northern Ireland, where violent clashes between Catholics and Protestants continued until 1998, with sporadic incidences of violence occurring even now. Though the majority of this chapter has focused on religion and nationalism in what would one day become the Republic of Ireland, Northern Ireland can serve as an important comparative case, even within the Irish experience. Northern Ireland is a state with a deeply divided cultural and political history. The Irish Boundary Com-mission's partition of Ireland created a Northern Irish state with a Protestant majority, but only just barely. Efforts to carve out as much land for Northern Ireland while maintaining the Protestant majority led to the inclusion of border-land regions with significant Catholic populations, and, concomitantly, a North-ern Irish population that was only 52 percent Protestant and 48 percent Catholic. Despite the near parity in numbers, the wealthy but tenuous Protestant majority held power from the partition of the island until the implementation of a power-sharing agreement in 1998.

In Northern Ireland, religion held significant political relevance. Protestants largely tended to be unionist in political orientation, convinced that Northern Ireland should remain a part of the United Kingdom. Catholics, in contrast, tended to be nationalists, convinced that Northern Ireland would be better off were it to be reintegrated into the Republic of Ireland. Tellingly, the agreement that resulted in the separation of Northern Ireland from the rest of the island included a provision that allowed for a referendum in which the Northern Irish population could vote to leave the United Kingdom and unite with the Republic of Ireland. Were this to happen, the unionist community would have gone from a slight majority in Northern Ireland to an extreme minority in the Republic of Ireland. Faced with a strong Catholic minority and the looming presence of the heavily Catholicized Republic of Ireland to the south, Protestant leaders, in almost complete control of the state, took several repressive steps to ensure a continued Protestant majority. The Protestant government enacted policies of electoral, housing, and job discrimination, along with gerrymandering political districts to disenfranchise nationalist voters and consolidate the thin Protestant majority.[103] Such was the strength of these identifications that many believed there was truth in the apocryphal words said to have been uttered by Prime Min-ister Lord Cragovan that Northern Ireland was to be "a Protestant state for a Protestant people."[104] These efforts created a Northern Irish society that was highly polarized along religious lines. Catholics and Protestants lived in different neighborhoods in Ireland, with social divisions sharply policed by societal pressure. Restrictions on jobs Catholics could hold helped further these divisions, as did a school system in which Protestants and Catholics had their own entirely segregated school systems.[105]

The continued focus on religion by Protestant unionists desperate to maintain political control and keep Northern Ireland within the United Kingdom made it almost inevitable that political opposition would coalesce behind the banner of religious identity. In the late 1960s, nationalist groups launched a civil rights movement, based on principles used by the African American civil rights movement in the United States, that was designed to garner equal rights for Catholics, who had long been disadvantaged. Though initially nonviolent, this movement saw escalating violence on both sides and, following the climactic events of Bloody Sunday in January of 1972, soon evolved into the Troubles, a conflict that shook the region until 1998 and whose echoes continue to manifest themselves in sporadic violent incidents to this day. With the increase in violence, British troops were sent into Northern Ireland, ostensibly to protect the Catholic population from Protestant reprisals for the civil rights movement, and the British government soon took direct control of governmental processes. This direct action by the British state had a powerful effect on the conflict and upon Northern Irish culture.

The imposition of British control and the decision to send British troops into Northern Ireland had profound repercussions. British troops were originally sent to protect the nationalist community and the civil rights campaigners from violent responses by loyalist mobs, but the relationship between nationalists and the British army soon became contentious and the troops began to support the unionist cause.[106] Nationalists, who already viewed the unionist community as illegitimate settlers and an expression of British dominance, saw British troops on Irish soil as just another example of British imperialism. British troops seemed a physical manifestation of the political and cultural repression that the civil rights movement had been designed to combat. The republican movement within the nationalist community, led by the Provisional Irish Republican Army (PIRA), soon began targeting British troops and army bases along with unionist targets. The Northern Irish police force, known as the Royal Ulster Constabulary (RUC), was drawn largely from the Protestant unionist population, and they and the British army often colluded with loyalist paramilitary organizations.[107]

This demographic makeup, when combined with the loyalist paramilitary groups that proliferated in Northern Ireland in response to actions by the PIRA caused significant resentment in the nationalist community. Nationalists, largely confined to Catholic ghettos and lacking the type of political power possessed by their unionist opponents, felt besieged on all sides and disenfranchised by what they considered to be an illegitimate government. The British answer to the PIRA campaign was firm and, in the eyes of the nationalist community, unjust. The British government, in direct control of Northern Ireland from 1973 onward, enacted several repressive measures under the aegis of the Special Powers Act and its successor, the Northern Ireland (Emergency Provisions) Act. Operation Demetrius, a policy of internment without trial for anyone suspected of being associated with the PIRA, was launched in 1971 but was ineffective and spurred significant negative backlash against Britain. Those arrested were almost entirely Catholics, though few had any significant ties with the PIRA, and rather than crushing the movement, many scholars credit internment for a groundswell of popular support for the PIRA and a direct rise in PIRA violence, sparking a "Long War" of intercommunal conflict that would last decades.[108]

Violence, intergroup politics, and struggles over social and political power have meant that religion continues to play a powerful role in group identity in Northern Ireland. Scholars such as Liz Fawcett and Jo Campling have argued that in Northern Ireland religion is as visible as skin color.[109] Religious difference is thus exceedingly important in everyday life. As Claire Mitchell has argued, "religion does not just mark out the communal boundary in Northern Ireland . . . it gives structures, practices, values and meanings to the boundary."[110] Interestingly, this seems to be true regardless of religious commitment, measured in terms of behavior, devotion, or belief in the supernatural.[111] Indeed, many of the paramilitaries most involved in the violence explicitly recognize that their actions run counter to the strictures of their religion, and describe being willing to set aside religious concerns, even at the cost of their souls, for the greater good of the religious community.[112]

The emphasis on religion as a social boundary marker that structures patterns of interaction reveals the extent to which religion has permeated political culture and works to transmit political ideas and social relationships. In this, religion in Northern Ireland functions as a "chain of memory" in Hervieu-Léger's formulation,[113] providing the fundamental cultural core of myths, memories, and symbols that provide the justification for social difference. The transmission of political culture via religion has led to a situation, as it did in the rest of Ireland during the nineteenth century, in which religious and national identity are explicitly fused. This has led to communities with low levels of social identity complexity, in-groups in which members must share all characteristics of identity, including religion, political orientation, and cultural background, in order to be truly considered members of the community. Polarization along religious lines has been matched by political polarization, and vice versa, as politics and religion have come to be two sides of the same coin. To be Catholic is to be a nationalist, and to be Protestant is to be committed to the union. This polarization meant that it was only after a long and tumultuous peace process, which culminated in the Good Friday Agreement in 1998, that the two sides were able to settle their differences and create a working form of government that could share power between Catholics and Protestants. Crucially, the government that was put into place has been explicitly described as a "power-sharing agreement," revealing that despite efforts to work together, intercommunal divisions between religious denominations in Ireland remained, even then, an issue of significant concern, and religion continued to serve as a means of defining the political players on both sides of the conflict.

CONCLUSIONS

This chapter has traced the development of a nationalistic sense of Irish religion, from its origins in the early nineteenth century through the Troubles in Northern Ireland at the end of the twentieth. Where the last chapter sought to understand how nationalistic politics took on a religious form, this chapter has sought to do the reverse, examining how religion in Northern Ireland became politicized, and how Catholicism became the fundamental social characteristic around which Irish national identity became conceptualized. From the mass politics of Daniel O'Connell, through the catastrophic trauma of the Great Irish Famine, to the political and religious ferment of the Gaelic Revival, Catholicism was a social phenomenon that could transmit a sense of difference, helping to craft a powerful dividing line between what would coalesce as a new Irish nation, and the assimilating power of English cultural and political imperialism. When Ireland finally gained its independence in 1922, Catholicism was firmly entrenched as the foundation of social life and collective identity, a situation that endured for decades. Only in the last thirty-five years or so, as the threat of the United Kingdom and Protestant ascendancy waned and decades of calm and peace have allowed centuries of oppression to fade, has religion too started to have less relevance in the lives of the Irish people.

Even so, most measures of religiosity continue to place Ireland among the most religious communities in the Western world, a legacy of Catholicism's role in the Irish nationalist movement and its foundational place in Irish national identity. This fading of religion has an exception, however, in Northern Ireland, where the last thirty-five years of the twentieth century saw religious affiliation rise to an unprecedented level as a marker of political and national belonging. Here the clash between Catholicism and Protestantism retained its power, serving as a proxy for political ideals of unionism and nationalism amid a struggle over political control of the conflicted region. This continued threat to both religious communities, and the repeated battles over political power, helped religious identity serve as a fundamental and foundational element of social identity.

This analysis of the religious dimensions of national identity in Ireland reveals the importance religion can hold for nationalist movements struggling to craft an independent state. At its most fundamental, religion served as a boundary marker in Ireland, differentiating who could be considered part of the nation from those who were seen as outsiders, dangerous to the political movement. This was particularly important in an Ireland that was rapidly Anglicizing, as the Irish language and traditional culture were replaced by English and Protestant political culture. An Ireland ruled by landlords based in England, whose population was excluded from most aspects of public life and political power on account of their religion, quickly rallied around religion as a central tenet of what made them different from English imperialists. O'Connell was the first to capitalize on such sentiments, fusing from a disconnected and uneducated mass population a political movement that would win rights previously denied to even the wealthiest and most educated of Catholics. In his efforts to achieve Catholic emancipation, O'Connell made religion matter to the population, revealing how ordinary and everyday policies of discrimination held powerful social and political effects on Catholics' role in Irish society and their continued impoverishment and disenfranchisement. Such arguments were brought brutally home in the Great Irish Famine, in which people's religion, as well as their socioeconomic status, played a critical role in whether they lived or died. That Protestant landlords occasionally boasted about the toll the famine was taking on Catholics, while exports of foodstuffs continued to leave Ireland destined for English tables, made clear the social and political divides that structured interaction in Irish society. Protestant efforts to proselytize, only giving out relief supplies in exchange for conversion or attendance at Protestant church services, further cemented religion's role as a key facet of identity in the minds of many. Catholics and Protestants became "us" and "them" in a way that polarized religious relationships that were none too civil to begin with.

The Gaelic Revival provides an interesting case of a nationalist movement that was sparked by Protestant nationalists concerned with gaining independence from England and its insidious language and culture. Protestant Revivalists felt that traditional Irish culture and language were distinct and worthy of protection, viewing such cultural elements as fundamental to their own belief that the Irish nation, represented by them of course, deserved political independence or at least a limited form of self-government. What such Protestant cultural and national entrepreneurs failed to realize, however, was the exceptional power that Catholicism had come to hold in the lives of the Catholic population. To many Catholics, to be Irish and to be Catholic were synonymous, and the revival of the ancient Irish culture and language fit comfortably in arguments that Ireland was unique because of its culture, language, and religion; after all, Catholicism was the first form of Christianity to prevail on the island, and traditional Irish culture was closely associated with traditional Irish Catholicism to many. This conflation of dimensions of identity represents what Roccas and Brewer have termed a lack of social identity complexity[114] and a belief that others must share all one's dimensions of identity in order to be truly counted a member of the national in-group.[115] This perspective found its greatest champion in the person of Patrick Pearse, who combined a fervent belief in the power of Irish culture with a personal Catholicism that was apocalyptic and centered on concepts of self-sacrifice, martyrdom, and the importance of blood. Pearse's vision reveals the extent to which Catholicism served as a "chain of memory," passing on a reservoir of cultural symbols and myths, most visible in the themes of sacrifice drawn from the death and resurrection of Jesus Christ. To Pearse, who combined Catholic themes of blood sacrifice and martyrdom with similar ideas drawn from Irish culture in the person of Cú Chulainn, the Irish nationalist movement might suffer and individual nationalists might die, but it would rise again in glory, the blood of the martyrs serving as not just the seed of the church, but of the nation as well.

The social and political context of the development of nationalism in Ireland closely associated it with the Catholic religion. Catholic nationalists, with the exception of the Protestants who led the Gaelic Revival, possessed a vision of Irish nationhood that merged political independence, Gaelic culture, and Catholic religion. Theirs was a vision of the nation that lacked social identity complexity; it was crucial to the nation that its members be all of these, and they took steps to revive the Gaelic culture and closely tie the nationalist movement to the hierarchy of the Catholic Church. The attempt was successful. The persistence of religion as a fundamental means of organizing society, visible in significant levels of religious affiliation, church attendance, and electoral success for Catholic social causes throughout most of the twentieth century, reveals the extent to which Catholicism continued to matter in the lives of most Irish people. This conflation of religion and nation was brought into even sharper focus in Northern Ireland, where religious differences served as fundamental markers of community identification in politics and political violence throughout most of that country's existence. As we will see, Ireland is not unique in this conflation of religious and national identity. Though the two cases vary significantly in context, the processes of nation formation in the Republic of Turkey took a similar path, drawing on religious conception of difference as a means of differentiating and gaining support for the nation. In Turkey, Islam provided a core component of ethno-religious identity around which national boundaries and a sense of nationhood could be formed, much as Catholicism did in Ireland. In both states everyday conceptions of religious identity came to serve as powerful markers of national identity and drivers of political action, serving as the foundation of claims to nationhood and national community.

4 · CONSTRUCTING THE NEW NATION
Official Nationalism and Religious Homogenization in the Republic of Turkey

The development of the Turkish nation has long been an object of fascination for scholars of nationalism. A nation with a majority Muslim population, yet seemingly modeled on Western secular forms of governance, Turkey is an intriguing study in contrasts. Yet it is these contrasts that have proved problematic for a Turkish nation that has struggled to find a balance between the religious beliefs of most of its populace and the secular arguments of its founding fathers. This dichotomy has led to some of the most important political debates and crises in Turkish history. Much of this turmoil dates back to the complicated history of the nation's founding. Rather than a slow, centuries-long process of national identity formation, such as that found in Ireland, Turkish nationalism burst on the scene as a consequence of the specific set of historical circumstances that accompanied the decline of the Ottoman Empire and the end of World War I in the Middle East. The Ottoman Empire's defeat by a coalition of Western powers proved a devastating blow to its already tottering political and social structure. The sultan's painful concessions in the Treaty of Sèvres and the subsequent partition of Ottoman territory among the victorious Allies proved too bitter a pill to swallow for a significant group of revolutionary political and military leaders.

The Turkish nationalist movement arose from this frustration, ignoring the strictures of the Treaty of Sèvres and seeking to reverse political capitulation by the sultan's government. The chief goal of the national movement was to unite scattered opposition movements to retain national sovereignty and create a unified state for the Turkish people. The Turkish nationalist movement can thus be seen as a struggle against external imperialism and the partition of the national community, but also as pushback against the failures of a decadent and out of touch empire that was seen as not properly representing the will of the Ottoman people. In contrast, the nationalist movement sought specifically to represent the Turkish people and craft a new nation that would more properly reflect their concerns. But this effort raised the question of precisely who the Turkish people were. The Ottoman Empire had been a multiethnic, multireligious, and multilingual polity. How should the complexity of the Ottoman Empire be transformed into a unified national community? Who should be counted a member of the new Turkish nation? On what characteristics should national identity be based, and how should national identification be determined? Such questions would prove of critical concern to the movement and the new state it would craft.

The origins of the official version of Turkish history lie in the work of Mustafa Kemal Atatürk. Rising to prominence in the Turkish nationalist movement by 1919, Atatürk became the first president of Turkey when the republic was proclaimed in 1923. Faced with the need to assemble a new national state out of the wreckage of the Ottoman Empire, as well as to subdue opposition within his own party,[1] Atatürk took it upon himself to lay out a vision of late Ottoman and early Turkish history that could serve as a new foundational narrative for the nascent Turkish state. Atatürk delivered this historical vision in a marathon speech that lasted for thirty-six hours over the course of six days. This "Great Speech" (Nutuk in Turkish) sought to illuminate the development of the new state of Turkey, describing the various struggles the nationalist movement had overcome and providing a historical foundation for a glorious new era of Turkish history. In Atatürk's own words, he hoped to "explain how a great nation, which was thought to have come to the end of its national existence, had gained its independence and had founded a national and modern state based on the latest principles of science and technology."[2] In this Atatürk was eminently successful: the Nutuk represents what is almost certainly the single most influential source in the development of Turkish history and historiography. School textbooks, popular writing, and much of the academic literature for most of Turkey's history have accepted and built upon the version of events Atatürk relates. Only since the 1970s has a steadily growing trend in Turkish historiography begun to question this acceptance, beginning to view Atatürk's Nutuk as not just historical, but as a political and ideological document as well.[3]

When understood as a political argument, rather than as a straightforward telling of objective history, the Nutuk reveals several key ideological preoccupations and foundational beliefs shared by both Atatürk and the political movement he founded. First, Atatürk's formulation of Turkish national history describes a distinct break between the collapsing Ottoman Empire and the newly formed Turkish state. The events of World War I, the Turkish War of Independence, and the founding of the new Republic of Turkey are presented as a distinct rupture, a watershed moment in the history of a primordial nation as the Turkish people rise up and seize their country back from the imperialistic ambitions of Western powers and the corrupt and inept sultan alike. Second, Atatürk believed that the Republic of Turkey would be a new, modern state, eschewing the traditional social and political formations of the old empire and instead adopting a more Western form of society and governance. According to this perspective, religiously oriented forms of social organization were backward and oriental, and social advancement and development could only be achieved by reconfiguring Turkey as a civic and secular state.

This particular mindset was echoed in some of the earliest scholarly examinations of the Turkish republic. Bernard Lewis's *Emergence of Modern Turkey* seems to portray a "spontaneous and gradual process,"[4] the birth of a sort of primordial nation as it *emerges* amid the fragments of the decaying shell of empire within which it had always lain dormant. Such an approach argues for the inevitability and naturalness of what was, instead, assuredly a creation and product of deliberate actions taken by a revolutionary elite. Explaining the development of the Turkish nation as the emergence of a primordial nation thus draws a strict contrast between the new nation and the old empire, portraying modern Turkey as the product of a teleological process and emphasizing the distinctly new, modern, civic, and secular characteristics of the newly founded state. Similarly, Niyazi Berkeş's *The Development of Secularism in Turkey* takes for granted that Turkey has managed to become a secular state. Berkeş places heavy emphasis on the processes of modernization and secularization that have long been seen to have defined Turkish history and its split with the Ottoman Empire. This perspective continues to downplay continuities between the two states as well as the continued role of religion in modern Turkey. Such approaches are typical of much of the historical and sociological scholarship on the development of Turkey. Though it reached its peak in the 1950s and 1960s, this emphasis on modernization and secularization remains the dominant historiographical perspective on the rise of the Turkish nation.[5] The assumptions made by those early scholars and their own particular areas of ideological emphasis drew upon Atatürk and the Kemalists' own arguments and gave them even greater academic weight.[6]

Ultimately, however, the mainstream historiographical tradition based on Atatürk's Kemalist ideology tells only part of the story of Turkish nationalism. As Erik Zürcher has argued, such works have tended to focus almost exclusively on interplays of ideas, emphasizing the spread of Western ideologies such as modernization, secularization, and nationalism.[7] This emphasis on a history of ideas and how they were incorporated into the political and social thought of Turkish ideologues and theorists has thus focused almost exclusively on the elite, the educated and powerful strata of Turkish society that assimilated these ideas and put them into practice in their efforts to modernize and Westernize the Turkish state. Emphasizing the experiences of intellectual and political elites of the late Ottoman and early republican era resulted for a long time in a concomitant disregard for other aspects of Turkish history. Looking only at the ideas and actions of the elite has presented a skewed picture of Turkish history, placing too much weight on many of the ideological ideas of a small (if powerful) percentage of the population while ignoring the beliefs, actions, and conditions of the vast majority of people living within the boundaries of the new Turkish state.

The emphasis on ideology and ideas comes at the expense of a depiction of social realities on the ground and how they impacted not just politicians and ideologues but common people in the cities and countryside of modern Turkey. Such analyses have thus portrayed a one-sided view of Turkish history. Differing perspectives on the nation and on the role of such important issues as religion or ethnicities were dismissed as simply backward resistance to the implacable march of historical progress, mere negative reactions of "Muslim conservatives" and the like to the rapid progress of Turkish society. Such blithe dismissals of the beliefs of significant portions of Turkish society are unsatisfactory, however. While the ideas and policies of the ideological elite are certainly important, they fail to capture a variety of powerful beliefs and movements from outside the small circle of Westernizing elites that significantly impacted the development of Turkish society.

A more complete history, moving beyond elite ideas and into an analysis of the conditions and beliefs on the ground among everyday residents of Turkey, reveals a far different picture of Turkey than the dominant historiographical narratives have offered, one that sharply questions the teleological visions of nationalism, modernization, and secularism that Kemalist rhetoric has so strongly portrayed. Instead, a more historically contextualized approach makes it clear that more of the social and cultural structure of the Ottoman Empire survived than has often been admitted, and earlier forms of identification based on religion and culture have played an important, if underrecognized, role in the development of Turkish national identity.

More recent examinations of Turkish nationalism have begun to provide just such a perspective, moving beyond traditional Kemalist narratives and producing works with significantly wider focuses. These studies have called the Kemalist historiographical tradition into question, problematizing traditional historical characterizations of the Turkish nation and opening a broad array of new research avenues. One consequence of this is that ideological depictions of Turkey as a civic and secular state have been tested empirically as scholars have begun to ask questions about the role of social formations such as religion and ethnicity and the ways the Turkish state dealt with them. Ultimately scholars have begun to dispute the simplistic narratives that depict a sharp break between the Ottoman Empire and Turkey, the unquestioned triumph of Westernization, secularization, and the characterization of the Turkish state as ultimately civic and secular in nature. These scholars have argued that the development of Turkey as a distinct national community was far more complex, involving a multitude of different strands of nationalist thought, many of which focused far more on ethnic and religious differences than earlier theorists had recognized. Hugh Poulton,[8] for example, has identified three distinct impulses operating in the first few decades of the Turkish republic: Kemalist secular Western nationalism, a pan-Turkic ethnic nationalism dedicated to constructing a unified Turkish race encompassing all Turkic peoples, and Islamic variants emphasizing religious identity. Tanil Bora[9] has added further nuance to the picture of Turkish nationalism, arguing that by the 1990s five distinct nationalist discourses, including official, Kemalist, liberal, ethnic Turkish, and Islamist religious versions of nationalism, had found purchase in the Turkish political arena. Other scholars have found similar results, recognizing linguistic,[10] ethnic,[11] and religious[12] dimensions of the Turkish national project. Here I examine these alternate facets of nationalization before turning to the processes by which religion became a defining characteristic of modern Turkish identity.

FROM EMPIRE TO NATION: RELIGION, POLITICS, AND THE DEVELOPMENT OF TURKISH IDENTITY

Religious Difference and the Rise of Nationalism in the Late Ottoman Empire

From the beginning, the Ottoman Empire was a multiethnic state encompassing a tremendous amount of ethnic and religious diversity. Founded in 1299 by Osman I in northwestern Anatolia, within a century the Ottoman Empire had conquered the Balkans and much of the rest of Anatolia. Over the next few centuries, the empire expanded throughout what is today the Middle East, North Africa, and southeastern Europe, reaching its greatest extent by the end of the seventeenth century. This rapid expansion and vast territorial reach made the Ottomans rulers of an array of peoples with different political, social, and religious backgrounds. Most importantly, the Ottoman sultans' power and control of the Middle East allowed them to lay claim to the title of Caliph, the political and religious successor to the Prophet Muhammad and leader of the entire Muslim community, or *ummah*. Thus, from early on in its history the political structure of the Ottoman Empire was intimately connected to notions of Islamic identity. As Bernard Lewis argued, "Among the different peoples who embraced Islam, none went farther in sinking their separate identity in the Islamic community than the Turks."[13] The close relationship between politics and religion in the Ottoman Empire was noted by contemporary observers in Christian Europe, for whom "Turk" came to serve as a generic term for Muslims of any sort.[14] With its control over vast swaths of the Middle East and North Africa, the Ottoman Empire certainly counted among its residents a number of Sunni Muslims, but it similarly contained large populations of religious minorities, including Jews, minority strands of Muslim belief, and Christians of a variety of ethnic backgrounds. This multiethnic and multireligious polity proved a recurring problem for Ottoman rulers who sought to incorporate minority populations within an overarching political system.

The Ottoman solution to the problem of diversity was the *millet* system, a form of governance that relied heavily upon religious affiliation. Rooted in Islamic teachings regarding the treatment of religious minorities under Muslim rule, power under this system was devolved, with confessional communities largely allowed to rule themselves under the overarching umbrella of the Ottoman central state. Separate confessional communities supported separate legal courts, and minority populations were allowed to set their own rules and practice self-governance with little interference from the central Ottoman authorities. Muslim authorities ruled under Islamic *shariat* (*shari'a*) law, while Christian and Jewish communities were governed according to Christian canon law and Jewish Halakha, respectively.[15] This system had significant benefits for Ottoman authorities and minority populations alike. For the Ottomans, decentralizing power relieved the central state of many of the most troubling aspects of ruling a pluralistic society, allowing the responsibility of governance to rest on the shoulders of the minority populations themselves. Similarly, by granting extensive autonomy to minority communities, and significant power to their leaders, the Ottomans bound minority populations more strongly to the Ottoman state, giving them and their leaders a vested interest in remaining Ottoman citizens rather than rebelling and pushing for independence or reunification with coreligionists outside the boundaries of the empire. For religious minorities, the *millet* system provided significant amounts of autonomy and allowed religious leaders to rule their communities according to religious principles. Leaders such as the Greek Orthodox patriarch prospered under this arrangement, attaining more power even than they would have outside of Ottoman control. In large part, this system worked well, and despite significant religious and ethnic differences, the Ottoman Empire saw relatively peaceful relationships between religious communities for significant stretches of time.[16]

This is not to say, however, that religious minorities had rights and obligations equal with those of Muslims in the Ottoman Empire. Relatively peaceful coexistence there may have been, but the Ottoman strictures regarding the treatment of non-Muslim minorities, based largely on Islamic teachings, clearly established the religious minorities' position as second-class citizens. Inequality in areas such as taxation, military service, and representation under the law all favored Muslim citizens over Christians and Jews. Non-Muslim minorities of the Ottoman Empire annually paid the *cizye* (*jizya*), a tax levied by the Ottoman state, nominally collected as a fee for protection provided by the Muslim rulers for non-Muslim subjects.[17] Though policies varied significantly across the history of the Ottoman Empire, such taxes were often much heavier than the *zakat*, the tax required of Muslim citizens of the empire. Theoretically, by virtue of paying the *cizye*, non-Muslim communities were also exempt from the requirement to perform military service for the Ottoman state, a requirement expected of many Muslim men within the empire. By the fourteenth century this had changed, however, as Sultan Murad I introduced the *devşirme* (literally a "gathering" of youths),[18] periodic conscription of Christian boys from the Balkan region. Conscripted before adolescence, these boys were converted to Islam, trained as soldiers, scribes, and officials, and incorporated into the Janissary (*Yeni Çeri*, literally "new soldier") corps or the Ottoman bureaucracy, within which they could often reach great heights. Instituted in large part because of the sultanate's need for a completely dependent vassal population of soldiers and administrators outside the control of the Ottoman nobles and thus not a threat for power, the status of these conscripts nevertheless reveals the precarity of non-Muslim populations within the Ottoman Empire. Similarly, legal relationships between Muslims and non-Muslims were unequal, and significantly favored the former, as any legal dispute involving a Muslim was required to be heard before an Islamic, rather than Christian or Jewish, court. Such regulations provided an important advantage for Muslim citizens of the Ottoman state and reveal another arena in which religious inequality played an important role in the lives of Ottoman religious minorities.[19]

Religion thus functioned as a key aspect of identity in the Ottoman Empire, a defining facet of social identity that served not only as a marker of ethnic identity but also to determine a person's class and social position. This arrangement, in which religion played such a powerful role in social life, was of course a common one in medieval and early modern societies, not just in the Ottoman case but throughout Europe as well. Traditional sociological theories argue that it was the transition from early modern to modern forms of social organization, brought about by the spread of European Enlightenment ideas of rationality and secularism, that prompted the transition from religious to bureaucratic and secular forms of government. Such systems relied upon civic characteristics such as volition, rather than ethnic or cultural characteristics such as religion for determining social position.[20] Indeed, this is precisely the argument that scholars have made regarding the transition from a religiously oriented Ottoman system to the nominally secular democratic republic of the Turkish nation-state.

Yet when nationalism came to Ottoman lands it did so under a religious guise. Most of the breakaway nationalist movements that occurred among Ottoman territories in Europe cited their Christianity, and unwillingness to be ruled by foreign Muslim sultans, as the primary distinguishing factor that qualified them as independent nations. The French Revolution and new ideas of self-determination and governance spread through Europe and eventually reached the Ottoman Empire. In part this flourishing of national ideas spread through interactions between Ottoman populations (Christians and Muslims alike) and European populations through trade and similar links. Christians and Jews in many ways served as the merchant class of the Ottoman Empire, providing crucial economic and intellectual links with European societies.[21] Ottoman Muslims themselves had significant dealings with European states, however. By the eighteenth and early nineteenth centuries, the Ottoman Empire, which had long held a techno-logical and military advantage over many of its neighbors, had begun to grow stagnant, its social and political system became too rigid, and the Ottomans faced a variety of significant social and political crises.[22] Realizing the economic, military, and geopolitical consequences of being left behind by technological and social progress in Western Europe, Ottoman rulers sought to act, and it became *en vogue* for Ottoman elites to study in France and other Western coun-tries. Similarly, Ottoman sultans such as Selim III (r. 1789–1807) and Abdülme-cid I (r. 1839–1861) imported French and Prussian military commanders to train and reform the Ottoman military in modern fashion.[23] Such interactions pro-vided valuable linkages between the Ottoman Empire and the West, allowing for the dissemination of new ideas throughout Ottoman lands. Such intellectual links were not the only means through which ideas of self-determination and nationalism spread, however, as European powers sought to intervene in Otto-man affairs, prompting ethnic communities of Christians under Ottoman control to develop nascent conceptions of national identity, and pushing and supporting them to declare independence from the Ottoman Empire. Nowhere was this truer than Greece, where French and British *philhellenes*, aghast at the notion of the Greek nation, cultural forebear of much of Western civilization, remaining under the control of Muslim conquerors from the East. These philhellenes urged Greek Orthodox Christians to declare independence from the Ottoman Empire, drawing upon ideas of cultural and religious difference and supporting the movement both ideologically and financially.[24]

The spread of revolutionary ideas of self-determination and nationalism, then, burst upon the Ottoman scene in the nineteenth century. Both organically derived from intellectual linkages with the West and purposefully nurtured and prompted by Western ideologues, newfound national communities began to develop throughout the Balkans and other parts of the empire. Such nationalist movements relied heavily on religion as justification for their independence efforts, arguing that Christian communities should no longer be under the rule of an oppressive and unequal Ottoman state in which Muslims took precedence in the social and political hierarchy. The Ottoman Empire's continued techno-logical and economic stagnation made it particularly vulnerable to these sorts of breakaway national movements, and a series of Balkan nations, led by Greece in 1821, managed to secure their independence. Nationalist sentiments similarly arose among Armenian populations in the east of the Ottoman Empire, though with less success. Tellingly, though Ottoman control over Arabia and Egypt fluctuated according to the strength of the Ottoman government throughout the nineteenth century, resistance to imperial control did not take the form of nationalism until they were prompted to do so by foreign powers in the twentieth century.[25] Indeed, though a vague concept of Arab identity appeared in Arab literature of the nineteenth century, it took on no political manifestations. Demands for independence among Arabs in the Arabian Peninsula and the Levant began only with the rise of interest in Arabic cultural identity in Syria in the late nineteenth century, and again placed religion at the forefront, becoming popular only among a small population of Arab Christians.[26]

From the beginning, then, experiences of nationalism in Ottoman lands were intimately intertwined with questions of religious identity. Growing nationalist sentiment among religious minorities added to a series of social and political crises that had severely weakened Ottoman power. Successful national movements pried off pieces of the empire, while military defeats at the hands of foreign powers such as Russia made obvious the increasing gap between the technological and military prowess of modernizing states and the ineffectiveness of the stagnant and corrupt Ottoman system. The Ottoman leadership recognized the serious social problems afflicting the empire and set about trying to save a state that Tsar Nicholas I of Russia had gleefully dubbed "a sick man, a man who has fallen into a state of decrepitude, a man gravely ill."[27] Faced with both internal and external pressures, the "sick man's" administrative doctors prescribed a strict regimen of reform and reorganization, seeking to simultaneously modernize a bloated and stagnant administrative system that was resistant to change and heal the rifts between the various religious, ethnic, and cultural communities of the empire.

Tanzimat

The Ottoman solution was a series of policies that came to be known as the *Tanzimat* (literally reorganization) reforms. The Tanzimat built upon earlier scattered efforts at modernization to introduce wholesale reform in a way that would allow the Ottoman state to match its rivals for imperial power. In a movement that lasted from 1839 until 1876, the Tanzimat reforms drew upon the knowledge of bureaucrats who had been educated in Europe, most often France, to create a social and political structure that was capable of supporting the needs of the Ottoman state in a new modern era. The chief areas of concern were the military, which had proved significantly overmatched in recent wars, and internal administration, which had long been decentralized and diffuse, with little true power consolidated in the hands of the sultan's government in Istanbul. With these goals in mind, Ottoman reformers produced a targeted series of policies designed to rapidly modernize, centralize, and Westernize the Ottoman state.

New Western-style uniforms and military standards and training sought to bring the Ottoman armed forces into the modern world. Critically, the Ottoman state moved away from the *devşirme* system of religiously targeted military conscription in exchange for a system of universal conscription across ethnic and religious lines. Changes to styles of dress among the aristocracy and efforts to change the administration of Ottoman territories represented efforts to change the stagnant attitudes of imperial officials and administrators, seeking to convince them of the benefits of adopting Western ways of thinking and governing. Other more direct policies instituted modern governmental apparatus such as the first Ottoman post office (1840), census (1844), universities (1848), and telegraph and railway systems (1847–1856).[28] Throughout, imperial reformers sought to strengthen the central Ottoman government and allow it to assert stronger control over the imperial periphery and stem the hemorrhaging of territory and population that had so weakened the Ottoman state. Reformers pursued these efforts by incorporating Western techniques of administration and governance that they hoped would prove as successful for the Ottoman government as they had for other powers. If the worst maladies facing the empire had come from the West in the form of increasingly powerful foreign states and the rise of Western-style national movements within Ottoman territory, they argued, perhaps the cure could be found there as well.

The Ottoman leadership made significant efforts to knit together the fractured polity of the empire, seeking to draw Muslim and minority populations alike back into accord with the central state. Only such a radical reform, they believed, could stem the tide of nationalism and ethnic and religious politics that was dismembering the territory of the Ottoman Empire piece by piece. Tanzimat reformers sought to advocate a policy of "Ottomanism," attempting to reaffirm the populace's attachment to the Ottoman state, subordinating ethnic and religious difference in favor of allegiance to an Ottoman ideal. Thus the imperial Edict of Gülhane issued by Sultan Abdülmecid I in 1839, which formally launched the Tanzimat reforms, included significant clauses relating to the status of religious minorities within the Ottoman state. The edict emancipated religious minorities, making them subject to the same laws and conditions as the Muslim majority, and guaranteed the right to life and property for all Ottoman citizens regardless of ethnic or religious background.[29]

A further Reform Edict in 1856 was even more specific, confirming and enforcing these changes. It explains that "All the privileges and spiritual immunities granted by my [Abdülmecid I] ancestors ab antiquo, and at subsequent dates, to all Christian communities or other non-Muslim persuasions established in my empire under my protection, shall be confirmed and maintained."[30] The Reform Edict reaffirmed that religious difference would no longer be used as a salient category of identity for administrative purposes and asserted equality for all Ottoman citizens regardless of class or creed. It explained that "Every distinction or designation tending to make any class whatever of the subjects of my Empire inferior to another class, on account of their religion, language, or race, shall be forever effaced from the Administrative Protocol. The laws shall be put in force against the use of any injurious or offensive term, either among private individuals or on the part of the authorities." It continued later, "As all forms of religion are and shall be freely professed in my dominions, no subject of my Empire shall be hindered in the exercise of the religion that he professes, nor shall be in any way annoyed on this account. No one shall be compelled to change their religion."[31] Further clauses established equal legal and property rights, taxation, access to education, and military service for Christians and other groups within the empire, elevating non-Muslim minorities to an equal standing with Muslim citizens and seeking to assuage many of the largest schisms within Ottoman society in a way that would unify the empire and provide a strong social base comparable to those of many of the European great powers.

Young Ottomans

Yet the efforts at reform, drastic and wide ranging though they may have been, were not enough for some segments of the Ottoman population. Established as a secret society in 1865, the Young Ottoman movement sought to extend the process of modernization, keeping the Ottoman state intact, yet proceeding further down the path blazed by European intellectuals.[32] To the Young Ottomans, only a modern Western-style constitutional government would provide the change necessary for the Ottoman Empire to remain competitive in the world at large. The Young Ottomans made their opinions known through a variety of publications, and key Young Ottomans such as Namik Kemal and Ziya Pasha published plays, newspapers, and magazines dedicated to their revolutionary ideas. Publications such as *Tasvir-i Efkâr* (Interpreter of Ideas) and *Hürriyet* (Freedom) achieved wide circulation.[33] In part, this strength grew due to the support of disgruntled Muslims who were humiliated at both the interference of Christian powers in Ottoman affairs and the economic and social power of Christian minorities in the empire, who prospered in the environment of official tolerance and equality brought about by the Tanzimat reforms. With this in mind, the Young Ottomans advocated for "the continuing and essential validity of Islam as the basis of Ottoman political culture."[34] The growing strength of the constitutional movement caught the attention of Sultan Abdülaziz, who cracked down on the leadership of the Young Ottomans and forced them to flee into exile in Paris. The Young Ottomans' ideas were not so easily suppressed, however, and they maintained significant support among the Ottoman Muslim elite.

The Young Ottomans managed to return from exile in 1871, and the condition of the Ottoman Empire made it ripe for their message. Financial hardship throughout the empire in the early 1870s, revolts among Christian populations of the Balkans in 1876, and Russia's declaration of war in support of those Christians in 1877 proved devastating blows to the sultan's government.[35] In May of 1876, Young Ottomans, bolstered by support among the political elite, launched a coup d'état, seizing control of the government and installing Murad V, nephew of Abdülaziz and supporter of the movement, on the Ottoman throne. Despite his promises to impose a new constitutional regime, Murad V refused to do so and soon became mentally unstable.[36] After only three months, Murad was replaced by his brother, who ruled as Abdülhamid II and quickly promulgated the first Ottoman constitution on December 23, 1876. The Ottoman constitution established the General Assembly of the Ottoman Empire, the empire's first parliament, setting the stage for what the Young Ottomans hoped would be a new era for the empire. This hope was to be in vain, however, as Abdülhamid II reasserted the power of the sultan, dissolving the General Assembly a mere two years later.

Yet this First Constitutional Period did provide precedent for the significant changes soon to come as the state transitioned from empire to republic. Chief among these was the rise of ideological politics among the elite of the Ottoman Empire, who began to take an interest in public opinion and the will of the masses of Ottoman society.[37] Also important, however, was the reassertion of the role of Islam in the self-definition of Ottoman identity. For the Young Ottomans, nationalism, loyalty to state and territory, and civic belonging were all important virtues that should be adhered to above and beyond allegiance to religious communities. The goal of Ottomanism was thus to transcend communal divisions between Christians and Muslims. Yet this seeming tolerance and multiculturalism urged by the Ottoman patriotism of the Young Ottomans had limits. The Young Ottomans believed that the new constitutional system should be developed within the framework of Islam, uniting liberal Western values of civic politics with traditional Islamic values in a new form of political organization.[38] In practice this was problematic, as despite its multicultural character the Ottoman Empire had never managed the civic equality to which the Young Ottomans were aspiring. These seemingly contradictory impulses, between the universalism of Ottomanism and the particularism of a focus on crafting a specifically Muslim view of culture and society in which Islamic ideals took precedence, was to become a key characteristic of the Turkish nation that would succeed the Ottoman state.

Young Turks

The goals and methods of the Young Ottoman movement served as inspiration for a second group of radical revolutionaries, the Young Turks.[39] Meeting in secret throughout the first decade of the twentieth century, the Young Turks organized themselves under the aegis of the Committee for Union and Progress (CUP), a secret society that soon evolved into a genuine political party and revolutionary movement.[40] In 1908, spurred on by war with Russia and fears of further loss of territory and partition in the Balkans, the Young Turks launched a revolution. With support from military units and elements of the military leadership, the Young Turks seized power, reinstated the 1876 constitution, and ushered in the Second Constitutional Period, the Ottoman Empire's first experience with multiparty politics. With this revolution the Young Turks and the CUP essentially ended the sultan's de facto control over Ottoman politics as power came quickly to reside in the Ottoman parliament, rather than the sultan's palace, for the first time.[41] The problem, of course, with installing multiparty politics is that sometimes public opinion runs in unexpected ways, and the CUP found itself faced with significant electoral challenges from the Freedom and Accord Party, which won the elections of 1911. Undeterred, the CUP consolidated its power in a series of moves, including a rigged election in 1912 (known as the "Election of Clubs," for its violence against Freedom and Accord members), and a coup d'état that involved a raid on the Sublime Porte, the center of Ottoman governance.[42] The CUP soon came to dominate Ottoman politics under the leadership of a triumvirate of officials, known as the Three Pashas: Mehmet Talat Pasha (Grand Vizier and minister of interior), Ismail Enver Pasha (minister of war), and Ahmed Djemel Pasha (minister of the navy).

In addition to the political changes their revolutionary actions catalyzed throughout the Ottoman Empire, the Young Turks inspired a crucial transition in the ideology of revolutionary movements in the Ottoman Empire, one revealed by the group's name itself. Though the Young Turks originally contained members of a variety of ethnic and religious backgrounds and placed a heavy emphasis on the maintenance and continuation of the Ottoman state, as their predecessors had, the Young Turks' emphasis gradually changed, taking on a nationalist character that placed more weight on ethnic characteristics and the primacy of Turkish ethnicity.[43] Young Turk ideologies thus shifted the focus of political loyalty away from a pan-ethnic and religious Ottomanism to a more restrictive vision of ethnic and religious nationalism. It was during this time that Turkish nationalist ideology acquired an exclusionist character. Emphasis on Turkish ethnicity drew new boundaries of belonging where those of Turkish ethnicity and Muslim religion were seen as being more representative of the "true" nation than those who did not meet both qualifications.[44] This exclusionist attitude culminated in the Armenian Genocide, the deportation and massacre of hundreds of thousands of Armenian Christians in eastern Anatolia.[45] This transition, from a pan-ethnic vision of Ottomanism to one that privileged specifically Turkish identity, would set the stage for new visions of Turkish nationalism that would arise following the collapse of the empire itself, providing the foundation of new nationalist ideologies that, despite rhetoric to the contrary, viewed religious and ethnic characteristics as central to national identity and belonging in the new national community.

The Shattering of Empire

The growing schisms between Muslim and non-Muslim minority populations of the empire soon took its toll. Nationalist movements throughout Ottoman territory continued to use religion as a key signifier of social and cultural difference and constituted a significant strain as breakaway movements in the Balkans and elsewhere tested central Ottoman power. Defeat in wars with Italy over the

Vilayet of Tripolitania in North Africa (1911) and four Balkan states (1912–1913) stripped the empire of nearly all its remaining European territories and further weakened imperial power, as did a monarchist countercoup attempt in 1909 and a coup attempt by members of the Freedom and Accord Party in 1912. The final blow, however, was the Ottoman Empire's entrance into World War I in 1914 and its subsequent defeat at the hands of the Allies. Pushed to the brink of collapse, the Ottomans surrendered in 1918, and the sultan's government was forced to sign the Treaty of Sèvres in 1920. The terms of the treaty were devastating, requiring the Ottoman Empire to surrender vast territories in the Middle East and even much of the Anatolian peninsula, shrinking what was once a vast empire to a rump state occupying only part of the north central region of Anatolia. Under the terms of the treaty the Ottomans were to surrender all "non-Turkish" land, which was to be divided up among the victorious Allied powers according to economic and demographic concerns.[46] France, Greece, Italy, and Britain were all to receive substantial regions to control in the west and south, and a sizable independent Armenian state was to be established in the east.

This devastating defeat and drastic partitioning of the Ottoman empire would have several significant consequences for the region. The government's agreement to the dismantling of the empire destroyed any faith in the sultan and the Ottoman governmental system. In addition to the de jure control the sultan surrendered to the Allies, the government lost de facto control of most of the rest of even the rump state that remained. Revolutionary leaders such as Mustafa Kemal Atatürk stepped into this gap and seized on it as an opportunity to establish a nationalist movement that could rally those opposed to the treaty and craft a new national state around the population and territory that remained. Furthermore, the defeat in the Balkan Wars of 1912–1913 and later the 1918 defeat in World War I increased tensions between the Christian and Muslim populations of the empire. The victorious Balkan states were largely Christian, and their victory over the Ottoman Empire created a wave of devastation and despair among the Muslim populations of the Balkans. Throughout the Balkan states, Muslims were killed or evicted from their homes and deported, setting off a wave of "ethnic unmixing" and religious migration as the newly formed Christian states purged their new territories of Muslim populations.[47] This wave of misery and migration was compounded by the Ottoman defeat in World War I, coming as it did at the hands of a coalition of Christian powers. Following the partition of the Empire, Greece invaded Anatolia, seeking to claim its newly acquired territory and consummate its irredentist *Megali Idea* (Great Idea), a policy seeking to unite all Greek Orthodox Christians under a greatly expanded Greek state modeled on the glories of the Byzantine Empire. These circumstances meant that religion, long an important facet of identity, once again took primacy as the category around which citizens of the former Ottoman Empire conceived of themselves and their national and ethnic identity.

The Turkish War of Independence

It was under these conditions that a truly powerful Turkish nationalist movement first began to form. Turkish revolutionaries under the leadership of Mustafa Kemal Atatürk were unwilling to accept the terms of the Treaty of Sèvres. The nationalists launched a revolution, ignoring the dictates of the now mostly defunct government of the sultan in Istanbul and beginning a military campaign designed to drive the Allied powers from the peninsula. The choice of which territory to defend was made for both nationalistic and practical purposes. Anatolia was considered the homeland of the Turkish people but also represented a defensible border that could be consolidated politically and militarily. As Atatürk himself would argue, "I tried to define the national boundaries somewhat according to the humanitarian purposes of [Woodrow] Wilson's principles [the Fourteen Points outlining the importance of ethnicity in defining national boundaries, but].... Poor Wilson, he did not understand that lines that cannot be defended by the bayonet, by force, by honour and dignity, cannot be defended on any other principle."[48] The Turkish revolution was remarkably successful, meeting the Greek advance near Ankara and driving it swiftly back. The initially successful Greek invasion soon turned into a rout, and Turkey's nationalist forces drove the Greek army completely out of Anatolia, leaving the Turkish nationalist movement in almost complete control of what is now modern-day Turkey, and significantly improving its negotiating position vis-à-vis the Allies.

In one decisive move, Atatürk and his fellow revolutionary nationalists succeeded in simultaneously wresting control of Anatolia from the ineffective rule of the sultan's government and driving out the foreign armies that sought to further claim Ottoman territory. The nationalist movement soon consolidated its gains and reached an accord with the Allied nations at peace talks in Lausanne, Switzerland, in 1923. Under the terms of the Treaty of Lausanne, the Republic of Turkey officially attained its independence as a sovereign nation and was formally recognized as the successor state to the defunct Ottoman Empire, marking the victory of the steadily growing nationalist movement and placing it in complete control of the newly formed Turkish state.[49]

CONCEPTIONS OF NATIONAL IDENTITY IN THE TRANSITION FROM EMPIRE TO NATION

This, then, was the situation the Turkish nationalist movement faced upon winning control of the territory that would become the Turkish state. While the Turkish nationalist movement was indeed nationalist in character, dedicated to the independence and sovereignty of the Turkish nation, this goal was complicated by the fact that there had been, to this point, no such thing as a distinctively Turkish nation. Turkish identity had simply been one facet, and not necessarily a positive one,[50] of a larger multicultural and multinational Ottoman identity that was quickly collapsing. Populations throughout the former Ottoman territory were forced to reconsider and reconceptualize their own ideas of identity and belonging, seeking new forms of self-identification on which they could construct new states and societies amid the collapse of the old.

For Turkish nationalists, it was of critical importance to construct an independent Turkish identity, one separate and independent from Ottomanism. To do this, nationalists undertook significant efforts to define and delineate precisely what it meant to be a Turk. Atatürk's own civic nationalist rhetoric sought to rely on territorial concerns, arguing that all those residing within the borders of the new Turkish state would be Turkish citizens, and thus part of the new Turkish nation. Though this rhetoric proved powerful and became the official stance of the state, the reality on the ground turned out to be much more complicated. Far from being the only version of nationalism to prosper in post-Ottoman Turkey, civic-oriented political nationalism faced significant challenges from alternate discursive constructions of the nation that sought to advance different characteristics to determine national identity. This section examines each of these competing strands of nationalist rhetoric in turn, examining how they intertwined throughout Turkish history, and showing how religion continued to be a powerful characteristic of even official Turkish identity long after the state had imposed a version of secular civic nationalism that seemed to counter-indicate this.

Political Nationalism

Following the French vision of civic allegiance to the nation, Atatürk argued for a conception of the nation that emphasized devotion to a common territory and set of political principles, regardless of ethnic or religious background. Even religious and ethnic minorities were to be included in this expansive definition of the state. Atatürk himself argued both that the new state would be tolerant and humane to the remaining Christian minorities in Turkey[51] and that clauses put into place at the Lausanne treaty to guarantee protection for religious and ethnic minorities were unnecessary, because all inhabitants would be members of the new state.[52] A new Turkish nation, it was thought, could be created out of a unification of a variety of races, much as the nations of France or Switzerland had.[53] Such a political program is evident in the policies and reforms Atatürk imposed on the new state following its founding, as he sought to enact a massive reorganization of the former Ottoman territory's political and social system, ushering out the early modern system of the sultans and paving the way for an utterly modern Turkish state.

Atatürk's priority following the founding of the republic was to create a strong state and nation, solidifying the conception of a distinctly Turkish state that would be manifestly different from the defunct Ottoman Empire. In his own discussions of the foundation of the Turkish nation, Atatürk explicitly rejected definitions of the nation that would unite all ethnic Turks, or all Muslims under the new Turkish banner. "I am neither a believer in a league of all the nations of Islam," he argued, "nor even in a league of the Turkish peoples . . . the government must be stable with a fixed policy, grounded in facts, and with one view and one alone—to safeguard the life and independence of the nation within its natural frontiers."[54] Elsewhere he laid out precisely the characteristics that members of the Turkish nation should share and around which national identity should form, explaining that "these are the historical and natural facts regarding the basis of the Turkish nation: a) Political unity; b) Linguistic unity; c) Territorial unity; d) Unity of lineage and roots; e) Shared history; f) Shared morality."[55] Such a neat delineation of the characteristics of national identity seems relatively straightforward. People who were born in Turkey, spoke Turkish, were of Turkish background, and participated in Turkish politics were theoretically to be accorded full membership in the nation. As in all such things, the situation on the ground was far more complicated, however, and religious and ethnic definitions of identity retained a powerful hold on a large segment of the Turkish population. Such an emphasis on religious and ethnic identities, though standard during the Ottoman Empire, elicited loyalties that, in Atatürk's mind, threatened allegiance to the national state, a circumstance that could not be tolerated. Atatürk's government went to significant lengths to foster commonalities of feeling and identity among the new Turkish populace. Two of these efforts, the creation of a new national historical narrative and language reform meant to craft a new purified form of the Turkish language, are of particular note.

Atatürk's government undertook several important reforms designed to inspire allegiance to the new Turkish state while at the same time modernizing and secularizing the country. The creation of the Directorate for Religious Affairs (1924) and the official abolition of the caliphate (1928) sought to both further limit religion's role in national identity and consolidate control over religion within the central state. The unification of the education system (1924), restrictions on traditional headgear and dress (1925), and other reforms sought to further bring Turkey into line with Western ideals and norms. Perhaps most important, however, was the decision to "purify" the Turkish language, stripping it of all foreign loan words from Persian and Arabic, and installing a new alphabet modeled on the Latin alphabet used in Western Europe. While linguistic nationalism has often been seen as a form of ethnic or cultural nationalism, in the Turkish case it represented an effort to craft a new political community in which all members of the state could partake, rather than an effort to return to a time of cultural purity, as in prototypical linguistic nationalist movements.[56]

This drastic change, accomplished in just three months, had many important effects on Turkish society. Prior to the language reform, the Turkish language was split between Ottoman Turkish, a literary language used in formal communication and high society, and everyday, or "rough" Turkish spoken by most Turkish language speakers. The language reform based the new modern Turkish language on this rough Turkish, the language of the people, providing far more access to politics and society for the majority of Turkish people and unifying the speakers of Turkish under the banner of one common language. Just as importantly, however, the transition from Ottoman to modern Turkish cut the new Turkish state off from its Ottoman past. The new language and alphabet were different enough that generations of Turks educated solely in modern Turkish soon lost the ability to comprehend the Ottoman language in which the documents of earlier periods were written. The general inaccessibility of the histories and documents of the past made Turkey fertile ground for the introduction of new conceptions of Turkish history, ones that would portray a very different vision of the state and nation than those espoused by the Ottomans.

At Atatürk's urging Turkish historians and nationalist ideologues crafted a vision of Turkish history that emphasized the virtues and advances, some real, others imagined, of a pre-Islamic proto-Turkish culture.[57] Such a vision had the advantage of rejecting not just the tainted and decadent Ottoman past, from which the new nation needed to emerge, but also removed the Ottoman focus on Islam as the key facet of identity. This narrative of Turkish history, which soon came to be known as the *Turkish History Thesis*, argued that proto-Turkish cultures were not simply the ancestors of the modern population of Anatolia, but in fact were the founders of the great civilizations of Iraq, Anatolia, Egypt, and the Aegean.[58] Political nationalism in the Kemalist era thus sought to reappropriate conceptions of Turkish national identity, removing ties to the Ottoman Empire and its religiously oriented system of governance in favor of a new model of Turkish history and society.

Atatürk's secular modernist Republican People's Party (CHP), which dominated the state's one-party political system in the 1930s and early 1940s, was explicit about this emphasis. In the program at their Fourth Grand Conference in 1935, the CHP argued in Article 1 that "The Fatherland is the sacred country within our present boundaries where the Turkish Nation lives with its ancient and illustrious history and with its past glories still living in the depths of its soil." The CHP continued, explaining in Article 41(b) that "The training of strongly republican, nationalist, populist, etatist and secular citizens must be fostered in every degree of education. To respect and make others respect, the Turkish nation, the Grand National Assembly of Turkey, and the Turkish State must be taught as a foremost duty," and that "Our Party lays an extraordinary importance upon citizens knowing our great history. This learning is the sacred essence that nourishes the indestructible resistance of the Turk against all currents that may prejudice the national existence, his capacity and power, and his sentiments of self-confidence."[59] The emphasis throughout on issues of history, language, and allegiance to the national cause reveal the rhetorical preoccupations of the Turkish state. To Atatürk and the Kemalists of the CHP, it was this political allegiance, fostered through residence in Turkey, speaking the language, and buying into modern secular conceptions of what it meant to be a national state, that truly made a Turkish citizen a member of the Turkish nation. Yet despite its power, rhetoric, and official backing, the political definition of the nation was not the only one that affected residents of the new Republic of Turkey as they struggled to form new modes of identity in the aftermath of the Ottoman collapse. Traditional identifiers of ethnicity and religion remained powerful forces and would help significantly shape what it meant to be a true member of the Turkish nation.

Cultural Nationalism

At the unification of the Kingdom of Italy, Italian statesman Massimo d'Azeglio is said to have commented, "We have made Italy, now we have to make Italians."[60] Such was the challenge facing Turkish nationalists upon the founding of the Republic of Turkey. Political unity and allegiance to the state were certainly important; however, efforts to create a new unified political state soon made it clear that issues of identity transcended the merely political. The Turkish state, after all, was to be the homeland of the Turkish people, and nationalists undertook significant efforts that sought to bind all people living in Turkey to a larger conception of Turkish nationalism. But how was the "Turkish people" to be defined? In their quest to invent a new Turkish nation, nationalists seized upon ethnic and cultural discourses of the nation to provide an "ethnic core"[61] around which the new nation-state could form. The official Kemalist version of political nationalism thus found itself incorporating ethnic and cultural characteristics into the new national community, becoming entangled with alternative discursive constructions of nationalism that placed characteristics other than territory and political allegiance at the forefront of national identity.

Discourses of nationalism that viewed the nation in racial, ethnic, and cultural terms were prevalent in the Ottoman intellectual milieu even before the rise of Atatürk and his victorious revolutionary movement. The Kemalists' melding of political and cultural variants of nationalism in the construction of the Turkish state can be seen as an acknowledgment of the power of ethnicity and culture in the mind of everyday Turkish citizens who, far from the elite debates of the nationalist intelligentsia, continued to view their identity in traditional fashion. Several of the most important nationalist thinkers during the last decades of the Ottoman Empire emphasized the primacy of Turkish ethnicity and culture. The power and influence of the ethnic and cultural focus of these nationalist theorists was such that, when political variants of Turkish nationalism did arise, they expressed themselves through a discourse that emphasized the power and history of the Turkish race and culture. It was ethnicity and culture on which the new Turkish state would be based, and the ethnically and culturally Turkish people whom it would serve. Those who did not fit such definitions of

Turkishness could conform or depart, but Turkey was to be a Turkish state for a Turkish people.

This effort to construct and define a new sense of Turkish identity and select key characteristics around which Turkish nationhood could form is visible in the work of Turkey's earliest nationalist thinkers. Yusuf Akçura and Ziya Gökalp, considered the two founding fathers of Turkish nationalist ideology, both devoted significant attention to this question, seeking to determine the proper relationship between civic, religious, and ethnic dimensions of identity in the new Turkish nation. In his 1904 *Three Kinds of Policies*, Akçura discussed the change in focus among early nationalists from an Ottomanist civic version of the nation, in which Muslims and non-Muslims would share membership in the new nation, to one emphasizing Islamic or ethnic Turkic identity as key signifiers of membership in the national ingroup. Akçura argued that earlier efforts to create a civic form of Ottomanism had been unsuccessful because reformers "had failed to grasp the significance of race and religion, and they had in particular failed fully to appreciate that it was too late for the creation of a new nation, that the various elements under Ottoman sovereignty, even if it were to their advantage, had no desire for such a union and blending, and that consequently the application of the French concept of nationality in the East was impossible."[62] Akçura argued that it soon became obvious to the Ottoman reformers that ethnic and religious minorities could not be adequately assimilated into the Ottoman nation, and so nationalist opinions toward them hardened. These attitudes resulted in hostility toward minorities, viewing them as outsiders to the national community.[63] Akçura himself advocated Turkish race and ethnicity as the proper foundation for the new Turkish nation, arguing that a policy of Turkism would tie together the Turks of the Ottoman territories more firmly than mere political or religious ties.[64] The creation of a new specifically Turkish nation was thus, to Akçura, a complex process. What we see in his discussion of Turkish nationalism, however, is the failure of a secular and civic-minded form of Ottomanism in favor of a more ethnically focused conception of the nation, an entanglement of political and ethnic modes of identity that would remain visible throughout the history of the Turkish nation.

Ziya Gökalp, the second key theorist of Turkish nationalism, made a similar argument about the role of culture in the Turkish nation. Gökalp, unlike Akçura, argued that it was a common sense of Turkish culture, not race or ethnicity, that should define the new Turkey. In his 1923 work *The Principles of Turkism*, Gökalp argued that an emphasis on ethnic purity is normal for nations in the early stage of social evolution but was "pathological" for the stage Turkey had reached. Instead, at the current stage, "social solidarity rests on cultural unity, which is transmitted by means of education and therefore has no relationship with consanguinity."[65] Gökalp argued that it is clear that a nation is not a racial, ethnic, geographic, or political group, "but one composed of individuals who share a common language, religion, morality, and aesthetics." After all, he continues, "In truth a man desires more to live with those who share his language and religion than with those who share his blood, for the human personality does not dwell in the physical body but in the soul."[66] Here too, Gökalp placed a key emphasis on the role of common culture in promoting national identity and solidarity. To Gökalp, in order to form a true community a modern state must become homogeneous in terms of culture and religion, and thus national identity.[67]

Gökalp's vision of the Turkish nation was thus a community that would share a common culture, defined explicitly in terms of language and religious identity. This was a definition of the nation that excluded the religious minorities of the former Ottoman Empire and those that would be present in the new Turkey. Despite its professed civic character, the growth of Turkish nationalism would rely significantly on Gökalp's theoretical approach to the Turkish nation.[68] It would be Gökalp's emphasis on culture, education, and like-minded thinking among the national populace that spurred many of the most important reforms of the Kemalist period. Likewise, the approach to governance taken by Mustafa Kemal Atatürk, and the development of Kemalist thought that would dominate the Republic of Turkey for much of its history, drew significantly from definitions of the Turkish nation that placed strict boundaries on membership in the Turkish nation, conflating political and ethnic identities in a way that belied the civic rhetoric of the nationalist movement.

Other Turkish nationalists picked up on the ethnic and cultural emphases of Akçura and Gökalp, and such definitions of nationalism became legitimate competitors capable of challenging the official Kemalist nationalism. Emigrés from Russia and Central Asia favored ethnic and pan-Turkic versions of nationalism that argued for the reunification of all Turkic peoples. Akçura himself helped launch a pan-Turkish *Journal of the Turkish Homeland* (*Türk Yurdu Dergisi*) in hopes of creating a sense of common identity among all peoples of Turkic descent, and notable figures such as Enver Pasha similarly supported an ethnic definition of the nation.[69] Gökalp also spread his own interpretation of Turkish nationalism, helping to found the Turkish Hearth (*Türk Ocağı*), an organization that sought to combat the two extremes of political Ottomanism on one hand and Islamism on the other in favor of his own personal cultural approach.[70] Chapters of the Turkish Hearth were established in cities throughout Anatolia, and they sought to develop awareness of a unified Turkish culture. Though the CHP dissolved the Turkish Hearth in 1932, it was revived in 1949 and again in 1986 and has taken various steps to try to promote the Turkish culture and "defend Turkish values."

A more virulent version of ethnic nationalism established itself in ultranationalist fringe parties and movements such as *Türk Kültür Ocağı* (*Hearths of the Turkish Culture*), which, founded in 1946, argued for the superiority of the Turkish race.[71] This ideology took a more strongly racially motivated view of the

Turkish nation, holding as its basic tenets ideas of Turanism (pan-Turkism), racism and racial unity, militarism, and obedience to a hierarchical society.[72] Proponents of this more radical ethnic nationalism often sought to emphasize the cultural rather than the racial aspects of their beliefs. The 1988 program of the Turkist Nationalist Workers Party (MÇP) argued, for example, that "Turkish nationalism because it is a cultural movement . . . rejects racism."[73] Less official publications were more overt, however. Politician Muhsin Yazicioğlu, for example, asserted that "We firmly believe in the theory of superior race. . . . Turkishness is an essence comprised of religion and race. . . . The Turkish race is more precious than all others."[74]

It is clear, then, that despite the government's officially inclusive version of nationalism, significant strands of nationalist thought in Turkey emphasized ethnic and cultural characteristics as defining traits of the nation. Such efforts represented a repudiation of efforts to create a pan-ethnic Ottoman nation and instead reflected a transition from multiethnic empire to monoethnic national state. Even though official nationalist rhetoric stressed inclusiveness, membership in the Turkish nation contained a strong ethnic and cultural component for even the most ardent of political nationalists. At the same time, the official political nationalism saw its dominance challenged by discursive constructions of the nation that were even more strongly racialized, arguing for ethnicity and culture as the only true defining elements of national identity rather than seeing them as an important component of a more inclusive political definition of nationhood. Though political and ethnocultural nationalisms proved powerful indeed, a third variant of nationalism, one focused on the unifying power of religion, played a similarly influential role in the construction of the Turkish national community. This strand of nationalism attracted the least attention from scholars captivated by the assertions of the secular and modernizing character of the new Turkish state, but would prove powerfully influential in its own right.

Religious Nationalism

The third variant of nationalism operating in Turkey during the founding of the republic viewed national identity in religious terms. To such nationalists, ethnicity and culture were crucial elements of national identity, but both Turkish ethnicity and culture were to be defined through their relationship with the Muslim faith. Only those who were Muslims could truly share in the full experience of being a "real Turk," or so these nationalists argued, because it was the Turkish people's special connection to Islam that differentiated them as a distinct ethnocultural group. And indeed, despite Atatürk's own personal dedication to a secular and civic form of nationalism, most of his new subjects did not view their own identity in such terms. Rather, the legacy of the Ottoman Empire's *millet* system meant that religion was the main component of group identity for large numbers of the new Turkish population.[75] This was true of most people outside of the small circle of the intellectual elite, but was especially prominent outside of Turkey's largest cities, in rural villages and isolated populations. Such is still the case in Turkey today, in fact, where rural populations report significantly higher religious belief than urban populations in cities such as Istanbul, Ankara, and Izmir.[76] Even among Atatürk's revolutionary nationalists, opinions on the role of Islam in the new Turkish state were mixed, as a variety of nationalist figures placed more emphasis on Islamic belief than did the official rhetoric.[77] The role of religion as the salient characteristic of identity was made even more important by the Ottoman Empire's collapse and the rise of intercommunal tensions between Muslims and religious minorities. The coalition of Western Christian powers opposing Turkey, and the Greek invasion of Anatolia in pursuit of irredentist goals, crystallized the differences between religious communities in the new Turkish state, and brought religion to the forefront as the most important signifier of national and ethnic identity.

As the new Turkish nation struggled to resist the imperialist ambitions of Western powers and form a new nation out of the wreckage of the Ottoman Empire, attention swiftly turned to the question of religious minorities within Turkish territory. The emphasis on religion and the perceived connection between religious minorities and outside Christian powers made Turkish Muslims extremely suspicious of the Christian and Jewish minorities within Turkey. Yusuf Akçura, writing before the founding of the republic, saw only one inevitable result of this sort of approach in the Ottoman territories. He argued that "the religious discord and enmity among Ottoman subjects would accentuate, and the non-Muslim subjects and the areas in which they constitute a majority would be lost."[78] Though the "Ottoman nation" would be temporarily weakened in such an eventuality, "it would be very tightly knit and it would, for all its shortcomings . . . give rise to a stronger community, an Islamic community."[79] Indeed, though he himself preferred a racial and ethnic definition of Turkishness, he saw the potential power of religion as a means of promoting national solidarity. "It should not be forgotten," he argued, "that the greater part of the Turks whose unification is envisaged are Muslims. From this point of view, the Islamic religion can be an important element of a great Turkish nation."[80]

The violence and homogenization that Akçura foresaw were not long in coming. Following the collapse of imperial power, many Turks viewed the remaining populations of religious minorities within Turkish territory as traitors. Turkish leaders took severe measures to deal with what they considered a significant threat during both the last years of the Ottoman Empire and the first few of the new republic. Hüseyin Cahit Yalçin, a journalist who often served as the mouthpiece of the de facto ruling Committee of Union and Progress, summarized their approach to Christian minorities by saying "For the State . . . [and] the Constitutional Regime, the greatest danger came from the non-Turkish elements within Ottoman Society"; thus, "the history of the Constitutional period is the history of the Turks, who perceived the danger, and struggled not to drown in the flood of peoples."[81]

Such efforts to stem the tide of minority peoples began in 1915 with the Armenian Christian population in eastern Anatolia. While estimates vary, somewhere between 800,000 and 1.5 million Armenians were deported and massacred in a series of actions now recognized as one of the first modern genocides.[82] Throughout, the Turkish nationalist movement's concern was for the homogenization of the Turkish homeland, removing a minority population that did not share Turkish culture or religion. As Halil Menteşe, an influential member of the CUP, argued, "Had we not cleansed our Eastern Provinces of Armenian revolutionaries collaborating with the Russians, there would have been no possibility of establishing our national state."[83] Here again, religion was seen as an integral part of Turkish culture and identity; ethnic, religious, and national identities were conflated in a way that strictly delineated in- and out-groups. To be a Turk meant being a Muslim; to be a Christian meant being a foreigner and a potential threat to the nation.

Similar motivations lay behind the 1923 population exchange between Greece and Turkey. Theoretically designed to "unmix" national populations, the exchange explicitly utilized religious affiliation as a proxy for national identity.[84] Greek Orthodox Christians were moved from Turkey to Greece, while Muslim populations from Crete and elsewhere in Greece were transplanted to Turkey. This exchange is a particularly useful example of the degree to which religious and national identities were fused in the newly forming Turkey. Despite the professed civic character of the new Turkish nation, populations were exchanged even when all other markers of identity—characteristics such as languages, ethnicity, and territorial origin—identified them more with their original country than the new "homeland" to which they were moved. This was particularly true of the Karamanli people of central Anatolia, for example, a Turkish-speaking group of Greek Orthodox Christians who Turkey made part of the exchange, despite expectations that they would be allowed to remain in place.[85] Similarly, Muslims from Greece, who, despite their centuries of ancestral roots and lack of any understanding of the Turkish language, were sent to Turkey, where their religious identity more closely matched that of surrounding populations.[86] Even Assyrian Christians and other small populations of other Christian communities were caught up in the exchange, making evident the exchange's focus on religion rather than nationality as a prerequisite for exchange.[87] Throughout, the concern of the Turkish government was to promote ethno-religious homogenization, separating "Turks" from "Greeks" and defining both national identities in explicitly religious terms. The supposed civic character of the nation professed in Turkish rhetoric thus proved problematic on the ground. Turkish policies at the very beginning of the nation consistently made it clear that the Turkish leadership viewed being a Muslim as a necessary prerequisite for membership in the Turkish in-group.

This conflation of religious and national identity lasted long past Turkey's founding period, however. As Turkey entered the high Kemalist years of the 1930s, religion continued to play a powerful role in defining national identity. As Soner Çağaptay has argued, this was particularly true in regard to immigration policy, where Turkish policy utilized religion as a litmus test when granting citizenship and allowing entrance to the country.[88] Turkey allowed some of the remaining Greeks in Istanbul to gain full citizenship rights if they were willing to convert to Islam.[89] Similarly, Turkey allowed wide-scale immigration of Muslims from former Ottoman territories, regardless of ethnic background, while denying entrance to Christians from similar territories and denaturalizing minority residents of Turkey who had left during the wars. As a resettlement law adopted in 1926 explained, "Those who don't share the Turkish 'hars' . . . will not be admitted as immigrants."[90] The Turkish word *hars* means culture, and is the same word Gökalp used to refer to Islam and a shared sense of cultural identity in his own efforts to define the Turkish nation. At the beginning, Turkey explicitly utilized religious terms in citizenship decisions, specifically describing those allowed citizenship as "Muslims." This slowly changed throughout the 1930s as the term "Turk" began to replace "Muslim" in official documents.[91] Significantly, while the term used to describe such immigrants changed, immigration policy itself did not. Citizenship and immigration priority were still determined on religious grounds, but the relationship between religion and national identities was such that the terms were interchangeable, members of the Muslim in-group and members of the Turkish in-group were considered one and the same, and those who fell outside of the Muslim in-group could not and would not be Turks.

Other policies put in place by the Turkish government similarly reveal an emphasis on religion in determining full membership in the nation. A law passed in 1931 established strict governmental control of the press in Turkey, permitting only Turks to own magazines or journals.[92] Similarly, a Law on Associations was passed in 1936 prohibiting the establishment of organizations and associations representing ethnic and religious minorities.[93] Most devastatingly, law number 2007, passed in 1932, banned non-Turkish citizens from a large variety of professions, both skilled professional ones and those requiring little formal training.[94] This law was aimed specifically at the remaining Greek Orthodox population in Istanbul, which had been exempted from the population exchange and remained a thorn in the side of Turkish efforts at homogenization. As Çağaptay explains, many of these Greek Christians were left unemployed, and more than 15,000 left the country as a result.[95] The burdens on the remaining religious minorities were made even heavier in 1942 when the Turkish government imposed a strict tax on non-Muslim citizens, a move widely understood to be an effort aimed at financially ruining the remaining non-Muslim minorities in Turkey.[96] Discrimination and mistreatment of the remaining religious minorities in Turkey extended beyond official government policy, however, and in September 1955 hostility toward Christians and Jews boiled over in violent riots targeting non-Muslims in Istanbul. Following the explosion of a bomb outside Atatürk's historic house in Salonika, later proved to have been planted by the Turkish Secret Service in an effort to rouse ethnic tensions, thousands of shops, homes, churches, and ceme-teries owned by Christians were burned and destroyed.[97] Here again, non-Muslims were seen as falling outside the Turkish in-group and fair game for acts of punitive violence, not considered fellow members of the Turkish nation but foreigners and traitors on account of their religious affiliation.

Religion, then, played a powerful role in the conceptualization of the new Turkish nation from its beginnings in the last decades of the Ottoman Empire onward. Forged amid the traumatic collapse of Ottoman society, the rise of intercommunal conflict between religious groups, and defeat and invasion by powerful Christian states with a vested interest in supporting Christians over Muslims, the Turkish nation soon came to take on a religious dimension. Mus-lim Turks were to serve as the core of Turkish society, and the threatening nature of intergroup interaction served to crystallize religious identity as a key facet of identity around which the new nation-state could form. The association of Turk-ishness with Islam persisted well past the founding of the nation-state, however, as perceptions of national belonging have continued to have a religious dimen-sion throughout Turkish history, proving that religious definitions of the nation were not "superfluous expressions which were incompatible with the modern character of the new Turkish State and our republican regime,"[98] as Atatürk had argued, but a powerful and long-lasting element of Turkish national identity.

CONCLUSIONS

This chapter has traced the evolution of nationalism in Turkey, examining its ear-liest beginnings during the last century of the Ottoman Empire, following it through the establishment of Turkey as an independent republic in 1923, and analyzing the ways that the new state expressed its own identity as nationalists sought to build a united nation and a homogeneous Turkish people. This approach reveals the multifarious nature of Turkish nationalism. Though the nationalist movement and the national government it created preached a strongly secular-ist, political, and civic form of nationalism, alternative discourses of what Turk-ish nationalist identity meant operated within, around, and in competition with the official Kemalist version of nationalism. In this, the experience of Turkish nationalism paralleled the Irish case, where complicated debates over the nature of the nationalist community also caused significant strife. In Turkey, such alter-nate discourses, placing more emphasis on ethnicity, race, and religion, played powerful roles in determining who qualified as a "Turk" and thus merited full inclusion in the Turkish nation. This analysis thus adds nuance to the dominant view of the relationship between religion, ethnicity, and nation in Turkey. Exam-

ination of the formation of national identity reveals that phenomena such as ethnicity and nationhood in Turkey, as in Ireland and many other places, were relational and processual, crafted as political projects rather than existing as static
social forms. The constellations of identities that came to serve as the foundation
of the Turkish state and nation were the product of boundary-making processes
that drew upon various categories of collective identity to construct a singular
and cohesive national identity.

Ultimately, all the various strands of Turkish nationalism sought to craft a
new and unified Turkish state and nation, constructing a new sense of national
identity upon which society could be based following the collapse of the multireligious and multiethnic Ottoman Empire. Political nationalists argued that
Turkey could bind together scattered members of diverse populations into an
overarching Turkish political identity. Ethnic and cultural nationalists took a different approach, arguing that the new state should be a Turkey for the Turks, and
that the residents of Turkish territory should assimilate or depart so that the new
state could attain ethnic and cultural homogeneity. Finally, religious nationalists
argued that Islam was at the center of what it meant to be ethnically and culturally Turkish. Thus, though the Turkish nationalist movement succeeded in
establishing an independent state in 1923, important debates over the foundational character of Turkish national identity that had begun during Ottoman
times continued well into the first several decades of the Republic of Turkey. The
nationalist movement had "made Turkey," but it was an entirely different matter
to "make Turks."

Despite the official nationalist movement's emphasis on secular nationalism,
religion played a powerful role in who was truly a Turk. In many ways, this
emphasis was a natural response to the circumstances in which the Turkish
nationalist movement arose. The Ottoman Empire had utilized religious affiliation as a key determinant of legal status, meaning that populations in the new
Turkey were predisposed to emphasize religion as the most salient characteristic
of their own self-identity. The rise of nationalist movements in the Balkans,
many justified through new conceptions of religious self-determination spread
by revolutionary intellectuals in Western Europe, made religion an even more
important area of concern for Ottoman and post-Ottoman populations. Finally,
the victory of the Allied Christian powers over the Ottoman state in World War I
and the partition and occupation of Ottoman territory by those same powers
brought religion into focus as Muslim populations increasingly felt themselves
under threat on religious grounds. Reliance on religion to craft a new sense of
identity reveals the construction of national and ethnic boundaries along a critical axis of difference, imposing a dividing line between the new Turkish community and the culture perceived to be the most direct threat to Turkish identity
and sovereignty, an oppositional Christian culture with which Turks had had
centuries of polarizing interaction and conflict.

This chapter has sought to show how the official Turkish nationalism became intertwined with religion, constructing a religiously homogeneous national society despite an inclusive civic rhetoric emphasizing membership in the nation for all. Despite their secular rhetoric, nationalist politicians have been very clear about the role of Islam in Turkey and Turkish identity. As with the case of Ireland, however, an emphasis on the official policies of the nationalist movement does only half the work of understanding religious nationalism as a social, cultural, and political project. The next chapter seeks to break such constructions down even further, examining what Islam and nationalism meant on a common quotidian basis, how such formulations operated in everyday life, and the conditions under which relationships between Muslims and Christians in Anatolia, often peaceful, broke down in a wave of intercommunal violence and expulsion. In essence, this chapter will seek to explain why intellectual elites abandoned their secular rhetoric in favor of religiously motivated policies and why such efforts garnered them mass public support.

5 · RELIGION AND NATION ARE ONE

Lived Experience and Everyday Religion on the Ground in Turkey

Though Turkish nationalism has garnered significant academic attention, scholars examining the development of the nationalist movement and the formation of the Turkish nation-state have often placed heavy emphasis on the ideology of Mustafa Kemal Atatürk and the Kemalist elites who followed him. Such a focus is understandable given Kemal's dominant position in the nationalist movement and the state it would found. The "Father of the Turks," as he would come to be called, held particular ideas about the proper construction of the nation, and it was his ideology, and that of his followers, that would shape the official rhetoric of the new Turkish nation. Yet Kemalist ideas of a secular, mono-ethnic, Western-style nation-state were not the only ones with significant appeal during the tumultuous transition from empire to nation. As the last chapter has shown, religious affiliation remained a prominent individual and communal identifying characteristic long after the founding of the supposedly secular Turkish state. Indeed, despite the rhetoric of the Kemalist elite, religion played the most important role in determining who would and who would not be considered "true" Turks and members of the Turkish nation.

Such religiously oriented conceptions of national identity found expression in official policies that excluded or disadvantaged religious minorities, but they did not start there. Rather, religiously focused policies that trickled through the officially secular governmental apparatus represented only the tip of the iceberg, a reflection of deeper conceptions of identity and belonging held by elites and commoners alike. This chapter focuses on these understandings of identity, examining how the relationship between religious, ethnic, and national identifiers interacted at the ground level, in the everyday experiences of not just elite policy makers, but in the lives and interactions of common people throughout Turkey.

Many scholarly analyses of Turkish nationalism have approached their topic through an analysis of the writings, speeches, and policy initiatives of the largely Kemalist elite.[1] This approach offers a variety of advantages for scholars. Official sources provided important insights into political ideology and maneuvering, revealing what the people who were crafting the theoretical foundation and governmental structure of the new Turkish state thought, or at least professed to think, about the processes they were undertaking and the goals they were pursuing. Yet, at the same time, this focus entails certain drawbacks, as it privileges the experiences of a handful of elite decision makers without regard for most of the population. Emphasizing as it does the experience of a highly selective elite group, such an approach often lacks nuance, failing to engage with many of the deeper social and political currents that drive policy efforts and political ideologies. Furthermore, examining the writings of a group of political victors, those who ultimately achieved control over the new Republic of Turkey and implemented their own political ideas, albeit with uneven results, risks presenting a teleological approach to history and society, taking political rhetoric at face value and, particularly where nationalism is concerned, accepting a vision of national history that is often reimagined and invented after the fact. These approaches thus often do not adequately take into account alternate formulations of the nation, and fail to incorporate both the voices of those who had different conceptualizations of what the nation could be, and those of minority populations who were excluded from the processes of nation formation, deemed too foreign and outside the boundaries of communal national identity.

As we have already seen, many of these blind spots were true of the first generation of scholarship on Turkish nationalism. An emphasis on the political strategies of elite Kemalists led scholars such as Bernard Lewis,[2] Niyazi Berkes,[3] and Feroz Ahmad[4] to produce works that, though enormously influential and classics in the field, reproduce the modernist, secularist, and teleological perspectives of their sources. Recent strides have been made in developing a social historical approach to Turkish nationalism, however, emphasizing the beliefs and perceptions of everyday people as they struggled to come to grips with the radical transformation from Ottoman Empire to Turkish Republic.[5] Such efforts have utilized collections of alternative sources such as provincial newspapers,[6] oral histories,[7] periodicals,[8] and memoirs[9] to supplement the official narrative of Turkey's elite nationalists and provide a more balanced and comprehensive picture of the end of the Ottoman Empire and the founding of the Republic of Turkey. This chapter follows such trends and utilizes similar sources.

Here I draw upon the writings of late Ottoman Muslim bureaucrats and military officers, who were in a position to write about religion, ethnicity, and nationalism, as well as the writings and oral histories of minority populations, who were even more likely to write about how religion interacted with ethnic and national forms of identification in everyday life. Such sources allow us to examine the ways in which people on the ground spoke and wrote of their own national and group identities and examine what membership in such groups meant to people in their everyday lives. Though such data certainly only reflect the experiences of those writing at the time, a subset of the population that tended to be wealthier, urban, and male,[10] they nevertheless provide perspectives from beyond the core of Kemalist nationalist elite who were dedicated to the official version of nationalism. Such sources allow us to examine how people on the ground spoke and wrote of their own national and group identities and examine what membership in such groups meant to people in their everyday lives.

At its core, this effort to understand the relationship between religion, ethnicity, and nationalism on an everyday level is essentially concerned with the complexity of social identity. Scholars interested in the construction and maintenance of social and group identities have paid increasing attention to the fact that most individuals are simultaneously members of a variety of social groups.[11] These social groups correspond to a variety of facets of identity, and individuals draw upon their perceived membership in such social groups to help conceptualize their own cohesive sense of self. Residents of the late Ottoman Empire and early Turkish republic were no different in this regard: people's understandings of their religious, ethnic, and national identities overlapped and intersected in complicated ways. It is the ways that these various facets of identity intersect, which social group engenders the strongest sense of allegiance at any given time, that helps determine the most salient characteristics around which an individual's overarching sense of self-identity is formed. Such constellations of identity play an important role in the ways people conceive of themselves, but also how they relate to others, laying the groundwork for interpersonal and intercommunal relationships and helping to determine how people respond to those around them. In turn, such relationships provide the foundation for policies of inclusion and exclusion at a societal and governmental level, as patterns of cognition drive patterns of social and political organization.

This chapter thus takes a social historical approach, drawing on sources produced by common people who were forced to negotiate the transformation between empire and republic, to examine the social complexity of identity in the late Ottoman Empire and the Republic of Turkey. Such sources provide a wealth of insights into the relationship between different facets of identity, among them religion, ethnicity, and nationalism, and the ways in which people understood their own senses of self. Ultimately, it was the confluence and interaction of these distinct facets of identity that helped shape the ways in which national identity in Turkey would develop. The relationship between religion, ethnicity, and nationalism, and the consequent negotiation of identity that their interaction entailed was most visible during periods of strife, situations in which people were forced to reexamine and reconceptualize their own identities and their membership in a variety of social groups. As in Ireland, these periods of strife represent several distinct "ruptures"—time periods and events in which common conceptions of ethnic, national, and religious identity were put under significant strain. At each rupture, it becomes clear that for most common Turks, conceptions of social and national identity have been explicitly mediated in religious terms. Thus, despite efforts to the contrary, the ostensibly secular Turkish nationalist movement developed a significantly religious component. In essence, if the last chapter traced the ways in which the Turkish nationalist movement picked up on and utilized religious concerns, this chapter in many ways tells the opposite story, examining how religious populations became nationalized and served as the foundation of a new national state.

BEFORE THE NATION: TOLERATION AND COMPROMISE IN PRE-REPUBLICAN ANATOLIA

During the late Ottoman Empire, religious affiliation played a powerful role in conceptions of communal identity. The *millet* system that the Ottoman Empire used for purposes of internal administration utilized religious categories as a means of determining social and political status and legal rights.[12] Far from simply an organizational system imposed from above, however, the *millet* system codified and made political a social system already in place on the ground, in which religious difference served to structure daily life within the multicultural and multireligious Ottoman polity. This was particularly true for religious minorities, populations of Jews, Greek and Armenian Orthodox Christians, and heterodox Muslim groups such as Alevis, who lived and worked within the boundaries of the Ottoman state. As Ronald Suny has argued, in big cities such as Istanbul or Smyrna, "Their social interactions were primarily with people in their own millet rather than with those outside with whom they were unlikely to worship or marry or even bathe in the same hamam. Members of Ottoman minorities developed social interactions with other non-Muslims or with Europeans resident in the larger cities."[13] In some ways, this segregation proved an asset for Christians and Jews. Members of religious minorities were often able to rise far in the Ottoman system, attaining economic and political success under a system of social organization that provided legal guarantees for even those who fell outside the bounds of Ottoman Sunni orthodoxy.[14] Their foreign connection eventually made some minorities so powerful that Christians and Jews largely dominated the economic system during the last decades of the empire. Such was their power that by the founding of the Turkish republic one member of the Committee for Union and Progress (CUP) felt it necessary to argue for the disenfranchisement of minorities because "The CUP could not have relied on the non-Muslim minority who controlled all the economic institutions of the country; it was necessary for some segment of the economic power to be transferred into the hands of the Turks."[15]

Despite the religious segregation and the tendency of coreligionists to keep to themselves in imperial centers like Istanbul, daily life outside of the largest cities of the Ottoman Empire often involved significant intercommunal contact. As William Ramsay, an Englishman who traveled extensively through Anatolia, noted, "In respect of religious feelings or intolerance there is a marked contrast between the village Turks and the city Turks. In the villages you rarely see any signs of bigotry or of dislike to Christians. The people seemed never to have the slightest objection to my going freely about their mosques."[16] Numerous oral history sources testify to good relations between Christian and Muslim communities in western Anatolia, with some Christians going so far as to say that "Before [World War I] we lived well with the Turks. We got on like brothers," and mutual concerns of village life led to strong intercommunal bonds and deep friendships across religious lines.[17]

Christians and Jews played an integral role in the economy of late Ottoman Anatolia. Successful businessmen, merchants, doctors, craftsmen, and farmers, religious minorities made up much of the middle class of the Ottoman Empire, so much so that the waves of population exchanges, interreligious violence, and emigration that would eventually purge Turkey of most of its religious minorities brought with them a devastating economic toll as whole sectors of the Anatolian economy vanished with the Christians and Jews who departed.[18] Religious difference was treated respectfully and Christians and Muslims often visited each other's places of worship and celebrated each other's holidays in a spirit of friendship.[19] For much of late Ottoman history, then, intercultural relationships were largely positive; Christians, Jews, and Muslims lived side by side within the multireligious Ottoman framework and religious minorities were treated far better in the Ottoman Empire than were Jews and other minorities in Western Europe.[20]

Yet despite, and perhaps because of, the significant interaction between different religious communities in Anatolia, there was little mixing of religious groups. Religious communities jealously guarded intergroup boundaries, and though commerce and fellowship were shared across religions, conversion, mixed marriage, and other forms of cultural blending were relatively rare.[21] Though it was not uncommon for members of different religious communities to attend each other's religious functions, they were careful not to take part,[22] being conscious and respectful of difference rather than blending aspects of multiple religious traditions. The strict enforcement of group boundaries was the result of the ways self and communal identity were conceptualized in the Ottoman Empire. Neither their friendly relationships with Muslim neighbors nor the legal position as accepted minorities within the Ottoman Empire guaranteed equality for members of religious minorities. Orthodox Muslims were given preferential legal positions and rights within society, and despite their relative wealth their status as "second-class citizens" within the empire reinforced the importance of religion and religious identity for many minorities.

Such concerns structured how people perceived their identity. For minorities in the Ottoman Empire the religious facet of identity was so dominant that ethnic and national categories of identification "meant little to the people in question. Western accounts often refer to Balkan peasants who seemed puzzled by the ethnic labels ascribed to them,"[23] a condition not uncommon in other areas of the Ottoman Empire as well. Similar conceptions of identity were found among the Muslims of Anatolia. "The word Turk, which referred to the lower classes of rural Anatolia was in the nineteenth century contrast to Osmanli, a term usually reserved for the ruling elite. Islam also had a far more positive valence among ordinary Muslims than identification with being Turkish."[24] The framework of the Ottoman Empire was such that people's religious faith directly determined their position in society, the avenues available to them, and the people they came in contact with on a daily basis. Social organization along religious grounds helped determine the most salient characteristic of identity in the everyday lives of the Ottoman population. Difference, and therefore collective identity, in the late Ottoman Empire was thus structured around religious grounds. People conceived of themselves as being "Christian," "Jewish," or "Muslim" rather than being "Turkish" or "Greek," and it was these religious identities that drove their sense of national and political belonging.

If Western conceptions of ethnic identity proved perplexing for peasants in Anatolia and the Balkans, Ottoman conceptions of communal identity proved equally confounding for Western audiences primed to view ethnicity and nationalism as obvious and natural characteristics, central to identity and serving as the cores around which communities form. Indeed, the complex interweaving of religion, language, ethnicity, and later nationalism, that structured daily life in the Ottoman Empire combined to produce Ottoman conceptions of group identity that differed significantly from the ways in which Westerners saw the world. This was particularly true of the ways religion combined with other facets of identity to create an overarching sense of identification and belonging. Infused with the spirit of Enlightenment rationality, Western politicians (and indeed many of the scholars who would later follow them) failed to comprehend the extent to which religion structured Ottoman identity.

In the Ottoman Empire, religious rather than ethnic or linguistic boundaries formed the core of social organization. It was these boundaries that were actively policed, leading to peculiar relationships between religion, language, and group identity. Such constellations of identity thus made it possible for, among other examples, one particular Turk to tell Bryer in 1969 that "this is [Roman] Rum country; they spoke Christian here,"[25] and for populations of Karamanli Christians in central Anatolia to practice Greek Orthodox Christianity while speaking a dialect of Turkish that was written using Greek characters. That the interaction between facets of identity such as religion, language, and ethnicity produced identities rife with what seems almost conceptual slippage to modern and Western audiences reveals the complexity of social identity during the late Ottoman Empire. This complexity would soon take center stage as nationalism gained a foothold among Ottoman populations. Nationalists and the nations they worked hard to create sought to carve distinct national communities out of Ottoman society. A multicultural system in which crosscutting facets of identity combined to create complex identities could have no place in a nationalizing world preoccupied with homogenization and unity.

CONFLICT, EXCLUSION, HOMOGENIZATION: FROM THE BALKAN WARS TO THE FOUNDING OF THE REPUBLIC

Though the *millet* system of the Ottoman Empire provided a framework in which Muslims, Christians, and Jews were able to get along peacefully, if not overly intimately or equitably, in Anatolia, events on the world stage during the first decades of the twentieth century would soon conspire to strain the relationships that guaranteed intercommunal civility. The rise of nationalism in Western Europe spread quickly to the east, and Christian populations in the Balkans revolted against the Ottoman Empire. Internal turmoil and the failure of much-needed efforts at reform weakened the Ottoman Empire significantly, and in 1912 and 1913 Bulgaria, Greece, Montenegro, and Serbia forged a successful alliance that, bent on the goal of liberating coethnics from Ottoman rule, stripped the Ottomans of most of their European territories. A catalyst for the significant political changes discussed in the last chapter, the disastrous defeat in the Balkan Wars, and in the Great War that would follow closely on their heels, proved devastating for common citizens throughout the empire as well, throwing communities into turmoil and shattering the bonds of neighborly tolerance that had allowed Christians and Muslims to live in peace.

The Balkan Wars were conducted under the guise of nationalism and ethnic reunification, but, as with so many things in the Ottoman territories, both ethnic and national identities were closely tied to religious affiliation. The breakaway nationalist movements that had succeeded in wresting territory from the Ottomans and establishing states of their own in Greece, Bulgaria, and Serbia often defined national identity in ethnic and religious terms. Significantly, Greek tradition holds that it was an Orthodox bishop, Germanos III of Old Patras, who blessed a Greek flag and proclaimed the national uprising that won Greece its independence in 1821,[26] and the Orthodox Church played a powerful role in shaping conceptions of Greek ethnic and national identity.[27] Similarly, the Syrian Revolution took religion as a central concern. Serbian leader Karađorđe Petrović's 1809 proclamation calling for a national uprising listed religious freedom and relief from the Ottoman Empire's religious taxes as central goals and equated Serbian nationalists with Christian priests spreading Christianity and national fervor in equal measure.[28]

The religious character of Balkan national states bled over into their quest during the Balkan Wars, almost a century later, to reintegrate ethnic populations of Greeks, Bulgarians, and Serbians who still fell under Ottoman rule into their respective national states. The violence that accompanied the Ottoman Empire's loss of its European colonies brought with it a wave of human misery as communities were polarized by national conflict expressed in sectarian terms. The Balkan Wars entailed significant amounts of ethnoracially motivated violence and terror, an ethnic, and therefore religious, "unmixing" of populations that had lived in close proximity for centuries.[29] Christians in the Balkan nations used their victory as an opportunity to pay back the Ottomans for what they saw as centuries of oppression. Such ethnically and religiously targeted violence had vast repercussions. Millions of Muslim refugees fled the former Ottoman possessions in the Balkans for safer conditions deeper within the empire.[30] The Muslims who arrived in Anatolia brought with them heartbreaking stories of Christian campaigns of brutality and ethnic cleansing against Muslims.

The influx of Muslim refugees from the Balkans and the perceived demise of the empire polarized Ottoman society. Religious identities, long markers of relatively benign difference, acquired an increasingly political charge. Religion became a powerful defining line between those considered loyal to the nation and those perceived to be a threat. The Ottoman government certainly reinforced sentiments that emphasized Muslim identity at the expense of Christian minorities to impart a new sense of solidarity and pro-Ottoman sentiment. As Hasan Kayali has argued, the Young Turks appealed to Islam to "safeguard the unity and continuity of what was left to the empire."[31] But much of this sentiment arose from the common people themselves. Contemporary accounts reveal the escalating level of despair among Ottoman Muslims as they watched their coreligionists suffer and encountered at first hand the victims of Christian atrocities. One account,[32] related by Fatma Müge Göçek in her superb study of Ottoman memoirs, explains that the escalating series of crises facing the empire made it feel as if "A nation was disintegrating, sinking into the darkness of history. . . . All we could do was . . . protest [to no avail] . . . sing bitter marches and shout 'vengeance, vengeance.'"[33] This vengeance was to be against Christians, those perceived to be the cause of the empire's decline and the greatest threat to its continued survival. As one Anatolian Christian who would survive this turmoil and eventually end up relocated to Greece related, before this time, "[t]he Turks did not pressure us. We loved them, they loved us. But the Macedonian Turks came through here and they were fanatics and they spoiled them."[34] Another argued that "The Turks were good people. Only after 1912 did our relations with them suffer, for the Turkish refugees from Macedonia and Crete would say 'they've pushed us out.' They'd say [to the Anatolian Turk], 'hey you. You have THESE people as your "brothers"? Do you realize what the Greek army did to us?'"[35] Such sentiments were shared by Muslim Turks, one of whom explained that "[t]he deadly news delivered by the convoys of [Balkan] migrants poisoned us."[36] Not only did the influx of Muslim refugees turn the sentiments of Anatolian Muslims against their neighbor Christians, the increasing polarization of identity and antiminority sentiments extended to physical violence as Muslims driven from their homes in the Balkans exacted revenge against Christians in their new land. As official campaigns against Christians in Anatolia got under way, Muslim Turkish refugees began "to slowly show the Greek Rum the torture they themselves had suffered in the Balkans."[37]

The Armenian Genocide

The worsening relationship between religious communities in the Ottoman Empire expressed itself in devastating acts of cross-communal violence. Foremost of these was the Armenian Genocide, a series of targeted killings, conscriptions into labor battalions, and death march deportations, in which 1.5 million of the approximately 2 to 2.5 million Ottoman Armenians would be massacred.[38] Though the facts on the ground remain politically contested, modern scholarship has convincingly concluded that the genocide of Ottoman Armenians was the result of a state-sponsored plan of elimination, driven by orders from the CUP government and carried out by Ottoman soldiers pursuing a centralized plan of religious and ethnic homogenization.[39] The Turkish government continues to protest this interpretation, arguing instead that the massacre of Armenians in eastern Anatolia was part of a much larger sequence of intercommunal religious and ethnic violence in which Armenians, bent on national self-determination and allied with the Ottomans' Russian enemies, were as much the perpetrators as the victims.[40]

The culpability of the Ottoman government in the Armenian Genocide now seems clear, however, and it is equally evident that imperial intervention and the actions of nationalist politicians played a role in growing interreligious tensions as they encouraged Ottoman Muslims to support violent policies. Anecdotal evidence abounds in the oral histories of genocide survivors and Muslim Turks and in the accounts of foreign observers who relate the extent to which local Muslim populations rose up against their Armenian neighbors. What had been a relationship that had largely been peaceful, though at times contentious and strained, soon devolved into full-scale violence as Ottoman soldiers and Muslim populations, fueled by a belief that Armenians were disloyal to the state and an imminent threat, unleashed a wave of violence focused on driving them from the empire's territory and eliminating a religious minority that was seen to be incompatible with new conceptions of the political and social community.

Faced with the loss of significant amounts of territory in Europe and desperate to find a reformulation of identity that would allow what remained of the empire to stay together, Ottoman leaders seized on religion as a central facet of identity around which to rally. The division of society along religious lines that had prevailed in the Ottoman Empire proved a useful starting point, as religion remained the fundamental characteristic most Ottomans used to conceptualize their identities. The polarization brought on by the influx of Muslim immigrants from the Balkans had reinforced the importance of religion in Ottoman society. At the same time, religious concerns provided additional opportunity for nationalists determined to rescue a more stable form of society from the decline of the empire. Successive waves of Muslim immigrants from the mid-1800s on made the control of arable land a central concern, and Armenian peasants in eastern Anatolia and Cilicia were seen as competitors usurping valuable resources from a Muslim population that had already faced significant challenges.[41]

Muslim populations in Turkey saw further evidence of their disadvantage in the financial success of Christians and Jews, many of whom leveraged international connections with coreligionists in Christian countries to become wealthy. Muslim resentment of Christian success further deepened the divides between religious communities. Göçek cites the experiences of a Muslim Turk in this time period who explained Muslim sentiment through the example of a trip to the theater.

> If you lived in [the Muslim part] in Istanbul . . . then you would have to go from [Muslim] Istanbul's mud covered streets immersed in darkness across the . . . bridge, climb the hills and, half penitent by this time, enter the theater. . . . But as you returned home, soiled [in mud], staggering in the dark with something twisted within your heart as you thought and as your heart ached about the foreigners, the Greek Rum, Armenians, Jews on the other side of the bridge leading a very pleasant life in their own magnificent mansions, while the Turk on the other side pulled the blanket of his deprived life . . . over his head to sleep.[42]

Similar sentiments were pervasive. Pamphlets circulating at the time described Christians as "vipers" who "have been sucking out all the life-blood of the nation. They are the parasitical worms eating into our flesh whom we must destroy and do away with."[43] The increasing economic success of Christian and Jewish populations, especially when placed in stark contrast to the poverty of Muslims fleeing religious violence in the West, spurred resentment among Muslims and furthered the deep schisms in Ottoman society.

Needing to create a new form of social organization and sensing the deepening divisions in Ottoman society, CUP politicians seized on persecution of Armenians as a means of homogenizing Anatolia. Seen as suspect because of potential links to coethnics in Russia, which had long held designs on the Ottoman Empire's eastern provinces, Armenians represented a tangible (if in reality largely fabricated) threat to social solidarity and the integrity of Ottoman territory. Religious conceptions of identity served as foundational distinctions of communal identification, and the CUP took steps to disentangle Armenian Christians from Muslims, first removing the Armenians' political influence and then the Armenians themselves. Armenians and other Christians were shut out of official centers of power. The Ottoman parliament had dozens of Christian and Jewish members, but when it was reformed as the Grand National Assembly of Turkey in 1920, there was not a single non-Muslim among the 337 members.[44] Indeed, members of parliament were elected on the basis of an electoral law that allowed only Muslims to vote or run for election.[45]

Similarly, during their purge of Armenians in 1915, the CUP issued orders removing Armenian officers and governmental employees from positions of power.[46] Suny recounts how, as the genocide unfolded, the Armenian patriarch attempted to meet with Talat Pasha, the Ottoman interior minister, "but the minister would no longer see him."[47] Even Grigor Zohrap, a prominent Armenian member of the Ottoman parliament who pled for the Armenians to be spared and played cards with Talat the night before Talat signed the Armenian deportation orders "as if the Ottomanist connections between Armenians and Muslims were still intact," was arrested and murdered shortly thereafter.[48] The breakdown in intercommunal contact only increased as time went on. The CUP contacted elements of the local governments in the eastern provinces of Anatolia who organized committees to carry out the deportations, conscripting men into deadly labor battalions and forcing Armenian women, children, and the elderly into death marches designed to winnow their numbers and relocate those who survived to inhospitable desert regions in which life would be nearly impossible.

The formal efforts undertaken by the CUP government heightened a process of boundary formation that was already occurring at an unofficial level. Sultan Hamid II's effort to enforce pan-Islamism as a means of social organization in the 1890s resulted in an outpouring of violence against Christian Armenians in which 80,000–300,000 people were massacred. These massacres differed from the 1915 genocide in that they were not centrally planned, but rather were instigated by local officials, intellectuals, and clerics who inflamed the passions of Muslims fearing attacks by Armenians.[49] One Armenian Christian priest related the experience in his memoirs, describing the perpetrators as "a wild mob" who, when they caught sight of him, broke off their assault on a Gregorian church and shouted "*İşte bir kafir! Acele eddin ve onu geberddin!*" (An infidel! Hurry and slay him like a dog!).[50] In 1909 political tensions in the province of Adana boiled over and Muslim villagers massacred between 20,000 and 30,000 Armenians, payback for Armenian involvement in the deposition of Hamid II and perceived loss of status Muslims would suffer in a new regime, when Christians and Muslims would be equal. Such sporadic incidents of mass violence were joined by lower levels of internecine conflict as Christians and Muslims clashed over property rights and economic concerns. In 1911, the Armenian patriarchate delivered a letter of grievance to the government, attesting that "Since the beginning of [1911], as many as fifty people have been killed in the Eastern provinces and there have been a great number of attacks and wrongful seizure [of property]."[51]

Contemporaneous sources similarly reveal the response of Muslim communities to the deportation and execution of Armenians during the 1915 genocide. Göçek relates one account of the local mayor of Kaseri tasked with carrying out part of the genocide, who preserved a detailed list of the violence Muslim Turkish villagers, including local notables, officials, and officers, inflicted on the deported Armenians and the plundering of the property they left behind. His list details murders "of many Armenians," rapes, beatings, seizures of abandoned goods, and profiteering.[52] Notably, most of the perpetrators, who it should be said were blamed not for the damage they did to the Armenians but because they usurped governmental processes for dealing with deportees and their properties, were never prosecuted. Throughout, such actions were portrayed as a legitimate effort of self-defense, a stance the Turkish government maintains to this day. What such accounts reveal is the polarization of social life, the conflation of facets of social identity down to a single overarching conceptualization such that to be Ottoman meant to be Turkish and to be Muslim. Victims of boundary-formation processes in which national and social identity were being remade, Armenian Christians were considered dangerous outsiders, and were brutally excised from the newly forming nation.

"Greeks" and "Turks" in Anatolia

If the Armenian Genocide was intended to cleanse the eastern portions of the Ottoman Empire of dangerous religious minorities deemed inimical to the national community, the persecution of Ottoman Greek Orthodox Christians and the Greco-Turkish population exchange that followed accomplished a similar goal in the west and north of Anatolia. Here too, Muslim Turks believed they faced a direct threat from minority populations bent on upsetting the social order and obtaining independence. In the case of the Greek Orthodox Christians, such a threat was made devastatingly real. It was Christians from Greece, Bulgaria, and Serbia who had committed the violence that drove so many Balkan Muslims from their homes, forcing them to relocate into Anatolia proper and providing the indelible scars that had dramatically increased intercommunal tensions in the Ottoman Empire, polarizing society along religious lines. Muslims feared continued violence at the hands of Christian populations who they believed had already caused them great harm. Muslim populations retaliated against Greek Orthodox Christians in Anatolia, organizing boycotts that were enforced with violence and the killing, looting, and burning of Christians and their properties.[53] The Ottoman Empire's devastating defeat in World War I and its international consequences further deteriorated relationships between Christians and Muslims. The sultan's capitulation in the peace talks heralded the breakup of the remains of the Ottoman Empire, and the Treaty of Sèvres granted significant Ottoman territories, including massive stretches of Anatolia itself, to the victorious Western powers. Among the most difficult of these to bear was the granting of Smyrna (now Izmir) and its surrounding territories to Greece. The Greek army occupied Smyrna in May of 1919 and used the city as a staging point for an invasion that pushed deep into Anatolia. The Greek invasion, and the social and political turmoil that followed it, would spell the end of intercommunal tolerance and cooperation in western Anatolia as local Christian and Muslim communities were caught up in the whirlwind of international politics.

When the Greek army landed in Smyrna it was met with celebrations by many of the Greek residents of the town.[54] Smyrna had a large Christian population, most of them ethnically Greek, and had an important role in both the history of Christianity and the history of the Greek people in the region. The rising sense of intercommunal tension and increasing violence by Muslim refugee populations and native Muslims dismayed at international events had made Christians in the region the target of Muslim irregulars and bandit gangs, violent actors who posed an increasing threat to non-Muslim communities.[55] Greek Christians interviewed for oral history archives after the war confessed that they understood why local Muslim populations had turned on them, viewing them as a fifth column in a struggle that had suddenly transcended local differences and become an issue of international concern.[56] Nevertheless, their sudden insecurity and rising levels of violence throughout the region led the Christian populations of western Anatolia to view the Greek army as a force of liberation, come to protect them from their dangerous neighbors. The arrival of the Greek army introduced a dangerous element into an already polarized political situation, however. Greek soldiers and leaders, drawn from the Greek mainland and tempered in the interreligious conflicts in the Balkans, had little conception of the complicated patterns of interreligious and intercommunal relationships that had long secured a relatively peaceful equilibrium between Christians and Muslims in western Anatolia. In their attitudes toward Muslims and their failure to accommodate long-standing patterns of interreligious tolerance and dialogue, the Greek army represented a Christian counterpart to the polarized Muslim refugees who had fled the Balkans in fear of Christian brutality. Neither population understood how society in western Anatolia functioned, and so they brought their own prejudices and predispositions to a complicated and increasingly tense situation already primed to explode into open conflict.

The invading Greek army, its leaders and soldiers steeped in the sort of nationalist ideology that drew strict boundaries between Christian "Greeks" and Muslim "Turks," committed savage atrocities against the Muslim populations they found in Anatolia. Western sources relate countless reports of the Greek army's violence against civilian populations. The Greek landing itself turned into a slaughter. When a single shot from the crowd killed a Greek soldier, the Greek army opened fire on the surrounding Turkish population, killing several hundred "beastly and wildly," in the words of an Italian naval officer who beheld the scene.[57] Plunder, detention, rape, beatings, and torture soon followed. Such

depredations were not confined to Smyrna, however. As the Greek army consolidated its control, Greek soldiers and the local Greeks who were "incited by
the Greek officers and clergy, committed innumerable atrocities against the
Turks"[58] in surrounding villages. British and Italian officers in the region would
later recount the mass execution of men who had surrendered in the villages of
Buluk Kaya, Menemen, and Aydin, and the massacre of so many Muslims that
though the Greeks "wanted to hide the proof of their guilt," the corpses were too
many to be successfully hidden in mass graves hastily dug for that purpose.
Other reports reveal efforts at ethnic cleansing of Greek-controlled areas near
Izmit and Yalova.[59] If anything, Greek treatment of Muslim populations became
even worse when revolutionary Turkish forces under the command of Ismet
Pasha mounted a defense outside of Ankara, stopping the invasion and routing
the Greek army. The Greek soldiers burned and looted as they fled west and were
quickly joined by Greek Orthodox Christians in the area who, fearful of expected
reprisals by Muslim populations and Turkish troops, fled with the troops they
had supported.

The Muslim populations did indeed retaliate against the remaining Christian
populations in the region. Muslims who had lived through the atrocities committed by the Greek army and those Anatolian Christians who supported it
viewed the remaining Christian populations as traitors to the nation who had
essentially chosen a side, picking their ethnic and religious connections with the
Greek state over their social and political ones with the Ottomans. The support
that some Anatolian Christians gave to the Greek army essentially made all
Christians enemy combatants in the eyes of many Muslims, and their retaliation
answered atrocities with further destruction.

Perhaps the most visible expression of this sentiment was the burning of
Smyrna. The site of the Greek army's landing and a city of deep historical significance to the Christian community, Smyrna was seen as a symbol of the Christian and Greek presence in the region. Four days after the Turkish army retook
the city, a fire started in the Armenian quarter of the city. Over the course of
more than a week, the fire spread until the entirety of the Greek and Armenian
quarters of the city was consumed and destroyed. Crucially, while the destruction of the city is still considered a tragedy among Greeks,[60] the Turkish national
narrative refers to it as the "liberation" of the city.[61] The cause of the fire remains
disputed. Many Turks argue that it was the Greeks and Armenians themselves
who started the fire, but reports from Western observers at the time lead most
scholars to place the blame squarely on Turkish soldiers, who were seen igniting
Christian-owned businesses in the city.[62] While the Turkish revolutionary
army was involved in the retribution against Christian populations, significant
amounts of damage were done by Turkish paramilitaries, units drawn from the
Muslim populations of the surrounding countryside who pursued vengeance for
offenses committed by their Christian neighbors. Murder, pillaging, rape, and

the eventual destruction of nearly the entire Christian presence in western Anatolia were all seen as fair reprisal for the similar atrocities committed by the Greek occupiers and the communities that supported them. What had once been a multireligious and multiethnic community in which religious differences mattered, but were tolerated, broke down completely into an all-out war between partisans of two different nations who no longer viewed each other as "brothers" but as mortal enemies.

The collaboration between local Christian populations and the invading Greek army, and the retaliation Muslims exacted against those Christians who were not able to flee, reveals the extent to which religious identities had become intertwined with nationalized conceptions of collective identity. Many survivors of this tumultuous period mark the Greek invasion as the moment when Christian and Muslim compromise and coexistence came to a decided and definitive end. In a 2004 interview, Ali Onay, a Cretan Muslim who was relocated to Ayvalik in the Greco-Turkish population exchange, explained that "The Rums [Greek Orthodox Christians in the Ottoman Empire] forgot the tradition of Christian-Muslim friendship after 1919. Before the Greek army came to Anatolia, the Rums were not nationalists, they were Christians who were loyal Ottomans. But when the Greek army came here and did terrible things to the Muslim community, and the Rums collaborated with them, then it was all over. If only those terrible things hadn't happened, the Rums would still be living here now."[63] Yet the Greek invasion also marked a distinct break in the relationship between various religious populations and the central, now nationalizing, state. Whereas before the Balkan Wars and World War I religious difference had served as a form of social organization within a single Ottoman system, it now differentiated between members of two national communities. Indeed, the Greek invasion brought to a boiling point tremendous levels of societal and interconfessional tensions, catalyzing what had been important, but small-scale, conflict into what was perceived as a true struggle between national peoples. The Greek army was expected to commit atrocities, because that's how they had acted in the Balkan Wars. It was therefore imperative for their survival as a people, Turkish nationalists argued, that Anatolian Muslims rally against the foreign occupiers. Such occupiers now included the Greek Orthodox population that had lived in Anatolia for centuries, considered outside the boundaries of a newly forming national community because of their religious difference. As Mustafa Kemal himself argued, "If the enemy had not stupidly come here, the whole country would have slept on heedlessly."[64] It was the Greek invasion and the sudden necessity to choose sides in a struggle between an independent Greece and a rapidly homogenizing Turkey that spurred the formation of these boundaries and helped "awaken," or in more academic parlance "construct" and "imagine," the national community.

The division between the new national communities of "Greek" and "Turk" was made final in 1923. A peace treaty at Lausanne, Switzerland, put an official end to conflict between the Turkish nationalists and the Western powers and established the Republic of Turkey as the sovereign successor to the now defunct Ottoman government. Among the provisions of the treaty was an agreement to exchange the remaining Greek Orthodox population of Turkey for the Muslim population of Greece. Ostensibly designed to "unmix" the entangled population of western Anatolia along national grounds, with Greeks in Greece and Turks in the new Turkey, the population exchange relied upon religious affiliation to determine who would be exchanged. Under the terms of the agreement, to be Christian was to be Greek, and to be Muslim was to be Turkish. Though the exchange was formally proposed by Fridtjof Nansen, the League of Nations high commissioner for refugees, the agreement had the strong support of both national governments, who believed that the separation of the two warring communities was the best course of action for both nations.[65] Such sentiments were echoed by the beliefs of many on the ground in western Anatolia and even Greece, where the relationship between the two religious communities had deteriorated long past the point of saving. Bruce Clark cites one Christian in Mytilene who told a treasured Muslim friend, "You should thank the leaders of Turkey for agreeing to the population exchange, otherwise those fighters would be coming to get you."[66] Indeed, many of the survivors of the population exchange and their descendants still believe that the disentangling of religious communities, devastating though it was for people who were exchanged, prevented further large-scale bloodshed. Ahmet Yorulmaz, a popular Turkish writer born in Ayvalik to Muslim parents who were expelled from Greece, makes a similar argument, conceding, "It's understandable if a Greek resents Mustafa Kemal for throwing the Greeks out of Anatolia, or a Turk resents Venizelos for invading Anatolia . . . but really we should be grateful to both men because they saved the Greeks from the Turks, and the Turks from the Greeks."[67] The persistent use of religion to determine who would be exchanged reveals the extent to which religious distinctions had come to form the boundaries of the nation in both Greece and Turkey. Religious difference had been replaced by national difference as an ordering characteristic of society, but what determined a person's national membership remained their religious affiliation, rather than the language they spoke or the territory they inhabited. In essence, religious difference was nationalized as a multicultural and multireligious Ottoman society fractured into discrete nations.

Ultimately, the survivors of the transition from multireligious empire to monoreligious nation emphasized the role of nationalist elites and their polarizing ideas in the breakdown of interreligious relationships. The oral traditions of all the groups most directly involved in the struggles in Anatolia—Muslim, Orthodox, Armenian, Cretan, and Rum alike—argue that it was the advent of wars and political turmoil brought about by high politics and the actions of leaders far removed from the everyday experience of daily life in the mixed commu-

nities that led to the polarization of Anatolian society and the sundering of tolerant interactions that had lasted for centuries. As one Anatolian Christian put it,
"it wasn't our Turks who brought about all the troubles and dangers . . . it wasn't
our Turks who started the massacres in the nearby villages"; rather, it was "wild
men, who knows from what part of Anatolia they came from,"[68] who committed
most of the violence. The violence in Anatolia thus reflects a gradual separation
of Christian and Muslim communities, one that would reach its greatest extent
with the genocide of Armenians and the compulsory exchange of the majority
of Greek Orthodox Christians. Christians and Muslims interacted less and less
as the twentieth century wore on, withdrawing into their own communities as
interreligious violence spread from clashes in the Balkans throughout Anatolia
proper. Social identity in Anatolia became less complex as a variety of facets
of identity combined to form a single overarching sense of collective identity.
Christians were Greeks or Armenians, Muslims were Turks, leaving no room for
the spectrum of identity that had prevailed in Ottoman times, in which religion,
language, and cultural background were more fluid and intertwined.[69] Christian
and Turkish, or Greek and Muslim, were now facets of identity that were mutually exclusive in a way that Anatolia had never experienced before.

The events of the first quarter of the twentieth century would have a powerful
impact on the development of Turkish society. Ottoman policies removing
Christians from positions of power, confining Christian soldiers to brutal labor
battalions, and eventually the genocide of Armenians and the removal of most
Greek Christians significantly strained intercommunal networks and left Sunni
Muslim Turks in complete control.

In large part, it was the political hierarchy in the Turkish social field that
determined which actions specific political actors were able to take. Faced with
constructing a new national community, Turkish nationalists, even those who
preferred a more secular system of government, were more than willing to go
along with the use of Islam as a cultural component on which to found a national
identity. Religion was a facet of identity that was already foremost in the minds of
the Turkish populace, both because of the Ottoman *millet* system and the recent
clashes between the Ottoman Empire, the nationalist movement that superseded
it, and various neighboring Christian powers. Religion was thus a powerful force
around which social cohesion could be rebuilt, and it could be used to construct
effective boundaries between the new Turkish state and its Christian neighbors.
The remaining Christians, Jews, and minority Muslim populations, now occupying rungs lower in the political hierarchy, would have only a partial place in the
new national community unless they were willing to cross the new boundaries—
converting to Islam, taking a new Muslim name, and learning Turkish—in a way
that would remove them as threats to the community.

ATATÜRK, NATIONALISM, AND THE PURSUIT
OF A SECULAR STATE

While the importance of religion as an organizing factor of society in the late Ottoman Empire is well recognized, the traditional narrative of Turkish history argues that modernizing reforms during the first two decades of the Turkish republic stripped religion of its place in society, forcing Islam out of the public sphere and making it an issue of private concern. Indeed, the 1920s and 1930s saw a vast effort to reshape Turkish society, transforming what many considered to be a backward Ottoman system into a new civic, secular, and democratic state that would be on par with the Western nations it strove to emulate. There is little doubt that Mustafa Kemal, known as Atatürk after 1934, and other members of the Turkish elite sincerely wished to construct a state in which religion would take a back seat to allegiance to the state and nation. On the surface, Kemal's reforms did indeed appear successful in secularizing society: laws and social structures changed, sometimes radically. Yet there is little evidence to show that such efforts penetrated much further into Turkish society than the small circle of elites who dreamed them up. For most Turks, Islam continued to play a central role in daily life and in their own definitions of identity. The continued salience of religion in the new state had its origins in two intersecting phenomena: the central role religion had played in the late Ottoman Empire, and the rhetoric of the earliest nationalists themselves, who had described the nationalist movement and the Turkish nation in explicitly religious terms, drawing upon the unifying potential of Islam as they strove to mobilize a large nationalist coalition to forge the new state. Such efforts meant that Islam gained a foothold as an important part of Turkish society even before the Turkish nation was officially founded, and was so deeply rooted in the lives of ordinary Turks that even the best efforts of elite nationalists could not entirely eliminate it.

In their efforts to rally the Anatolian population behind the efforts of the nationalist movement, many of the earliest Turkish nationalists drew upon the contrast between the Ottoman Empire's traditionally Islamic identity and the Christian identity of many of the new Turkey's most dangerous enemies. The nationalist Committee for Union and Progress, which held substantial political power during the last decades of the Ottoman Empire, had pushed the sultan to declare *jihad*, a holy war, against the Christian Allied powers in World War I. The CUP's formulation thus explicitly framed the Ottoman Empire's final struggle in religious terms. Such a formulation would prove powerful. Mustafa Kemal, one of the Ottoman Empire's heroes in the war, where he first rose to prominence as a military leader, would use the honorific title Ghazi, or "a Muslim warrior who has participated in jihad," for much of the rest of his life.[70] Kemal drew on popular conceptions of religious identification in more than just his title, however. In his *Nutuk*, the Great Speech recounting, and in many ways formulating the official history of, the Turkish nationalist revolution, Kemal explicitly describes the danger of the collapsing Ottoman Empire's Christian minorities. In the speech Atatürk describes how after the defeat of the Ottoman Empire in World War I and the occupation of various parts of its territory, "Christian elements were also at work all over the country, either openly or in secret, trying to realize their own particular ambitions and thereby hasten the breakdown of the State."[71] Elsewhere, Kemal described the religious dimension of the struggle for independence, arguing that "God's help and protection are with us in the sacred struggle which we have entered upon our fatherland and independence."[72]

Other nationalists, too, relied upon religion in public statements describing Turkish identity. In an address to the Lausanne convention in which he discussed the situation of minorities in Turkey, İsmet İnönü, lead Turkish negotiator and the general who led the victorious campaign over the Greek army in the Turkish War of Independence, described the debate over Christian minorities in Turkey as a historical problem, a primordial clash of civilizations dating all the way back to the Turkish conquest of Constantinople in 1453. İnönü proceeded to lay out at length the ways that tsarist Russia and other Christian powers had interceded in Turkish affairs, instigating and supporting various heinous rebellions by Christian populations who had previously been content to live in peace under the beneficent leadership of the Turkish (Ottoman) state. İnönü summed up by arguing that in light of such continued foreign interventions on behalf of Christian minorities, and the tendency of those minorities, once instigated, to rebel violently, an enforced population exchange was necessary for the security and development of both the minorities and Turkey itself.[73] Such statements reflect a genuine recognition on the part of nationalist leaders that religion served as one of the important constituent elements of Ottoman social structure and a willingness to utilize religious sentiments for political gain. That their efforts to found a new secular state relied on mobilizing religious populations to the nationalist cause, however, ensured a conflation of religious and national identity in the new Turkey as well.

To combat the ways in which Islam and nationalism had become intertwined, Kemal undertook a vast series of reforms seeking to revolutionize and modernize Turkish society. Kemal ended the caliphate in 1924 and established the state-controlled Directorate of Religious Affairs in a move meant to distance the affairs of the state from the control of religious authorities and end the centuries-long affiliation between state and religious power. Similarly, reforms sought to strip the ulema, a body of Muslim religious scholars with political power, and a ban on tarikats, Sufi religious orders, both in 1925, worked to limit religious power in public society. Reformation of the dress code followed, including promoting Western clothing, discouraging veiling among women, and banning the traditional and religiously linked fez for men in favor of Western hats. The official ending of the millet system in 1926, and the reformation of educational policies including the transition from Arabic to Latin script in written Turkish and the purging of non-Turkish loan words in 1928, worked to further distance the new modern Turkish society from its religious past and drive religion from the public sphere. Yet the very necessity of imposing such a vast array of social reforms in an effort to promote secularism reveals the continued salience of religious definitions of identity in Turkish life well after the founding of the nation-state. Having emphasized the connection between Islam and political identity already existing under the Ottoman Empire, Turkish nationalists now took steps to sever it, seeking to reformulate Turkish society in a way that removed the "superfluous formulations" of religion that were "incompatible with the modern character of the new Turkish state and of the republican regime, even though the revolution and the republic saw no harm in allowing them as a concession at the time" of the national movement.[74]

Indeed, more recent research reveals that despite such far-reaching efforts, Kemalist reforms likely had a less drastic effect on most of the Turkish populace than previously supposed. The modernization efforts may have "changed the face of Turkey,"[75] but it seems to have had little effect on its heart and soul. Though the government officially banned *tarikats* in 1925, newspapers frequently reported the arrest of people who associated with them well after that, revealing their continued presence and popularity despite being in full violation of the law.[76] The implementation of the Swiss Civil Code in 1926, long cited as an example of the transition from a religiously focused government to a secular Western-style one, was a far looser interpretation of the original and did not mark a wholesale replacement of existing laws, as once assumed. Even in those areas in which the law was reformed, the new strictures were not consistently enforced by local officials in charge of law and order on the ground.[77]

The changes in style of dress imposed by nationalist reformers are a particularly useful example of the interaction between the state and local populations. In many ways, Turkish reformists saw the imposition of these measures as efforts not just to enforce modernization and Westernization, but as part of a broader process of socialization into a national culture.[78] Sami Efendi, inspector general of the CUP, writing from Van in 1925, argued that the clothing reforms were "needed not only for Westernization and modernization, but also to facilitate our policy of assuring that the other nations [in Turkey] wear the same modern clothes as Turks do and of gradually Turkifying them."[79] Yet here too, the reforms may not have been as comprehensive as nationalist reformers intended. In questioning the impact of the dress reforms, some scholars have argued that government reforms penetrated little into the daily life of the Anatolian peasants who made up the vast majority of the Turkish population. As Erik Jan Zürcher put it, "A farmer or shepherd from Anatolia had never worn a fez, so he was not especially bothered about its abolition. His wife wore no veil anyway, so the fact that its use was discouraged did not mean anything to him or her."[80] Yet more recent research has revealed that the transition from Ottoman to European styles of dress had powerful cultural and social dimensions that transcended simple economic access to Ottoman and European headgear and class-based styles of dress.

While some contemporary observers in the Turkish government argued that those who had not immediately adopted Western forms of dress, a particular problem in more rural Anatolian villages far from the state's centers of power, did so out of a lack of economic resources,[81] significant evidence exists of a variety of cases in which failure to conform to clothing reforms represented cultural and social resistance to the new order. On the extreme side of the spectrum, at least a few men sought to avoid the necessity of wearing the Western-style hat (and the indecency of appearing bare-headed in public) by simply refusing to leave their homes, vacating the public sphere entirely in favor of the private, where traditional norms of clothing and behavior could remain unchanged.[82] More common were the cases of men who would wear hats only when visiting the city, sometimes borrowing a communal village cap, while resorting to more traditional headgear in their home towns. Similarly, others purchased hats whose Western-style brims could be snapped up or drawn down over the ears in a way that resembled the more traditional fez.[83] Hale Yilmaz suggests that such efforts and the mixed reaction to the clothing reforms reveals the superficial effect the reforms had on the majority of the populace. Adhering to dress codes only when visiting the city, or altering Western items of clothing to fit a more traditional Ottoman standard "meant it did not challenge the local, tribal, or ethnic identities of the wearers, at least not immediately."[84] Rather, such superficial adherence to the law reveals a recognition of the state's efforts, but the continued prominence of traditional ways of defining and maintaining a core sense of identity, one that continued to rely on religion and ethnicity, rather than secularism and allegiance to the state, as its core element.

More prominent was the clash between modernists seeking to impose a more secular state and Islamic authorities, who sought to maintain traditional religious forms of dress and behavior. In the lead-up to the passing of the 1925 Hat Law, one Islamic scholar, Iskilipli Atif Efendi, published a book describing the adoption of the hat and other forms of Western dress as not acceptable according to the Quran and *hadith*.[85] Those who dressed in a Western manner, he argued, would soon lose their Islamic identity.[86] Though there was never an official national law regulating women's dress in the way men's clothing was limited, Western clothing for women was still encouraged. But here too, religious sentiments encouraged pushback against secularist policies. Atatürk himself argued that though many people urged a law banning women from veiling, "You can't catch me doing that. When religious prejudice and men's jealousy over their women's faces being seen in public are coupled in this problem, it becomes most difficult to cope with. No legislation about veils!"[87] In cities where local authorities had banned certain forms of Islamic dress for women, restrictions were met with a lack of enthusiasm, reluctance, and resistance.[88] Those women who did unveil or dressed in more Western fashion often faced harassment, assault, and social pressure from more conservative members of Turkish society.[89]

Other sources reveal a significant degree of noncompliance among Turkish imams, who continued to prefer traditional dress even while performing more secular duties, such as tending store, or pursuing other forms of economic activity. This was problematic to Turkish reformers, who did not object to imams wearing traditional robes and turbans during religious activities, but who sought to draw a strict boundary between religious and secular spheres. Imams were thus to wear religious garb only while performing their religious duties and Western garb at all other times. As Yilmaz recounts, Turkish authorities dedicated significant attention to the problem of recalcitrant imams who wore strange combinations of religious and secular clothing at all times, thus refusing to maintain the honor of the religious functionary and intentionally blurring the religious and the secular in the public sphere.[90] Here, in the religious core of the populace, efforts at reform met with dedicated, if not organized, resistance as religious scholars continued traditional practices or significantly modified the clothing mandated by the government in a way that made clear their rejection of the new separation between religion, society, and the state.

Such everyday forms of common resistance, "weapons of the weak" to use James C. Scott's celebrated phrase,[91] reveal a significant undercurrent of adherence to traditional norms and resistance to the government's policies of Westernization and secularization. Where the Turkish reforms did succeed was in bringing to the forefront the issue of religion and its role in the traditional lifeworlds of the Turkish people. By enacting legislation that forced the issue, Turkish nationalists created a situation in which the official rhetoric of the nation-state contradicted the ways most people viewed their own identity as members of the nation. A leading group of elite nationalists were prepared to overthrow the traditional system in favor of a secular and civic state, but such ideas were confined to a small elite, albeit one that controlled the official policies of the state. While Turkish reformists were thus successful in creating a national state system that was formally divorced from religion, the reforms' lack of penetration into Turkish society and Islam's continued prominence in the lives and self-identification of most Turks meant that religion did not fade from public or private consciousness in the ways secularists intended. In this regard, Islam's traditional role in the Ottoman Empire and nationalists' emphasis on religious definitions of identity as they sought to rally Anatolian Muslims to the national cause played a key role in cementing the intersection of religion and politics in the new Turkish state. While Turkish leaders sought to enforce the creation of a secular state, for most of the population of Turkey identification as a Turk in reality meant being a Muslim, and despite the efforts of leading Turkish nationalists, religion survived the years of Kemalist reforms and continued to serve as a fundamental organizing characteristic of Turkish society, strongly shaping opinions toward and interactions with politics.

POLITICAL LIBERALISM AND CULTURAL CONSERVATISM: THE 1940S AND 1950S

Mustafa Kemal Atatürk's death in 1938 brought with it a fundamental change in the structure of Turkish politics. Long the dominant figure in the Turkish political sphere, Kemal had presided over a rigidly single-party political system in which Kemal's own Republican People's Party (CHP) held complete control. Though Kemal had made overtures toward a multiparty system as early as 1930, early opposition parties such as the Progressive Republican Party and the Free Republican Party were quickly shut down by the government for being too tainted by the Islamist ideas of traditionally oriented reactionary elements within the country.[92] The speed with which such parties quickly took on religiously oriented elements, though they were founded by loyal secular nationalists, reveals in itself the continued appeal of religious norms among the Turkish population. When Turkey finally succeeded in transitioning to a multiparty system, with the establishment of the National Development Party in 1945, elements of the population who did not completely support the secularist and modernist orientation of the government found more room to make their opinions heard. Turkish voters consistently supported parties that prioritized religion and viewed religion as a core driver of political policy. The Democrat Party (DP), established in 1946 and elected to government in 1950, became the first party to unseat the reigning CHP, establishing a series of policies that loosened the restrictions on the practice of Islam in the public sphere. Notably, the DP undertook significant efforts to reach beyond the secular Western elite in major urban areas, canvassing for votes among rural villagers and incorporating the peasantry into the political process for the first time.[93]

Such was the strength of the populace's religious focus that Adnan Menderes, who had been elected prime minister from the DP in 1950, felt comfortable arguing in a 1952 speech that "The Turkish nation is Muslim, and it will remain Muslim."[94] The electoral success of more conservative political parties and the concomitant loosening of restrictions on public religious practice have led many scholars to label the 1940s and 1950s a period of religious revival in which religious practice took on a bigger role in Turkish society.[95] Yet as the preceding section has shown, religious practice and traditional forms of dress and behavior never truly disappeared. Religious observance certainly continued unabated in the private sphere, but even in public, cultural forms linked to a traditional and religious milieu remained prominent enough for a variety of contemporary observers to note them. For many people, Islamic identity had been, and would remain, a key facet of their own self-identity as Turks, regardless of the official efforts to separate religion from the nation.

Rather than a revival of religion, then, what the liberalization of religious policies during the 1940s and 1950s reveals is a new stage in the relationship between Islam and the state. In many ways, the 1940s signaled a surrender on the part of secular nationalists who had struggled to make Turkey a strictly secular state. Such efforts had never really succeeded even among the government's own policies, which had continued to draw on religious conceptions of national identity in determining national membership, even when it directly contradicted nationalist rhetoric. With the rise of more religiously oriented parties, the de facto religiosity of Turkish nationalist policies and the significant religious orientation of the Turkish population was finally matched by de jure statutes that allowed religion in the public sphere.

Social historian Gavin Brockett has argued that it was only in this period, in which popular expressions of national identity were given room to flourish, that a true national culture developed in Turkey. For Brockett, who builds on Benedict Anderson's famous theory of nation formation,[96] it was the development of a popular print media that "contributed to the crystallization of an increasingly widespread national identity"[97] one in which all levels of society could take part. Brockett's evidence is convincing, and he cites a wide variety of print materials published in Turkey's provinces, far from the secularized urban centers, that served as fora in which religious and secular definitions of identity could be debated and negotiated. Regional and provincial periodicals such as *Büyük Cihad* (Great Struggle), *Yeşil Nur* (Green Light), *Vicdan Sesi* (Voice of Conscience), *Büyük Doğu* (Great East), and *Sebilürreşad* (The Straight Path), among others, provided outlets in which religious nationalists and other figures could express the continued importance of a core Islamic identity to Turkishness. In these more popular and provincial print outlets, religiously focused Turks sparked fierce debates over the role of Islam and secularism in society and pushed for religiously oriented public policies. Issues such as the teaching of religion in schools; the language in which the *ezan*, the Muslim call to prayer, would be proclaimed; instruction on how to properly practice Islam; and issues of public morality all featured prominently in religiously oriented popular media during this time period. A variety of popular sermons also circulated, providing religious instruction and guidance for Turks who were thought to have lost the details of Islamic orthopraxy, if not their faith, in the two decades of Kemalist reform.[98]

The popularity of religious print media and the flourishing of a culture in which religious issues were debated publicly and in a large variety of periodicals around the country reveals the continued importance of religion in the lives of many Turks, who welcomed the opportunity to more closely engage with religious materials and practices in the public sphere. Crucially, some print sources explicitly denied that their proliferation reflected any sort of dangerous "religious reactionism" as feared by secular Kemalists, but rather sought to encourage a form of Islam that could help bolster the strength of the Turkish nation, protecting it from communism and other dangers that threatened from both within and without.[99] Indeed, this popularity makes it clear that "the so-called Islamic revival after 1945 did *not* reflect the death throes of the last generation of Ottomans. Rather, these individuals were linked by a commitment to Islam and to utilizing print media to appeal to, and harness, the religious sentiments of the people,"[100] religious sentiments that remained strong despite two decades of enforced secularity. The efforts to devise political policies that followed religious beliefs reveals a strand of religious nationalism in Turkey that prioritized a public approach to religion.

Public sentiments toward religion and the extent to which religious affiliation had become intertwined with conceptions of the nation were visible again in the pogroms that swept Istanbul in early September of 1955. Debates over the disposition of Cyprus during the early 1950s ramped up tensions between Greece and Turkey, which both considered the island part of their national territory. On September 6 and 7, these tensions boiled over into a mass riot in which organized Turkish mobs attacked the remaining Greek Orthodox population of Istanbul, destroying more than 5,000 homes and businesses, killing more than a dozen people, and beating or raping countless more in a series of attacks that some commenters have compared to the *Kristallnacht* assault on Jews in Nazi Germany.[101] Sparked by an unfounded rumor that Greeks had bombed the Turkish consulate in Thessaloniki, Greece, which also happened to be the house in which Atatürk grew up, the riot was encouraged by both the governmental intelligence organization and the Turkish press. As *Hürriyet* (Liberty), a popular daily newspaper, put it a week before the riots, "If the Greeks dare touch our brethren, then there are plenty of Greeks in Istanbul to retaliate upon."[102] Though the bomb turned out to have been placed by a Turkish secret service operative, popular sentiment quickly turned against the remaining Greek Orthodox population in Istanbul, who were still considered foreign and not true members of the nation to many Turks. As Omar Sami Cosar, writing in the nationalist newspaper *Cumhuriyet* (Republic), phrased it only a week before the riots, "Neither the Patriarchate nor the Rum minority ever openly supported Turkish national interests when Turkey and Athens clashed over certain issues. . . . Do the Phanar Patriarchate and our Rum citizens in Istanbul have special missions assigned by Greece in its plans to annex Cyprus?"[103]

Spared from the 1923 population exchange after intense negotiations, Istanbul's Greek Orthodox population represented one of the last significant concentrations of Christians in the new Turkey. The riots, which aimed to destroy the livelihoods of non-Muslim minorities and limit their ability to survive in Turkey, served as a continuation of processes of religious homogenization that had begun with the genocide of the Armenians in 1915 and the exchange of the Greek

Orthodox in 1923. Focused on a historically and still numerically significant population of religious minorities, the effort to drive the remaining Orthodox Christians from Istanbul reveals the extent to which non-Muslims continued to fall outside the boundaries of the Turkish nation. Critically, though the riots were instigated by the government, they saw mass popular support as people bused in from the surrounding countryside and mobilized within Istanbul itself. As Ali Tuna Kuyucu has argued, such efforts thus cannot be seen as either "spontaneous rioting caused by over-excited masses nor as solely a government conspiracy that eventually got out of control."[104] Rather, the popular riots against minorities that took place in 1955 represent a moment in which the meaning of Turkish nationality, strained as it was by the debate over Cyprus, came once again into question. The Turkish population responded emphatically, targeting non-Muslim populations in a way that made clear that neither residence in Istanbul nor Turkish citizenship was enough to qualify as a "true" Turk. True Turkishness was to be found in culture and in religion, and those who were more closely tied to a foreign power were dangerous enemies who once again needed to be driven from the Republic.

In many ways, the Istanbul pogroms, which occurred at the same time as the Turkish government was taking significant steps to limit the rights of the remaining religious minorities in Turkey, were a successful move for nationalists seeking to further homogenize the Turkish nation. The Greek Orthodox population, which had numbered around 120,000 in 1927, four years after the population exchange with Greece, had fallen to about 7,000 in 1978. Between 1955, the year of the Istanbul riots, and 1960 the population of Greek Orthodox Christians in the city of Istanbul decreased from 65,000 to 49,000, while by 2008 it had fallen to somewhere between 2,000 and 4,000.[105] The decline of the Orthodox population in Turkey was so precipitous that it has sparked fears for the continued existence of the Greek patriarchate. The patriarch must, under the terms of the 1923 population exchange agreement, be a natural born citizen of Turkey, a condition that has been increasingly hard for candidates to fulfill. In their quest to make membership in the Turkish nation synonymous with Islam, Turkish nationalists have largely succeeded. The actions of the Turkish government, which officially privileged Muslims over religious minorities despite rhetoric to the contrary, reflected and enhanced the popular understanding of national identity as an essentially religious distinction. Religion and nation had been conflated to the extent that existing interreligious differences that predated the founding of the republic served as organizing characteristics decades later.

RELIGION AND THE STATE: THE 1960S, 1970S, AND 1980S

The electoral success of religious parties, liberalization of rules restricting religion in the public sphere, and popular efforts to remove religious minorities from the national community did not, however, represent a complete victory for religious nationalists over the forces of secularism and modernism. The complex interaction between religion and the state continued to be an area of concern in Turkey. In 1960, a coalition of young army officers launched a coup that drove the Democratic Party's Adnan Menderes from power. Though the instigators described their coup as explicitly anticommunist, it was also, in many ways, anti-Islamist in outlook. Organized by Colonel Alparslan Türkeş, the National Unity Committee (NUC) that took power sought to return Turkey to the republic of Atatürk's time, in which a powerful centralized state enforced rigid boundaries between religion and the state. Türkeş sought to substitute allegiance to ortho-dox national ideology for reliance on Islam, and the NUC took steps to bolster a secularist version of national identity. In the aftermath of the coup, Prime Minis-ter Menderes and two other members of the government were executed, while President Celal Bayar and four others were sentenced to life in prison. The DP, which they had founded and which proved so influential in returning Islam, always a fundamental element of Turkish culture, to the public and political sphere, was suppressed early in 1961 as the NUC sought to limit religion's role in politics once again.

This first intervention of the Turkish military into politics set the stage for an antagonistic relationship between the military, which had long considered itself the guardian of modernism, secularism, and progress in the republic, and the common people, many of whom continued to place Islam at the center of their cultural and political identities and who repeatedly voted in parties that took conservative approaches to the role of religion in society. The 1960s saw an alter-nation of power between the CHP, which continued to hold to the secularist tenets of its founder, Mustafa Kemal Atatürk, and the newly formed Justice Party, which gained support as a descendant and successor of the now defunct DP. The Justice Party drew upon the grassroots support of the DP, which had served as a party of the peasantry and had dedicated itself to slowing the pro-cesses of social change that Kemal's CHP had driven through during the single-party period. The Justice Party and the DP both based their platforms on poli-cies of economic liberalization and modernization, seeking to draw Turkey into the larger world economy, while adhering to more traditional cultural, religious, and social norms. The success of these parties reveals the complex mélange of liberal and conservative attitudes held by Turkey's peasants and villagers. By the 1950s and 1960s, most Turks had accepted the inevitability of moderniza-tion and Westernization, and indeed had come to recognize the many material gains that could accrue from a more Western style of economic production and exchange.[106] Yet, again, in the social and cultural sphere, religion remained powerful in the lives of most Turks. Those outside the cities and the political elite continued to prefer a traditional form of social organization shaped by their religious values, and so, as one contemporary scholar put it, "the Justice Party, as did the Democrat Party before it . . . responded to the obvious desire of many Turks for a relaxation of the militant antireligious campaign carried out by republican reformers."[107]

Clashes between the more secular and liberal military and the conservative parties elected by the people reached a peak again in 1971, when on March 12 the military conducted a "coup by memorandum," in which the military delivered a demand for the resignation of the government rather than resorting to a direct military takeover. Reacting to the rise of a new, explicitly religious National Order Party, as well as a loss of political control and the rise of political violence between the left and the right in Turkey, the military overthrew the Justice Party government of Prime Minister Süleyman Demiril. In this intervention, the military sought again to return the state to the principles that Kemal's government had been founded upon and which the 1960 coup had sought to revitalize. Two years of continued violence and political repression followed, however, as the military cracked down on resistance and strengthened the state's control over society, instating a variety of measures to try to quell dissent. The army relinquished control over the government in 1973, having achieved what it believed to be success in creating a system of courts, media restrictions, and restrictions on association meant to curb radical behavior. The 1970s saw an escalating series of conflicts as parties on the right and left clashed, often violently. Support from the United States and the Soviet Union, respectively, meant that these clashes and the increased level of political violence on both sides took on the aspect of a proxy war as both superpowers tried to assert control over Turkey and its crucial geopolitical position straddling the Turkish Straits. A third coup followed, in 1980, as the Turkish military stepped in again in an effort to assert control and end the fractious violence that the elected government seemed unable to deal with. The military's National Security Council ruled Turkey for another three years, eventually rewriting the constitution before relinquishing power to an elected government in 1983.

RISE OF THE "NEW TURKS": PUBLIC ISLAM IN THE 1990S AND BEYOND

The 1980 coup brought with it social and economic changes above and beyond the radical transformation of the political landscape that accompanied the military intervention. The first party elected after the coup, Turgut Özal's Motherland Party (Anavatan Partisi) opened up the Turkish economy, abandoning the state-led efforts of earlier governments and opening Turkey to competition in the world market.[108] This transformation brought with it a significant influx of wealth, spurred by foreign investment and a new outlook on economic concerns. It was this influx of wealth, much of it ending up in the hands of the pious Muslim owners of small and medium-sized businesses, that spurred renewed interest in public religion.[109] Whereas for much of Turkish history wealth and economic power had largely been concentrated in the hands of a more secularized urban elite, the economic opening of Turkey created a new Muslim middle and upper class, one that could make its own tastes and preferences known. Indeed, "their wealth created a market for Islam-friendly bourgeois products and lifestyles (an Islamic economic sector) and initiated a Muslim cultural renaissance in fashion, lifestyle, leisure activities, novels, media, and music."[110] The rise of economic and cultural power among more pious, traditionally oriented Muslim Turks resulted in a concomitant surge in the success of not just conservative, but overtly religious political parties. In essence the 1980s saw the rise of a new economic and cultural elite, one that was unabashedly religious in its outlook and saw no contradiction between being Muslim on one hand and a Turk on the other. This, then, represented in some ways a rejection, in their opponents' opinion, or at least a reinterpretation of the ways in which elites had traditionally considered Turkishness. As anthropologist Jenny White argued, "One of the most revolutionary consequences of these changes . . . has been a contestation of the nature of Turkishness not seen since the founding of the Republic."[111]

The status quo in Turkish politics lasted for another decade and a half before the military stepped in a fourth time, with a coup in 1997. Here again, the military took power to, in their minds, protect the state from the unchecked growth of Islamist movements that abandoned the state's official secularist policies in exchange for a religiously focused social agenda. Yet again the ruling party, this time the Welfare Party, which led a governing coalition, was suppressed. The repeated election of parties supporting a stronger role for Islam in the public sphere, and the continued belief on the part of the military that it should step in and protect the country's traditional secular ideals from the wishes of the people, reveal the continued struggle over the position of religion in the Turkish nation. While the official position of the state was that the government should maintain strict secularity, the majority of Turkey's population consistently elected political parties that challenged the orthodox secularism of the government, revealing a continued desire for policy based on religious precepts. Turkish secularism was challenged again in 2002 with the founding of the Justice and Development Party (Adalet ve Kalkinma Partisi, AKP). In many ways, the AKP served as the successor to an Islamist strain in popular politics that had struggled to gain a foothold in the secularist state. The AKP followed, in succession, the National Order Party (Milli Nizam Partisi, MNP), the National Salvation Party (Milli Selamat Partisi, MSP), the Welfare Party (Refah Partisi), the Virtue Party (Fazilet Partisi), and the Felicity Party (Saadet Partisi), all but the last of which were banned from Turkish politics by the country's Constitutional Court for violating restrictions on the separation of religion and politics.

The AKP was founded in 2002 after the suppression of the Virtue Party, which had been disbanded in 2001. At the center of the new party was a core group of

Virtue Party members, who had argued for a reformed, more moderate version of religiously oriented politics, and now took the opportunity to form a new party of their own. In fact, the frequent suppression of religiously oriented political parties meant that many of the AKP's leaders had been members or leaders of not just the Virtue Party, but many of the earlier Islamist parties. The AKP swept to electoral success in 2002 and has remained in power ever since under the leadership of Prime Minister and later President Recep Tayyip Erdoğan. The AKP reveals the danger of relying on easy binaries and facile classifications when examining the complex nature of Turkish politics. Despite its conservative religious orientation, the AKP claims not to be an Islamist party, but rather presents itself as a moderate center-right conservative party. The party insists that those members who had once been members of Islamist parties have changed their minds, recognizing the importance of secularism in Turkish society.[112]

Initially portraying itself as pro-Western and pro-American, the AKP advocates a liberal market economy, and its regime has led to significant economic successes. Similarly, the AKP has, under Erdoğan, made significant efforts to join the European Union, revealing a commitment to integration with the West that would do credit to Atatürk's modernizing and Westernizing principles. Yet it was under the banner of the AKP that Islamist-oriented policies found their greatest open success. While various policies and procedures throughout Turkish history have utilized religion to define the nation, and indeed many Turks themselves have often used Islamic identity as a key facet of Turkishness, it was only under the AKP in the early 2000s that the government moved in a direction that explicitly rolled back Atatürk's secular reforms in a way that privileged Muslim social and cultural codes. Erdoğan's government has taken steps such as reforming the education system in a way that privileges religious schools, repealing bans on women's headscarves in universities and public offices, and tightening rules on internet use, abortion, and alcohol sales and consumption.

The AKP's turn to a more open brand of Islam has forced a renegotiation of what it means to be Turkish. Under Erdoğan's leadership, the practice of Islam and traditional Islamic virtues have become far more visible, leading to what some observers have called "the second revolution after the establishment of the Republic by Atatürk."[113] Traditional religious Turks have greeted the AKP's reforms with enthusiasm, lauding their newfound freedom to express Islam and new governmental policies designed to strengthen Islamic systems of education and bolster Islamic sentiments throughout Turkish society. Yet, though the AKP has won power with significant electoral majorities,[114] this opening of the public sphere to religion has not gone unchallenged. Such efforts have raised the ire of Turkey's staunch secularists, those who cling to Atatürk's more restrictive official interpretation of relationship between religion and the state, and the AKP has faced legal challenges in 2002 and 2008 as their opponents sought to have the party disbanded. Most notably, the 2008 challenge failed by just one vote. The closure request received six votes of the necessary seven from an eleven-member panel of judges empaneled to rule on the party's status. Ten of the eleven judges ruled that the AKP had become a "center for anti-secular activities," and the party was stripped of 50 percent of its state funding in response. Moreover, the ways Erdoğan has gone about imposing his vision of a more openly religious Turkish society has struck many secularists as an overreach of political power. Erdoğan's rule has been marked by a series of scandals and accusations of corruption.[115] In response, Erdoğan, mindful of the fate of many of his religiously oriented predecessors who ran afoul of the secularist military in their efforts to liberalize religious policies, has taken significant steps to blunt the Turkish military's role in politics. Simultaneously, Erdoğan has worked to reform the Turkish judiciary, long considered the second bastion of secularist thought in the Turkish system, taking steps to increase political control over the courts by purging judicial officials he accused of acting in consort with his political enemies.[116]

The debate over the role of religion in social and political life has thus again burst with full force into Turkey's public discourse. This time, with the rise of a Muslim elite, the success of the AKP, and the dismantling of secularist barriers to religious practice, Islamically oriented approaches to politics, society, and the nation have gained the upper hand. Interestingly, the position of secularist and Islamist political strains has thus reversed, with secular members of society protesting against political overreach and authoritarian behavior by Erdoğan in the ways he has sought to impose his vision on Turkish society. This dissatisfaction has expressed itself, among other ways, in the 2013 Gezi Park protests against Erdoğan's rule and the 2016 coup attempt by a faction within the Turkish military. In 2013 protests spread throughout Turkey following the Erdoğan government's decision to remove Istanbul's Taksim Gezi Park, one of the city's last green areas. Under the government's plan, the park would be the site of a newly rebuilt Ottoman-era Military Barracks that would serve as both a historical and cultural center as well as a shopping center that would cater to tourists. Though initially confined to Istanbul and focused on perceived government overreach in destroying the park, the protests soon spread throughout Turkey, and took on a pointedly anti-Erdoğan character. Soon protesters, who called themselves *çapulcu* (looters) after Erdoğan's own dismissive term for them, began expressing their discontent over Erdoğan's authoritarian tendencies and his policies restricting sales of alcohol, kissing in public, and other behavior deemed to fall outside of Islamic moral propriety.

The government responded with force, physically clearing the park through the use of tear gas, rubber bullets, and water cannons to remove protesters. Amnesty International reported that it received consistent and credible reports that protesters were beaten by the police, and authorities cracked down on journalists and access to the internet in an effort to break up the demonstrations.[117] In the end, the protests eventually subsided, and the government dropped the plans to destroy the park, but the heavy-handed nature of the police response and the government's efforts to quell public dissent and reassert control brought lingering tensions into sharp relief. Though the Gezi Park protests initially had very little to do with religion, the reinterpretation of the movement in a way that called attention to Erdoğan's conservative religious agenda, as much as the authoritarian tactics with which he pursued that agenda, once again raised the question of national identity, and whether the essential characteristic of Turkish-ness was to be Islam or the secularist vision of Atatürk's dream.

The coup attempt that took place on July 15, 2016, represented yet another clash between religious and secular elements in the Turkish government. Though the Turkish government blamed the coup on the Gülen movement, a religious organization led by reclusive cleric Fethullah Gülen, once a close ally of Erdoğan and the AKP, the Peace at Home Council, which served as the executive com-mittee of the coup, officially cited the erosion of secularism as the fundamental justification for the coup attempt. Erdoğan's effort to dismantle the secularist power of the military, which included a series of purges and trials of high-ranking military officers, incensed members of the military who remained committed to the secularist cause. As part of these purges, 275 people, including senior military officers, lawyers, and journalists, were convicted of being part of a secret society, named "Ergenekon," that was allegedly involved in plotting a coup attempt against the government. The elimination of many higher-ranking military offi-cers who were caught up in the purges provided an opportunity for more reli-giously minded officers to rise quickly through the ranks and assume high-level military positions. While such actions ensured that the majority of the Turkish military would be personally dedicated to Erdoğan and to his ideals, it created friction within the military between Islamist and secularist factions. This was particularly true after April 2016, when the original convictions in the Ergenekon case were overturned by the government's Court of Cessation, which ruled that they were invalid because the Ergenekon network had never been proved to actually exist.

Nevertheless, such efforts served as yet another example of what secularists considered Erdoğan's authoritarian overreach in the service of religious ideals. The conspirators in the coup struck quickly at Erdoğan himself, military head-quarters, and media broadcast stations. Troops and tanks occupied Istanbul's Atatürk Airport, Taksim Square, and bridges across the Bosporus, while military aircraft flew over Ankara and helicopters bombed police special forces, air force headquarters, and even the Turkish parliament building. Turkish forces loyal to the government eventually beat back the conspirators, and the coup attempt served as justification for another round of purges, this time extending far beyond the ranks of the military and the judiciary. To date, more than 125,000 civil servants, officials, soldiers, and academics have been detained or suspended. During his first speech after the coup, Erdoğan remarked on the opportunity that the conspirators had provided, arguing, "This uprising is a gift from God to us because this will be a reason to cleanse our army."[118] In this, the 2016 coup attempt served as yet one more front in the struggle between secularist and Islamist sectors of Turkish society. Consumed, yet again, by questions of what it means to be a Turk, and the proper philosophical and moral center around which to construct the Turkish nation, Turkish politics has entered a fractious and difficult new period. With the rise of the AKP and Erdoğan's success in consolidating control over the political system and purging his ideological opponents, religious definitions of the Turkish nation have achieved a powerful position, more openly accepted than at any time since the last years of the Ottoman Empire, before the founding of the nation itself. Yet a careful historical examination has revealed that, contrary to official claims, a religious definition of Turkish identity has always held a powerful position in Turkish politics and society, making the current ascendance of religiously oriented policies shaping public ideas and political practices less a religious resurgence and more an emergence into the public sphere of a strand of ideological thought that has long guided Turkish social and political policies.

CONCLUSIONS

In this chapter I have examined a broad spectrum of historical evidence to analyze the relationship between religion, ethnicity, and nation in the Republic of Turkey. I traced this relationship across roughly a century of Ottoman and Turkish history. The chapter began with the turmoil that accompanied the decline and collapse of the Ottoman Empire in the first two decades of the twentieth century, a time period encompassing Ottoman defeat and the rise of ethnoreligious conflict in the Balkans and that culminated in the perpetration of the Armenian Genocide and efforts to homogenize the national community. A close look at the situation on the ground reveals that these were the cataclysmic consequences of struggles between nationalizing states in the Balkans that polarized preexisting relationships between religious communities. An influx of power politics and suffering refugees had a devastating effect on communal life in Anatolia, collapsing finely balanced traditions of interfaith dialogue and compromise in a way that invariably led to violence between different communities. Religion, which had long served as a means of defining self-identity among Ottoman peoples, took on an increasingly political and nationalized role, as religious affiliation became a key marker of national identity and political affiliation. Christian and Muslim communities in Anatolia suffered alike, as grieving and fearful neighbors lashed out against those who had long been considered different from themselves but were now considered alien and foreign as well. Moreover, this potent emphasis on religion set the stage for Turkish national policies for decades to come. The conflation of religious and national identity redrew communal boundaries such that Turkish nationalists, even those who officially supported the construction of a secular state, utilized religion as a shorthand for the new national community, seeking to construct a Turkey whose core constituents would be exclusively Muslim Turks.

From the climactic events of the Ottoman breakup, this chapter then followed such issues through the reform period of the 1920s and 1930s, when Turkey sought to consolidate itself as a distinct national community and worked to further eliminate minority populations and ethnic and religious challenges to the new state. Such policies sparked a concomitant resurgence of public religion during the more open multiparty period that followed. The results of such policies were visible during the 1940s and 1950s, most notably in the pogroms against religious minorities that shook Istanbul in 1955, in which common Turks lashed out against the small population of religious minorities still extant in the former imperial capital. The events and policies of this time period reflect an effort to come to grips with the lingering problems of secularism and the relationship between religion and the state. While the Kemalist nationalists of the 1920s and 1930s continued to pursue reforms that would theoretically bolster the cause of secularism, religion was never far from their minds, nor from the minds of the vast majority of Turks, who continued to see Islam as a fundamental cornerstone of their own identities. The loosening of regulations on the practice of public religion that accompanied the transition from a one-party to a multiparty political system reveals the extent to which religious practice had never really gone away, even during the strictest periods of secularist reforms, but rather continued unabated as an important element of public life. Though the political parties that sprang up to support this population were often suppressed by the core secularist elite that controlled the military, their continued success and resurgence in different forms is testament to the popular support such religiously focused ideas received among the majority of the Turkish population. The electoral success of religiously focused parties throughout the 1940s and 1950s was matched by the success of print media catering to religious Turks interested in making their voices heard in the national government, marking a resurgence in the public sphere of religious elements that had long been present, but which had been actively suppressed under the one-party government.

Finally, I extended this analysis through the continued flourishing of religiously oriented political parties in the 1970s and 1980s, their battles with the holdout elements of the Kemalist elite, and their culmination in the success of Recep Tayyip Erdoğan and his AKP in the early 2000s, when religion took on a more explicit role in political rhetoric, and conservative religious parties achieved mass support across Turkey. Such an approach reveals the continued salience of religious dimensions of national and group formation well into the Turkish republic, and even into the present day. In contrast to the official narrative, this analysis shows that the religious considerations that dominated Ottoman society in its last years did not subside with Mustafa Kemal's modernizing reforms. Rather, conceptions of religious, ethnic, and national identity that were fused in early modern times continued to shape ideas of Turkish nationhood and Turkey's national policies long after they were supposed to have disappeared. In large part, this persistence was due to the reservoir of religious feeling and identification among members of the Turkish population who were outside the elite core of nationalist secularists. For the common people, religion and affiliation with the Muslim faith continued to shape what it meant to be a Turk, serving as the salient facet of identity that drove all other conceptualizations of what membership in the nation should mean. Though such an emphasis on religion was not always explicit, a closer look at historical sources reveals its continued power, a strength evident in the increasing role of religion in the Turkish public sphere today.

This analysis has revealed that, far from fading from the public eye with the advent of Kemalist secularism, religion played, and continues to play, a powerful role in shaping the fundamental boundaries of Turkish identity. The role of Islam as a foundational element of personal and communal identity in the late Ottoman Empire was only strengthened with the tumultuous transition from empire to nation and the growth of a new Turkish identity. In part this was due to the social structure of the Ottoman Empire, but it also was the result of deliberate strategies of boundary making pursued by Turkish political actors as they struggled to define the new Turkish state and differentiate it from both the failed Ottoman Empire that had gone before, and the threatening presence of Western Christian powers. Conditions during the first few decades of the twentieth century, and the early efforts by Turkish nationalists to draw upon religious motifs to further explicitly political goals, thus conflated religion, ethnicity, and nationalism in a way that would have powerful repercussions throughout the next century of Turkish history. In this regard, Islam served as a sort of chain of memory, in Danièle Hervieu-Léger's formulation, a fundamental reservoir from which Turkish society could draw its own sense of identity. This centrality of religious belief is evident in the testimonies of common people on the ground in Turkey as they weathered the intercommunal violence that accompanied the rise of nationalism in the Balkans and Anatolia amid the collapse of empire. Religious sentiments in the Turkish case did not represent ancient superstitions destined to disappear under the light of modernization and Enlightenment rationality, as so many theories of secularization had predicted. Rather, in the Turkish case, the religious character of most of the population served as the building block on which the entire project of Turkish nationalism was constructed. In their continued everyday practice of traditional Muslim behavior and dress, in their distaste for the small populations of religious minorities that continued to dwell among them, and in their repeated electoral support for religiously oriented parties despite continued suppression by a small core of secularist elites,

Turks demonstrated time and time again the centrality of Islam to their fundamental conceptions of self and other. It is this function as a key component of
national identity that made religion such a powerful means of boundary formation in the early Republic of Turkey, providing an important differentiator
between those who belonged and those who didn't, and providing the foundation for a religious form of nationalism that continues to prevail in Turkey to this
day, despite secularists' best efforts to the contrary.

6 · CONCLUSION

This book has examined the development of religious nationalism in both Ireland and Turkey, tracing the ways that nationalist movements in both countries drew upon religious definitions of the nation as a way of crafting social cohesion and homogeneity. In Ireland, this analysis began with a survey of official forms of Irish nationalism, seeking to understand how elites and those involved in the official politics of the state viewed the issue of identity. From the first English invasion of Ireland in the twelfth century, through the wars of religion that sought to determine the religious character of the English crown and its kingdom, to the Irish Penal Laws that suppressed Catholicism in favor of the official Protestantism of England, religion played a powerful role in politics on the British Isles.

Different conceptions of the nation, and even different national communities, formed in Ireland in response to historical and social conditions, as various parts of the Irish population sought to nationalize in ways that provided the most benefit to their own segment of society. It was not until the nineteenth century, however, that a true form of nationalism began to rise in Ireland, a product of dissatisfaction with English misrule of Ireland and a reflection of a growing sense of independent identity among an elite subsection of the Irish populace. This nationalist movement took three distinct forms, with some nationalists focusing on political concerns, others seeking to create a cultural movement based on an ancient Gaelic Irish identity, and still others striving to use religious frontiers between Britain and Ireland to argue for the distinct character of the Irish national community. Ultimately, it was the strength of this last movement, which was catalyzed by the failed 1916 Easter Rising and the blood sacrifice of Patrick Pearse, James Connolly, and their fellow revolutionary leaders that sealed the Irish community's Catholic character, a character it would retain as an independent state.

From there, the analysis turned to examine how religion and national identity interacted on the ground in Ireland. Daniel O'Connell's efforts at religious emancipation and the repeal of the most stringent Irish Penal Laws helped nationalize the Catholic population, tantalizing them with the idea that even Catholics could play an important role in political processes. Though religion had played a powerful role in the lives of common Irishmen throughout much of its history, it wasn't until O'Connell's movement that such conceptions of difference were mobilized and turned to concerted nationalist purposes. From then on, religion would play a more powerful role in social organization and in conceptions of collective identity. The devastating effects of the Great Famine that struck Ireland in 1845 only consolidated this trend and brought religion home in a more immediate and urgent way than it ever had before. During the famine years, religious identification played a crucial role in determining life chances, helping to dictate who would live and who would die. Poor Catholics, the vast majority of the Irish population, lacked the resources to survive the famine, and millions died or emigrated as a result. Protestants, in contrast, weathered the famine relatively well, but the decrease in the Catholic poor concentrated what little wealth the Catholic community had in the hands of a few, crafting a new Catholic middle class that could take on a much more powerful role in politics. The rise of the Catholic middle class, rising resentment over British failure to ameliorate the famine, and rising religiosity as a response to the tragedy of the famine led to a powerful role for Catholicism in the formation of new concepts of national identity. The Gaelic Revival of the late nineteenth century, the 1916 Easter Rising, and the division, on religious grounds, of a new Irish Free State from Northern Ireland, which remained in the United Kingdom, only served to further the connection between Catholicism and Irishness. To be Irish had become synonymous with being Catholic, a conflation of religious and national identity that helped structure the new national community.

Just as in the Irish case, the juxtaposition of official definitions of Turkish national identity with those that prevailed on the ground prove instructive. Though the official rhetoric of the Turkish nationalist movement described it in explicitly secular terms, a closer look reveals that Muslim identity played a powerful role in determining who could be considered a Turk. Secularists such as Mustafa Kemal Atatürk sought to craft a new national community that would be modern, Western, and secular, but the importance of religion to the everyday understandings of identity among most of the Turkish populace necessitated a role for Islam. In this, the new Turkish nation fell back on social distinctions predicated on religion that had structured intercommunal relationships during the Ottoman Empire. Nationalists codified these differences, moving from a cosmopolitan Ottoman system in which disparate minority religious populations were treated differently but were still considered part of the overall imperial society, to an exclusionary understanding of the new Turkish nation, one that took religion as its fundamental dividing line. In its expulsion and massacre of religious minorities at the founding of the nation, immigration policies privileging Muslims over other religions during the national period, and legislation specifically targeted to disadvantage religious minorities, the new Turkish nation made clear the extent to which Islam was the religion of the new nation and the characteristic around which national identity was centered.

An examination of the ways people on the ground conceived of the relationship between their religious and national identities reveals the extent to which, despite the best efforts of Turkey's early secularizers, religion was always a fundamental element of national identity. In the ways they thought about their neighbors of different religions, in the ways they pushed back against secularist reforms designed to reduce religion's role in the public sphere, and in the enthusiastic ways they voted for Islamically oriented political parties and candidates in the multiparty period, common Turks demonstrated again and again that they considered Islam a fundamental element of their political identity and what it meant to be a Turk. This relationship has continued even into the most recent period of Turkish history, as the religiously motivated AKP, under the leadership of Recep Tayyip Erdoğan, has achieved significant levels of success over the last two decades. Recent efforts to dismantle the secular social architecture first put in place by Mustafa Kemal at the founding of the republic have been met with significant support among rural Turks and AKP supporters but have also proved controversial. In continued battles before the courts, in protests across Istanbul's streets, and even in a 2016 coup attempt, struggles over the role of religion and the relationship between Islam, secularization, and the state have continued to dominate Turkish politics. In this, the religious conceptions of national identity that first helped shape the early years of the Turkish republic have found an echo in the movements and controversies of the last few years, revealing the crucial role of Islam in defining Turkish national identity.

Ireland and Turkey, then, are both nations that have been fundamentally shaped by religious concerns. In Ireland, this took the form of Catholic agitation first for equal rights and then for political independence. Catholicism represented the faith of the majority of the population, but was very much a religion of the powerless, and so came to represent a path toward freedom from foreign domination and self-determination for a national community that came to center its identity on its distinct religious and cultural elements. Islam in Turkey served a different function. Though also a majority religion, Islam was the religion of the powerful, rather than the powerless. Yet Turkish nationalism was also beset by insecurity and struggle, as the nascent national community fought to establish itself as a new state, free of the last vestiges of the Ottoman Empire and independent and powerful in the face of repeated attempts at colonial intervention by Western powers. Islam thus served as a means of reasserting unity and control over a fracturing society, providing a road map for social cohesion in the face of structural breakdown and rapid social change. Despite their varied contexts, in both cases religion functioned in similar ways. Both Irish Catholicism and Turkish Islam provided a central core of cultural symbols, memories, and attitudes around which national identity could form. Part and parcel of this nationalizing process was the formation of group boundaries, forms of social differentiation that would determine who would, and who would not, be considered members of the new nation. Both Islam and Catholicism provided a comfortable and exclusive characteristic that could make simple what were complicated questions of belonging and membership.

Though they varied in their context and circumstances, both nations coalesced as a result of a variety of complicated processes of boundary formation. In Ireland, nationalists pursued all of the strategies enumerated in Andreas Wimmer's typology of boundary formation. Within the structural and institutional context of the nineteenth-century British Isles, Irish nationalists at various times worked to (1) expand the number of people included, (2) contract boundaries and thus reduce the number of people they enclosed, (3) change the meaning of existing boundaries by challenging ethnic hierarchies, (4) cross boundaries by changing their categorical positioning, and (5) overcome ethnic boundaries by emphasizing other crosscutting levels of identity through strategies of "boundary blurring."[1] In their struggle to define who would constitute the "true" members of the Irish national community, nationalists such as Daniel O'Connell sought to expand what had once been relatively limited understandings of the nation to members of all walks of life, holding massive meetings in a way that brought poor Catholics from rural areas into the nationalist fold. The dissemination of political ideas through the use of print media such as *The Nation* and reading rooms set up so that political ideas could be read even to the illiterate members of the community likewise expanded the reach of the nationalist cause.

At the same time, political struggles between nationalist organizations of all stripes in Ireland created a situation in which other nationalists sought to shrink membership in the nation, restricting the definition of those who could count themselves as true members of the Irish nation to just Catholics, or Irish speakers, or even property-owning, mostly Protestant landlords, depending on political orientation. Cultural nationalists, too, sought to transvalue existing ethnic categories, arguing that the ancient Gaelic culture, long thought a primitive and uncivilized culture by British power brokers, in fact constituted an ancient and glorious cultural heritage, one worthy of a unique and distinctive national community. Finally, individual Irish actors sought to cross and blur social and cultural boundaries in an effort to better their position within the institutional hierarchy of the British and Irish social systems. By "converting" to Protestantism in order to secure famine relief, but still attending Catholic mass in order to protect their immortal souls, for example, common people in Ireland demonstrated the malleability of social and cultural boundaries, but also their unique ability to structure social interaction. In Ireland, then, what it meant to be Irish was a product of both large-scale boundary-formation strategies as different nations and political movements sought to define membership in the national community, but also countless everyday interactions and negotiations as people sought to find their place in the world.

In Turkey, too, nationalists and common people pursued similar strategies of boundary formation to determine the edges of the national community. Institutions, power, and networks all played a critical part in the development of Turkey's national boundaries. The rise of nationalism as a potent political ideology throughout the eastern Mediterranean in the late nineteenth and early twentieth centuries spurred ethnogenesis and forced minority and majority populations in the region to reconceptualize their own ethnicity and nationality. The hierarchy of power within the late Ottoman Empire and actors' political positions within that hierarchy played a powerful role in determining which strategies were available to various political actors. Finally, the extent of political networks determined which populations would be considered part of the new nation and which would fall outside it, separating the former Ottoman population into "Turks" and "others."

Within such constraints, political actors in Turkey pursued all of the various strategies of ethnic boundary formation that Wimmer enumerates. Nationalist politicians in Turkey sought to expand the boundaries of the new nation by crafting a new sense of Turkish identity, while at the same time contracting the boundaries of the nation by excluding Christians and Jews from the new national community. Similarly, actors sought to transvalue social categories, privileging a new positive definition of the term "Turk" and arguing for the inversion of the political and ethnic hierarchy in a way that would lead to political advantage. Meanwhile, individual actors sought to move between ethnic and national groups through processes of conversion and reidentification with alternate social groups, blurring the boundaries between them. Ultimately, political actors at both the collective and individual levels utilized boundary-making strategies that could help them secure advantages in political and social power. The seemingly contradictory nature of Turkey's various efforts to develop both civic and ethnic conceptions of the nation was a consequence of such attempts, as Turkish political and social actors sought to craft a new conception of Turkish national identity, establishing ethnic and national boundaries in a way that would maximize individual and collective social and political power.

The wide variety of different strategies that Irish and Turkish nationalists pursued confirms that national identity in these states, as in so many other places, is contextual, processual, and dynamic in the way Rogers Brubaker identified.[2] National identities in Ireland and Turkey were the product of long and complicated processes as people selected strategies of action and modes of identification that were most advantageous to their individual social and historical circumstances. In both Ireland and Turkey, the growth of nationalist movements was the result of periods of crisis, structural breakdown in which traditional social and cultural bonds were sundered and people struggled to make sense of the rapid changes occurring in the world around them. Faced with tremendous levels of insecurity and stress, people were forced to reconceptualize their own identities in order to find a new place in a world they no longer recognized. In part, this frantic reconfiguring of identity was brought about by changing relationships between the populace and the state. The nationalist movements in both Ireland and Turkey arose at moments in which an imperial system of governance and control was deteriorating. In Ireland, English control over Ireland had long been a contentious and complicated issue. By the nineteenth century, as the British Empire began to fade, powerful movements from a variety of sources rose to challenge British control over its closest colony. Movements for Catholic emancipation and political independence in Ireland represented the beginning of the end to British imperial control over most of the island, as newfound national concepts of self-determination and cultural distinctiveness challenged the foundations of London's claim to the island.

The Turkish nationalist movement, too, took place amid the decline of imperial power. The shattering of the Ottoman Empire amid various breakaway nationalist movements and the intervention of foreign powers radically changed the power structure of the eastern Mediterranean. Faced with the collapse of an imperial system that had structured Ottoman society for centuries, political actors in the former Ottoman territories were forced to craft a new social and political system. In constructing their new society, Turkish political actors took their cue from Europe, where new currents of nationalism and ethnic and political self-determination had begun to dominate the political theory and ideological thought of the day.

In both cases the political relationship between the imperial state and its subject populations proved decisive. As Frantz Fanon argued, colonialism and imperial power is a force that constitutes and defines the identity not just of the colonized but of the colonizer as well.[3] Identity is thus formed through opposition between the dominant and the dominated, the powerful and the powerless. In both Ireland and Turkey, this dialectic process of identity formation resulted in national identities deeply tied to the experiences of empire as nationalists sought to craft new national communities in response to the changing social conditions. In Turkey, nationalists first sought to re-create Ottoman cosmopolitanism in a new national form. Such efforts quickly failed, however, as nationalists soon came to realize that deep schisms between the many ethnic, religious, and cultural groups that called the former Ottoman Empire their home would make a unified form of governance impossible. In response, nationalist politicians abandoned efforts at creating an overarching national version of Ottoman identity and turned instead to constructing a bounded and exclusionary national community, one that would be centered on the Turkish ethnic group, as exemplified by the Muslim Turkish-speaking community of Anatolia. In Ireland, the relationship between the island's population and the British crown significantly shaped the ways in which nationalists and common people conceived of their own identities. While early efforts at achieving political power for the residents of Ireland focused on a wealthy upper class's efforts to influence British politics, rather than be relegated to the political backwaters of Ireland's rural countryside, subsequent efforts extended the idea of the Irish nation beyond its origins. The history of Irish nationalism is a complicated story of efforts by various segments of the Irish population, Protestant and Catholic alike, to earn a say in political decisions that directly affected them. When efforts to achieve self-determination within the decentralized system of British imperial control failed, nationalists in Ireland turned to the idea of separation and complete independence from the British Empire, and the subsequent creation of a national community that could define itself as free from the grasping control of London's imperial power.

In both cases, these efforts at making sense of a senselessly changing anti- and postimperial world settled upon religion as a fundamental characteristic of the social systems they would build. The identities that became most prominent in the aftermath of empire relied upon religion as a means of helping people find their place in the new world. As Danièle Hervieu-Léger has argued, this is one of the strengths of religion. Religion serves as an important reservoir of cultural symbols, beliefs, and attitudes, one that connects everyday life to a higher cosmic sense of order and structure derived from the divine. Such cosmic forms of organization represent an appeal to an authentic tradition centered in a deep and immutable past. By linking newly formed social structures, such as those created during the formation of nations, to such ancient and theoretically unchanging cultural forms, political actors sought to borrow legitimacy in a way that allowed them to argue that their new nations, too, were ancient and enduring, safe from the vagaries of social breakdown and rapid change. In this regard, the religious focus of nationalism in both Ireland and Turkey was a reflection of deep-seated concerns about the ways in which Irish and Turkish societies had suffered from rapid and ontologically threatening social change. In both cases, national communities settled on social identities that conflated multiple facets of identification into a single overarching in-group, merging national and religious identities in a way that led to a national identity with a low level of social identity complexity, but one that provided an important buttress against the stress and in-group threat that accompanied rapid social change.

While Hervieu-Léger identifies such destructive change with the transition to modernity itself, both Ireland and Turkey suffered from far more direct episodes of destruction and social breakdown. In Ireland, the catastrophic toll of the Great Famine that struck during the middle of the nineteenth century so revolutionized Irish society that it forced a radical reformation of everyday life and collective understandings of social identity alike. In Turkey, the devastating effects of successive defeats in the Balkan Wars and World War I combined with internal strife, breakaway nationalist movements, and a sense of creeping Western imperialism forced a reconsideration of the ways in which various population groups interacted with each other and conceived of their own identities in late-Ottoman Anatolia. In both places, religion served as a powerful force for social integration. Irish nationalists called upon Ireland's majority, drawing strength from a tremendous rise of religious fervor that followed the famine and redefining the Irish nation as a Catholic one. Turkish nationalists took a similar approach, crafting a new sense of Turkish national identity in opposition to the Western Christian powers and native Christian minorities within Ottoman territory itself.

Interestingly, religious conceptions of national identity were not the only ones with political power in Ireland and Turkey. In both cases, the first push toward nationalization was made by secular political theorists, academics, and political figures who drew upon Enlightenment ideals in an effort to craft a new and modern version of society. In Ireland, the first stirrings of the nationalist movement were led by a Protestant elite, who sought to transcend Ireland's religious schisms by arguing for a united movement based on political independence rather than religious homogeneity. In Turkey, Mustafa Kemal Atatürk and other early nationalist leaders worked to create a new modern state that would be modeled after Western ideas of secularism and liberalism. There too, religion was not meant to be a major concern, as nationalists believed it was necessary to move on from traditional forms of identification predicated on religious difference. In both cases, however, nationalists advocating a new secularist form of society quickly faced significant opposition, as the vast majority of the populace in both Ireland and Turkey continued to structure their own identities in religious terms. Common members of both communities, it seems, were unwilling to accept the arguments of social theorists that theirs was a secular age. The failure of some states to follow the expected path of secularization and modernization that scholars have predicted has often been seen as a backlash, a pushback against a new model of the secular state.[4] The cases of Ireland and Turkey, however, reveal a different story. Rather than a backlash, I argue that the strength of religious bonds and religious identification was so powerful in both countries that secularists failed to achieve sufficient purchase in the popular imaginary. Despite secularists' best efforts, religious communities in both countries accepted the new ideas of nationalism and self-governance but selectively adopted only the parts they were interested in, rejecting the new doctrine of secularization that came with them.

This selective appropriation of social thought has important implications for the study of nationalism, secularism, and religion. Rather than a straight-line teleological approach to modernization and secularization, as predicted by traditional social theories, a closer look at the Irish and Turkish experience reveals a process of negotiation, compromise, and selectivity as nationalists and common members of society interpreted the rapidly changing nature of society and sought to reconceptualize their own senses of identity and place within the world. As postcolonial theorists have argued, it is critically important to recognize that political ideas and theories generated in Europe are not always general-izable to other contexts around the world.[5] Rather, the experiences of different societies are powerfully shaped by their own social and historical contexts. This is particularly true of theoretical arguments about modernization, seculariza-tion, and the role of religion in society. Instead of accepting secularization and modernization wholesale (though admittedly some nationalists did just that), the vast majority of people in both Ireland and Turkey drew upon the ideals of nationalism and self-determination pioneered by the European Enlightenment and interpreted them to better fit their own particular circumstances.

Comparative results from two case studies both within and beyond the "Western" world thus provide important insights for the study of religion and nationalism. First, they help to specify the types of conditions in which religious nationalism forms. Religion serves as a powerful foundation for collective iden-tity, and political entrepreneurs often draw on the deep reservoir of meaning reli-gion offers when it is advantageous to do so, when religious diversity provides a ready-made scaffolding on which to construct political and national divisions. Such efforts are most necessary at moments of social and political crisis when a reconsideration of political bonds is required. This pattern is visible in other cases of religious nationalism as well. In India, for example, the nationalist move-ment seeking to gain independence was led by secularists, yet the borders and identity of the new state drew explicitly from a sense of the Hindu populace as a distinct political entity.[6] The United States,[7] Israel,[8] and Greece,[9] too, among others, have seen religious nationalist movements that flourished in moments of perceived crisis. The sense of in-group threat, whether from external forces or the vague creeping dread of an internal "other," has spurred nationalist move-ments to summon up religious identities as bulwarks around which political bor-der lines are formed. Examining these types of conditions can provide scholars with insights into where and how religion and nationalism are likely to intersect, in these cases and many others.

Just as important as the conditions within which religious nationalist move-ments form, however, are insights into the processes by which they become successful: the tactics and strategies by which religion becomes politicized and politics becomes part of religious practice and identity. Here I've discussed these as boundary-making processes—efforts to construct well-defined in-groups and out-groups. Nationalist and religious entrepreneurs manipulate the boundaries of such identities, stretching them, shrinking them, or reconceptualizing them to encompass or exclude target populations to craft homogeneous or distinct com-munities. In cases of religious nationalism, this is often done in a way that places primacy on religious identity, but links it explicitly to other differentiating facets of identity such as race, ethnicity, language, and geography. This analysis thus speaks to the necessity of approaches that emphasize the dynamic and inter-related nature of such efforts. By juxtaposing the cases of Ireland and Turkey and examining the efforts of political elites on one hand and the experiences of common populations on the other, this book demonstrates how complicated nationalist movements can be. Full of false starts and differences of opinion, debates, and even full-fledged conflicts, the Irish and Turkish nations that we know today were each just one among a number of possibilities that could have prevailed. Far from the smooth and triumphant story many nationalist movements tell about themselves, the reality is often far messier. Religious nationalism can, and does, develop in concert and dialogue with secular political and ethnic versions of nationalism within the same state. This book has sought to shed light on this process, an approach that could prove fruitful in examining a wide array of other cases, in which much work remains to be done.

Indeed, while this book has focused largely on historical processes of religiously focused national boundary making that took place during the first formation of nationalism, it is important to note that such processes continue to this day. Ireland and Turkey serve as just two examples of an intersection between religion, nationalism, and the state that has proved powerful in societies around the globe. Efforts to reconcile this relationship continue in both cases to this day. In Turkey, complicated questions about the role of religion in society have led to repeated struggles between secularists and religious populations. The 2013 Gezi Park protests against Recep Tayyip Erdoğan's religiously oriented government, recent political clashes between secularist and Islamist elements throughout Turkey, and 2016's attempted coup in which the Turkish army, long considered a bastion of secularism, struck back against Erdoğan's government are only the latest chapters of a long and conflicted debate. The role of religion in the nation has reared its head again even in Ireland, where such conflicts had been thought long buried, first in the Republic of Ireland and then even in Northern Ireland, where the 1998 Good Friday Agreement brought an end to the internecine struggle for political control between groups who identified themselves in religious terms. The 2016 "Brexit," in which the United Kingdom voted to leave the European Union, has threatened to reopen conflicts between communities in Northern Ireland. Despite the Brexit campaign's success in England, people in Northern Ireland voted overwhelmingly to stay in the EU. Complicated questions of the disposition of the border between Northern Ireland and the Republic of Ireland, as well as the significant economic benefits Northern Ireland has accrued as a member of the EU, have made the Brexit plans deeply unpopular there. Political figures from Sinn Féin and other former members of the nationalist movement have raised the specter of yet another nationalist campaign, urging Northern Ireland to finally break away from the United Kingdom and rejoin the Republic of Ireland once and for all. That such political opinions continue to break down along religious lines, with most nationalists members of the Catholic population of Northern Ireland and most unionists Protestants, reveals the continued strength of religion in the Irish national imaginary.

The experiences of Ireland and Turkey, as well as other movements, such as those in the United States, India, Israel, and many others, make it clear that religion continues to be a key element of national identity and a powerful force around the world. Despite theories to the contrary, religious nationalism, and the use of religion to determine membership in the national community, has continued to play a role in processes of identification in societies all around the globe. Rather than a new secular age in which religion slowly disappears, national boundary making along religious lines has helped define what it means to be a member of the national community in nations throughout the world. The continued prevalence of conflicts over identification, nationalism, and religion in the Middle East, Europe, the United States, and elsewhere makes it unlikely that this situation will change in the near future. Complicated patterns of group boundary making driven by religious and historical concerns have helped shape the modern world, and such processes seems likely to continue to structure the ways in which communities view themselves even in today's globalized and seemingly secularized world.

ACKNOWLEDGMENTS

I am deeply indebted to the many family members, friends, mentors, and colleagues who have supported and guided me through the creation of this book. Writing a book, especially a scholarly one, can at times feel isolating, yet I have had the privilege of a social support network that has made every step of the process possible. This book is based on my doctoral dissertation, which I wrote in the Sociology Department at the University of California, Santa Barbara. Its origins, however, lie in work I did in the History Department at UCSB before switching fields. I am deeply grateful to both of my supervisors and mentors, Simonetta Falasca-Zamponi in sociology and Beth DePalma Digeser in history, for their indispensable guidance, incisive comments, and unceasing support as I struggled to combine insights and methodologies from both disciplines. Thanks are especially due to Beth for continuing to support me in so many ways despite my transition from the History Department over to sociology. Other faculty in both departments were instrumental to my success. James F. Brooks and John W. I. Lee in history helped nurture my interests in borderlands and supported this project despite its being well out of both of their fields. In the Sociology Department, Fernando Lopez-Alves helped refine my sense of comparative historical methodology and always encouraged me to consider the big questions that underlay the cases I was interested in. The late John W. Mohr is also due special thanks both for his patience in teaching particularly complex bits of social theory, but especially for always having faith that historical questions could also be deeply sociological and helping to shore up my own belief that such projects could bear great fruit, even when I doubted myself. Thanks are also due to my first two academic mentors, Michele Salzman and John Christian Laursen at the University of California, Riverside, who fostered my love of research and helped set me on the path to large-scale comparative projects even then.

Great thanks are due the many friends from UCSB and my position at Aurora University who made both institutions welcoming places. At UCSB, special thanks are due Ryan Abrecht, Sarah Watkins, Ryan Horne, Viktor Shmagin, Brianna Bricker, Jessica Ambler, Peninah Wolpo, Joe Figliulo-Rosswurm, Dustin Walker, Jason Lin, Tracey Watts, Alison Turtledove, Elijah Bender, Travis Seifman, Malek Guerbaoui, and so many of my colleagues in the Ancient Borderlands program and the History Department. In sociology, Onur Kapdan, Kristen Bryant, Chandra Russo, Lauren Alfrey, Megan Tabag, Sara Rios, Katelynn Bishop, Maryam Griffin, Daisy Gonzales, and Lillian Jungleib all heard versions of this project in an array of seminars. At Aurora, Jonathan Fernand, Chris George, Meaghan Rowe-Johnson, Sarah Mead-Jasperse, and

David Roaché have all made the first few years on the tenure track immensely rewarding.

I'd also like to thank my editor at Rutgers University Press, Elisabeth Maselli, for believing in and supporting this project, as well as the production team for their efforts on the book's behalf. Thanks as well are due the two anonymous reviewers for RUP whose comments have significantly improved the final manuscript.

Last, but most importantly, my family means everything to me, and I would like to thank them for their ceaseless faith. My partner, Avery, has stuck with me through graduate school, dissertating, a move away from sunny California, pandemic-postponed weddings, and more. She has my eternal gratitude for making my life better in every way. Indy, who is the best research assistant any puppy owner could hope for, never fails to jump on my keyboard at precisely the right momenaelkag;herhger;wlfwa. . . . My parents, Robert and Pamela, have nurtured in me a love of learning for as long as I can remember and are still always there for me. My sisters, Jacqueline and Alanna, who have always been strong and supportive, but remind me not to take myself too seriously. Joel, who is always ready for so many deep conversations. And little Nora and Ezekiel, who are everything. Nothing would be possible without you all.

NOTES

1. BORDERS AND BOUNDARIES OF THE NATION

1. Padraic Pearse, *Political Writings and Speeches* (Dublin: Talbot Press, 1952), 55, 59.
2. Pearse, *Political Writings*, 64–75.
3. Thomas Burke, *Lectures on Faith and Fatherland* (London: Cameron and Ferguson, 1874), 117.
4. Article 44, Bunreacht Na Héireann, "Constitution of Ireland," Stationery Office, Dublin, 1937.
5. Yusuf Akçura and Ismail Fehmi, "Yusuf Akçura's Uç Tarzi Siyaset" [Three Kinds of Policy], *Oriente Moderno* 61, no. 1/12 (1981): 7.
6. Ziya Gökalp, *The Principles of Turkism*, translated by Robert Devereaux (Leiden: E. J. Brill, 1968), 192–193.
7. Gökalp, *Principles of Turkism*, 15–16.
8. Article 2, translated and reproduced in Edward Mead Earle, "The New Constitution of Turkey," *Political Science Quarterly* 40, no. 1 (1925): 73–100.
9. Mustafa Kemal Atatürk, *The Great Speech* (Ankara: Atatürk Research Center, 2005), 1.
10. Philip W. Barker, *Religious Nationalism in Modern Europe: If God Be for Us* (London: Routledge, 2009).
11. Andrew L. Whitehead and Samuel L Perry, *Taking America Back for God: Christian Nationalism in the United States* (New York: Oxford University Press, 2020).
12. Mark Juergensmeyer, *Global Rebellion: Religious Challenges to the Secular State, from Christian Militias to al Qaeda* (Berkeley: University of California Press, 2008).
13. J. Christopher Soper and Joel S. Fetzer, *Religion and Nationalism in Global Perspective* (Cambridge: Cambridge University Press, 2018).
14. Fredrik Barth, "Introduction," in *Ethnic Groups and Boundaries: The Social Organization of Culture Difference*. (Boston: Little, Brown, 1969).
15. Rogers Brubaker, *Ethnicity without Groups* (Cambridge, MA: Harvard University Press, 2004); Rogers Brubaker, *Nationalist Politics and Everyday Ethnicity in a Transylvanian Town* (Princeton, NJ: Princeton University Press, 2006); Rogers Brubaker, "Religion and Nationalism: Four Approaches," *Nations and Nationalism* 18, no. 1 (2012): 2–20.
16. Andreas Wimmer, *Ethnic Boundary Making: Institutions, Power, Networks* (New York: Oxford University Press, 2013).
17. See, among many others, William H. Swatos and Kevin J. Christiano, "Secularization Theory: The Course of a Concept," *Sociology of Religion* 60, no. 3 (1999): 209–228; Philip S. Gorski and Ateş Altınordu, "After Secularization?," *Annual Review of Sociology* 34 (2008): 55–85.
18. Barbara-Ann J. Rieffer, "Religion and Nationalism: Understanding the Consequences of a Complex Relationship," *Ethnicities* 3, no. 2 (2003): 215–242; Philip S. Gorski and Gülay Türkmen-Dervişoğlu, "Religion, Nationalism, and Violence: An Integrated Approach," *Annual Review of Sociology* 39 (2013): 193–210; Soper and Fetzer, *Religion and Nationalism*.
19. Ernest Gellner, *Nations and Nationalism* (Ithaca, NY: Cornell University Press, 1983); E. J. Hobsbawm, *Nations and Nationalism Since 1780: Programme, Myth, Reality* (Cambridge: Cambridge University Press, 1990); Benedict Anderson, *Imagined Communities: Reflections on the Origin and Spread of Nationalism* (London: Verso, 1983); Anthony D. Smith, *The Ethnic Origins of Nations* (Oxford: Blackwell, 1987).
20. Brubaker, "Religion and Nationalism."

21. Anthony D. Smith, *Chosen Peoples: Sacred Sources of National Identity* (Oxford: Oxford University Press, 2003).

22. Juergensmeyer, *Global Rebellion*.

23. Roger Friedland, "When God Walks in History: The Institutional Politics of Religious Nationalism," *International Sociology* 14, no. 3 (1999): 301–319; Roger Friedland, "Religious Nationalism and the Problem of Collective Representation," *Annual Review of Sociology* 27, no. 1 (2001): 125–152.

24. John Alexander Armstrong, *Nations before Nationalism* (Chapel Hill: University of North Carolina Press, 1982).

25. Anthony W. Marx, *Faith in Nation: Exclusionary Origins of Nationalism* (New York: Oxford University Press, 2003).

26. N. Jay Demerath III, "The Rise of 'Cultural Religion' in European Christianity: Learning from Poland, Northern Ireland, and Sweden," *Social Compass* 47, no. 1 (2000): 127–139.

27. Steve Bruce, *Religion in the Modern World: From Cathedrals to Cults* (Oxford: Oxford University Press, 1996), 96.

28. John Coakley, "Religion and Nationalism in the First World," in *Ethnonationalism in the Contemporary World: Walker Connor and the Study of Nationalism*, edited by Daniele Conversi (London: Routledge, 2002).

29. Barker, *Religious Nationalism*.

30. Philip Gorski, *American Covenant: A History of Civil Religion from the Puritans to the Present* (Princeton, NJ: Princeton University Press, 2019), 18.

31. Geneviève Zubrzycki, *The Crosses of Auschwitz: Nationalism and Religion in Post-Communist Poland* (Chicago: University of Chicago Press, 2009).

32. Gorski, *American Covenant*.

33. Barker, *Religious Nationalism*.

34. Smith, *Chosen Peoples*.

35. Juergensmeyer, *Global Rebellion*.

36. Daphne Halikiopoulou, *Patterns of Secularization: Church, State and Nation in Greece and the Republic of Ireland* (Farnham, UK: Ashgate, 2011); Barker, *Religious Nationalism*.

37. Peter van der Veer, *Religious Nationalism: Hindus and Muslims in India* (Berkeley: University of California Press, 1994); Baruch Kimmerling, "Religion, Nationalism, and Democracy in Israel," *Constellations* 6, no. 3 (1999): 339–363; Rosemary Radford Ruether and Herman J. Ruether, *The Wrath of Jonah: The Crisis of Religious Nationalism in the Israeli-Palestinian Conflict* (Minneapolis: Fortress Press, 2002).

38. Courtney Bender et al., eds., *Religion on the Edge: De-Centering and Re-Centering the Sociology of Religion* (Oxford: Oxford University Press, 2012).

39. Dipesh Chakrabarty, *Provincializing Europe: Postcolonial Thought and Historical Difference* (Princeton, NJ: Princeton University Press, 2009).

40. Gorski and Altınordu, "After Secularization?"

41. Brubaker, *Ethnicity without Groups*, 17.

42. Brubaker, *Ethnicity without Groups*, 9.

43. Brubaker, *Nationalist Politics and Everyday Ethnicity*, 6.

44. Brubaker, *Nationalist Politics and Everyday Ethnicity*, 7.

45. Brubaker, *Nationalist Politics and Everyday Ethnicity*, 14.

46. Hobsbawm, *Nations and Nationalism Since 1780: Programme, Myth, Reality*, 10.

47. Samuli Schielke, "Second Thoughts about the Anthropology of Islam, or How to Make Sense of Grand Schemes in Everyday Life," *Zentrum Moderner Orient Working Papers* 2 (2010); Rogers Brubaker, "Categories of Analysis and Categories of Practice: A Note on the

Study of Muslims in European Countries of Immigration," *Ethnic and Racial Studies* 36, no. 1 (2013): 1–8.

48. Karen Armstrong, *Fields of Blood*, 2014.

49. At present, such a reality is all too often visible in repeated efforts in America and Europe to categorize all Muslims as perpetrators of violence and supporters of religious terrorism. In contrast, see the wide variety of Muslim religious and political leaders who publicly condemn such acts and routinely call for peaceful coexistence and dialogue. For further discussion, see, for example, Nathan Chapman Lean and John L. Esposito, *The Islamophobia Industry: How the Right Manufactures Fear of Muslims* (London: Pluto Press, 2012).

50. Paul Lichterman, "Religion in Public Action: From Actors to Settings.," *Sociological Theory* 30, no. 1 (2012): 83–104.

51. The gold standard here remains, of course, Samuel Huntington's roundly criticized, though still politically influential, "clash of civilizations" model. Lichterman, however, identifies other examples of this in what he terms the "Unitary Actor Model." Samuel P. Huntington, *The Clash of Civilizations and the Remaking of World Order* (New York: Simon & Schuster, 1996); Lichterman, "Religion in Public Action."

52. Bender et al., *Religion on the Edge*.

53. Bender et al., *Religion on the Edge*; James V. Spickard, *Alternative Sociologies of Religion: Through Non-Western Eyes* (New York: NYU Press, 2017).

54. Brubaker, *Ethnicity without Groups*, 41.

55. Nancy Tatom Ammerman, *Everyday Religion: Observing Modern Religious Lives* (Oxford: Oxford University Press, 2007).

56. Kanchan Chandra, "What Is Ethnic Identity and Does It Matter?," *Annual Review of Political Science* 9 (2006): 397–424.

57. Joseph Ruane and Jennifer Todd, "Ethnicity and Religion: Redefining the Research Agenda," *Ethnopolitics* 9, no. 1 (2010): 3.

58. Pierre Bourdieu, *Language and Symbolic Power*, translated by John B. Thompson (Cambridge, MA: Harvard University Press, 1991).

59. Barth, "Introduction."

60. Fredrik Barth, "Boundaries and Connections," in *Signifying Identities: Anthropological Perspectives on Boundaries and Contested Values*, edited by Anthony P. Cohen (London: Routledge, 2000), 19, 23.

61. Anna Triandafyllidou, "National Identity and the 'Other,'" *Ethnic and Racial Studies* 21, no. 4 (July 1998): 593–612.

62. Barth, "Boundaries and Connections," 30.

63. Pekka Hämäläinen and Samuel Truett, "On Borderlands," *Journal of American History* 98, no. 2 (2011): 338–361; Ryan Abrecht, "My Neighbor the Barbarian: Immigrant Neighborhoods in Classical Athens, Imperial Rome, and Tang Chang'an" (doctoral dissertation, University of California, Santa Barbara, 2014); Victoria Reyes, *Global Borderlands: Fantasy, Violence, and Empire in Subic Bay, Philippines* (Stanford, CA: Stanford University Press, 2019); Gregory J. Goalwin, "Bandits, Militants, and Martyrs: Sub-state Violence as Claim to Authority in Late Antique North Africa." *Journal of Historical Sociology* 34, no. 3 (2021): 452–465.

64. Wimmer, *Ethnic Boundary Making*, 205.

65. Andreas Wimmer, "The Making and Unmaking of Ethnic Boundaries: A Multilevel Process Theory," *American Journal of Sociology* 113, no. 4 (2008): 986.

66. Wimmer, "The Making and Unmaking of Ethnic Boundaries," 990.

67. Andreas Wimmer, "Elementary Strategies of Ethnic Boundary Making," *Ethnic and Racial Studies* 31, no. 6 (2008): 101.

68. Pierre Bourdieu, *Distinction: A Social Critique of the Judgement of Taste* (Cambridge, MA: Harvard University Press, 1984).
69. Max Weber, *Economy and Society; An Outline of Interpretive Sociology* (New York: Bedminster Press, 1968).
70. Brubaker offers a notable exception, although even there, he concludes that nationalism is an essentially secular phenomenon. Brubaker, "Religion and Nationalism."
71. Brubaker, *Ethnicity without Groups*, 31.
72. Anthony D. Smith, *Myths and Memories of the Nation* (Oxford: Oxford University Press, 1999).
73. Shmuel Noah Eisenstadt, *Tradition, Change, and Modernity* (New York: John Wiley & Sons, 1973); Brian Heaphy, *Late Modernity and Social Change: Reconstructing Social and Personal Life* (London: Routledge, 2007).
74. Danièle Hervieu-Léger, *Religion as a Chain of Memory* (New Brunswick, NJ: Rutgers University Press, 2000), 123.
75. Hervieu-Léger, *Religion as a Chain of Memory*, 123.
76. Hervieu-Léger, *Religion as a Chain of Memory*, 83.
77. Hervieu-Léger, *Religion as a Chain of Memory*, 86.
78. E. J. Hobsbawm and T. O. Ranger, *The Invention of Tradition* (Cambridge: Cambridge University Press, 1983); Anderson, *Imagined Communities*; Smith, *Myths and Memories of the Nation*.
79. Hervieu-Léger, *Religion as a Chain of Memory*, 87.
80. Eugen Weber, *Peasants into Frenchmen: The Modernization of Rural France, 1870–1914* (Stanford, CA: Stanford University Press, 1976).
81. Smith, *The Ethnic Origins of Nations*.
82. Armstrong, *Nations before Nationalism*.
83. Anderson, *Imagined Communities*.
84. Gellner, *Nations and Nationalism*.
85. Sonia Roccas and Marilynn B. Brewer, "Social Identity Complexity," *Personality and Social Psychology Review* 6, no. 2 (2002): 88–106.
86. Roccas and Brewer, "Social Identity Complexity," 89.
87. Roccas and Brewer, "Social Identity Complexity," 93.
88. Roccas and Brewer, "Social Identity Complexity," 94.
89. M. B. Brewer and K. P. Pierce, "Social Identity Complexity and Outgroup Tolerance," *Personality & Social Psychology Bulletin* 31, no. 3 (2005): 428–437.
90. Roccas and Brewer, "Social Identity Complexity," 99.
91. Brewer and Pierce, "Social Identity Complexity and Outgroup Tolerance"; K. Schmid et al., "Antecedents and Consequences of Social Identity Complexity: Intergroup Contact, Distinctiveness Threat, and Outgroup Attitudes," *Personality & Social Psychology Bulletin* 35, no. 8 (2009): 1085–1098.
92. Bruce, *Religion in the Modern World*.
93. Grace Davie, *Religion in Britain since 1945: Believing without Belonging* (Oxford: Blackwell, 1994).
94. Hervieu-Léger, *Religion as a Chain of Memory*, 162.
95. Rieffer, "Religion and Nationalism"; Soper and Fetzer, *Religion and Nationalism*.
96. Van der Veer, *Religious Nationalism*; John Zavos, *The Emergence of Hindu Nationalism in India* (New Delhi: Oxford University Press, 2000); John Hansen and Thomas Blom Zavos, *Hindu Nationalism and Indian Politics* (New Delhi: Oxford University Press, 2004).
97. Aviad Rubin, "The Status of Religion in Emergent Political Regimes: Lessons from Turkey and Israel," *Nations and Nationalism* 19, no. 3 (2013): 493–512; Ruether and Ruether, *The Wrath of Jonah*.

98. Gorski, *American Covenant*; Samuel L. Perry and Andrew L. Whitehead, "Christian Nationalism and White Racial Boundaries: Examining Whites' Opposition to Interracial Marriage," *Ethnic and Racial Studies*, no. 1 (2015): 1–19; Whitehead and Perry, *Taking America Back for God*.

99. John McGarry and Brendan O'Leary, *Explaining Northern Ireland: Broken Images* (Oxford: Blackwell, 2000).

100. Hobsbawm, *Nations and Nationalism since 1780*.

2. THE GOSPEL OF IRISH NATIONALISM

1. Bunreacht Na Héireann, "Constitution of Ireland," Stationery Office, Dublin, 1937, 44.1.2.

2. J. Burley and F. Regan, "Divorce in Ireland: The Fear, the Floodgates and the Reality," *International Journal of Law, Policy and the Family* 16, no. 2 (2002): 202–222; Chrystel Hug and Jo Campling, *The Politics of Sexual Morality in Ireland* (New York: St. Martin's Press, 1999).

3. Philip W. Barker, *Religious Nationalism in Modern Europe: If God Be for Us* (London: Routledge, 2009), 46.

4. Daniel Webster Hollis, *The History of Ireland* (Westport, CT: Greenwood Press, 2001).

5. M. A. Busteed, Frank Neal, and Jonathan Tonge, *Irish Protestant Identities* (Manchester: Manchester University Press, 2008).

6. James Loughlin, "The Irish Protestant Home Rule Association and Nationalist Politics, 1886–93," *Irish Historical Studies* 24, no. 95 (1985): 341–360.

7. David George Boyce, *Nationalism in Ireland* (London: Routledge, 1995), 15.

8. Robert Kee, *The Green Flag; A History of Irish Nationalism* (London: Weidenfeld and Nicolson, 1972); Barker, *Religious Nationalism*.

9. Barker, *Religious Nationalism*.

10. Thomas Bartlett, *The Fall and Rise of the Irish Nation: The Catholic Question, 1690–1830* (Savage, MD: Barnes & Noble Books, 1992).

11. John Coakley, "Mobilizing the Past: Nationalist Images of History," *Nationalism & Ethnic Politics*, no. 10 (2004): 531–560.

12. Hollis, *The History of Ireland*, 15.

13. Boyce, *Nationalism in Ireland*, 27.

14. F. J. Byrne, *Irish Kings and High-Kings* (New York: St. Martin's Press, 1973), 56–57.

15. Boyce, *Nationalism in Ireland*, 29.

16. Boyce, *Nationalism in Ireland*, 30.

17. Edmund Curtis and R. B. McDowell, eds., "The Statues of Kilkenny," in *Irish Historical Documents: 1172–1922* (New York: Barnes & Noble, 1968).

18. James Muldoon, *Identity on the Medieval Irish Frontier: Degenerate Englishmen, Wild Irishmen, Middle Nations* (Gainesville: University Press of Florida, 2003).

19. Boyce, *Nationalism in Ireland*, 31.

20. Éamonn Ó Ciardha and Micheál Ó Siochrú, *The Plantation of Ulster: Ideology and Practice* (Manchester: Manchester University Press, 2012).

21. Aidan Clarke, *The Old English in Ireland, 1625–42* (Ithaca, NY: Cornell University Press, 1966).

22. Clarke, *The Old English in Ireland*.

23. See, for instance: Micheál Ó Siochrú, *God's Executioner: Oliver Cromwell and the Conquest of Ireland* (London: Faber & Faber, 2008). Yet in England, Cromwell is thought of far more positively as a champion of liberty, and a 2002 BBC poll even named him one of the top ten Britons of all time. Maurice Ashley, *The Greatness of Oliver Cromwell* (New York: Macmillan, 1958).

24. Gregory Goalwin, "The Art of War: Instability, Insecurity, and Ideological Imagery in Northern Ireland's Political Murals, 1979–1998," *International Journal of Politics, Culture, and Society* 26, no. 3 (2013): 189–215.

25. Charles Ivar McGrath, "Securing the Protestant Interest: The Origins and Purpose of the Penal Laws of 1695," *Irish Historical Studies* 30, no. 117 (1996): 25–46.

26. Patricia M. Schaffer, "Laws in Ireland for the Suppression of Popery Commonly Known as the Penal Laws," 2000, http://library.law.umn.edu/irishlaw/intro.html.

27. Busteed, Neal, and Tonge, *Irish Protestant Identities*.

28. Hollis, *The History of Ireland*, 25.

29. Peter Berresford Ellis, *Hell or Connaught! The Cromwellian Colonisation of Ireland, 1652–1660* (Belfast: Blackstaff, 1988).

30. For a discussion of the concept of "ethnic core," see Anthony D. Smith, *The Ethnic Origins of Nations* (Oxford: Blackwell, 1987).

31. Muldoon, *Identity on the Medieval Irish Frontier*.

32. S. J. Connolly, *Contested Island: Ireland, 1460–1630* (Oxford: Oxford University Press, 2007).

33. John Thomas Gilbert, *History of the Irish Confederation and the War in Ireland, 1641–1649*, 7 vols. (New York: AMS Press, 1973).

34. Clarke, *The Old English in Ireland*, 182.

35. Bartlett, *The Fall and Rise of the Irish Nation*.

36. McGrath, "Securing the Protestant Interest."

37. William Molyneux, *The Case of Ireland Stated* (Dublin: Cadenus Press, 1977), 19–21.

38. Busteed, Neal, and Tonge, *Irish Protestant Identities*.

39. Edmund Curtis and R. B. McDowell, eds., "Poyning's Law," in *Irish Historical Documents: 1172–1922* (New York: Barnes & Noble, 1968), 83.

40. Bartlett, *The Fall and Rise of the Irish Nation*, 35.

41. Muldoon, *Identity on the Medieval Irish Frontier*.

42. Henry Grattan, *Memoirs of the Life and Times of Henry Grattan*, vol. 1 (London: Henry Colburn,1839), 8.

43. Seán Moore, "Our Irish Copper-Farthen Dean: Swift's *Drapier's Letters*, the Forging of a Modernist Anglo-Irish Literature, and the Atlantic World of Paper Credit," *Atlantic Studies* 2, no. 1 (2005): 65–92.

44. Molyneux, *The Case of Ireland Stated*; Jonathan Swift, *A Modest Proposal and Other Satires* (Amherst, NY: Prometheus Books, 1995); James Kelly, *Henry Flood: Patriots and Politics in Eighteenth-Century Ireland* (Notre Dame, IN: University of Notre Dame Press, 1998).

45. Henry Grattan, *The Speeches of Henry Grattan, in the Irish, and in the Imperial Parliament* (London: Longman, Hurst, Rees, Orme and Brown, 1822), 123.

46. Society of United Irishmen, "The Organization of the United Irishmen," in *Irish Historical Documents: 1172–1922*, edited by Edmund Curtis and R. B. McDowell (New York: Barnes & Noble, 1968).

47. Society of United Irishmen, "The Organization of the United Irishmen," 238.

48. Edmund Curtis and R. B. McDowell, eds., "An Act for the Union of Great Britain and Ireland," in *Irish Historical Documents: 1172–1922* (New York: Barnes & Noble, 1968), 208.

49. Kee, *The Green Flag*.

50. Kee, *The Green Flag*, 208.

51. Kee, *The Green Flag*, 215.

52. John Hutchinson, *The Dynamics of Cultural Nationalism: The Gaelic Revival and the Creation of the Irish Nation State* (London: Allen & Unwin, 1987), 62.

53. Busteed, Neal, and Tonge, *Irish Protestant Identities*.

54. Hutchinson, *The Dynamics of Cultural Nationalism*.

55. Hutchinson, *The Dynamics of Cultural Nationalism*, 21.

56. Hans Kohn, *The Idea of Nationalism: A Study in Its Origins and Background* (New York: Macmillan Co., 1944); Ernest Gellner, *Nations and Nationalism* (Ithaca, NY: Cornell University Press, 1983).

57. Hutchinson, *The Dynamics of Cultural Nationalism*, 30–31.

58. Hutchinson, *The Dynamics of Cultural Nationalism*, 87.

59. John Hutchinson, "Archaeology and the Irish Rediscovery of the Celtic Past," *Nations and Nationalism* 7, no. 4 (2001): 505–519.

60. Hutchinson, *The Dynamics of Cultural Nationalism*.

61. "Editorial, Unsigned Article from *The Nation* (1842)," in *Ireland and England, 1798–1922: An Anthology of Sources*, edited by Dennis Dworkin (Indianapolis, IN: Hackett Publishing, 2012).

62. Richard P. Davis, *The Young Ireland Movement* (Dublin: Gill & Macmillan, 1988).

63. Thomas Wyse, *Historical Sketch of the Late Catholic Association of Ireland* (London: H. Colburn, 1829).

64. Edmund Curtis and R. B. McDowell, eds., "Roman Catholic Relief Act," in *Irish Historical Documents: 1172–1922* (New York: Barnes & Noble, 1968).

65. Curtis and McDowell, "Roman Catholic Relief Act," 228.

66. Diarmaid Ferriter, *The Transformation of Ireland* (Woodstock, NY: Overlook Press, 2005).

67. Cormac Ó Gráda and Andrés Eiríksson, *Ireland's Great Famine: Interdisciplinary Perspectives* (Dublin: University College Dublin Press, 2006).

68. Michael Foy and Brian Barton, *The Easter Rising* (Stroud, UK: Sutton, 1999).

69. Boyce, *Nationalism in Ireland*, 311.

70. Padraic Pearse, *Political Writings and Speeches* (Dublin: Talbot Press, 1952), 64–75.

71. Pearse, *Political Writings and Speeches*, 375.

72. Indeed, images of death and resurrection have become a key facet of Republican visual ideology in Northern Ireland, symbolic of the constant rebirth of the persecuted Republican movement. This motif is most obvious in depictions of the 1981 hunger strikers, and of both phoenixes and the risen Christ. See, among others, Martin Forker and Jonathan McCormick, "Walls of History: The Use of Mythomoteurs in Northern Ireland Murals," *Irish Studies Review* 17, no. 4 (2009): 423–465.

73. Provisional Government of the Irish Republic, "The Proclamation of the Irish Republic," in *Irish Historical Documents: 1172–1922*, edited by Edmund Curtis and R. B. McDowell (New York: Barnes & Noble, 1968).

74. Pearse, *Political Writings and Speeches*, 53–57, 364–371; Gregory J. Goalwin, "The Curious Case of Cú Chulainn: Nationalism, Culture, and Meaning-Making in the Contested Symbols of Northern Ireland," *Studies in Ethnicity and Nationalism* 19, no. 3 (2019): 307–324.

75. Pearse, *Political Writings and Speeches*, 255.

76. Karen Stanbridge, "Nationalism, International Factors and the Irish Question in the Era of the First World War," *Nations and Nationalism* 11, no. 1 (2005): 21–42.

77. Michael Laffan, *The Resurrection of Ireland: The Sinn Féin Party, 1916–1923* (Cambridge: Cambridge University Press, 1999).

78. Edmund Curtis and R. B. McDowell, eds., "Articles of Agreement for a Treaty between Great Britain and Ireland," in *Irish Historical Documents: 1172–1922* (New York: Barnes & Noble, 1968).

79. Susan McKay, *Northern Protestants: An Unsettled People* (Belfast: Blackstaff Press, 2000).

80. Conor Cruise O'Brien, *Ancestral Voices: Religion and Nationalism in Ireland* (Chicago: University of Chicago Press, 1995), 128.

81. Diarmaid Ferriter, *Judging Dev: A Reassessment of the Life and Legacy of Eamon de Valera* (Dublin: Royal Irish Academy, 2007).

82. O'Brien, *Ancestral Voices*, 129.

83. Héireann, "Constitution of Ireland."

84. Hug and Campling, *The Politics of Sexual Morality in Ireland*.

85. Tom Inglis, "Individualisation and Secularisation in Catholic Ireland," in *Contemporary Ireland: A Sociological Map*, edited by Sara O'Sullivan (Dublin: University College Dublin Press, 2007), 69.

86. Government of Ireland Central Statistics Office, "2016 Irish Census," 2017, https://www .cso.ie/en/media/csoie/newsevents/documents/census2016summaryresultspart1/Census 2016SummaryPart1.pdf.

87. Barker, *Religious Nationalism in Modern Europe*.

88. Rogers Brubaker, *Ethnicity without Groups* (Cambridge, MA: Harvard University Press, 2004).

3. RELIGION ON THE GROUND

1. Isaac Ariail Reed, "Between Structural Breakdown and Crisis Action: Interpretation in the Whiskey Rebellion and the Salem Witch Trials," *Critical Historical Studies* 3, no. 1 (2016): 27–64.

2. William H. Sewell Jr., *Logics of History: Social Theory and Social Transformation* (Chicago: University of Chicago Press, 2005).

3. Andrew Murphy, "Bringing the Nation to the Book: Literacy and Irish Nationalism" (Lecture, Trinity College Dublin, May 18, 2015), https://www.tcd.ie/trinitylongroomhub/events /details/2015/2015-05-18bringing_the_nation.php.

4. Maureen Wall, "The Rise of a Catholic Middle Class in Eighteenth-Century Ireland," *Irish Historical Studies* 11, no. 42 (1958): 91–115.

5. Kevin B. Nowlan, *The Politics of Repeal: A Study in the Relations between Great Britain and Ireland, 1841–50* (London: Routledge & Kegan Paul, 1965).

6. Roisín Higgins, "The Nation Reading Rooms," in *The Oxford History of the Irish Book*, vol. 4 (Oxford: Oxford University Press, 2011), 262–73.

7. "Repeal Education," *The Nation*, May 10, 1845.

8. Huston Gilmore, "'The Shouts of Vanished Crowds: Literacy, Orality, and Popular Politics in the Campaign to Repeal the Act of Union in Ireland, 1840–48," *Interdisciplinary Studies in the Long Nineteenth Century* 19 (2014): 7.

9. Charles Gavan Duffy, *Young Ireland: A Fragment of Irish History, 1840–1850* (London: Massell, Petter, Galphin, 1880), 387.

10. Thomas Ray, "First Quarterly Report upon Repeal Reading Rooms," in *Reports of the Parliamentary Committee of the Loyal National Repeal Association of Ireland*, vol. 2 (Dublin: Browne, 1845), 329.

11. Gilmore, "'The Shouts of Vanished Crowds," 9.

12. Thomas Wyse, *Historical Sketch of the Late Catholic Association of Ireland* (London: H. Colburn, 1829), 339.

13. Benedict Anderson, *Imagined Communities: Reflections on the Origin and Spread of Nationalism* (London: Verso, 1983).

14. Thomas MacNevin, "Custom House Ward: Repeal Reading Rooms," *The Nation*, February 8, 1845, 295.

15. Cited in Gilmore, "'The Shouts of Vanished Crowds."

16. Gary Owens, "Nationalism without Words: Symbolism and Ritual Behaviour in the Repeal 'Monster Meetings' of 1843–5," in *Irish Popular Culture 1650–1850*, edited by James S. Donelly Jr. and Kerby A. Miller (Dublin: Irish Academic Press, 1998), 256.

17. *Galway Vindicator*, June 17, 1843. Cited in Maura Cronin, "'Of One Mind'? O'Connellite Crowds in the 1830s and 1840s," in *Crowds in Ireland, c. 1720–1920*, edited by Peter Jupp and Eoin Magennis (Houndmills, UK: Macmillan Press, 2000).

18. Cronin, "'Of One Mind'?," 149.

19. Cronin, "'Of One Mind'?," 149.

20. Cited in Cronin, "'Of One Mind'?," 152.

21. Christine Kinealy, *The Great Irish Famine: Impact, Ideology, and Rebellion* (Houndmills, UK: Palgrave, 2002), 2.

22. Jeremy Rifkin, *Beyond Beef: The Rise and Fall of the Cattle Culture* (New York: Dutton, 1992), 56–57.

23. Cathal Póirtéir, *Famine Echoes* (Dublin: Gill & Macmillan, 1995), 216.

24. Póirtéir, *Famine Echoes*, 230.

25. Joseph Lee, *The Modernisation of Irish Society, 1848–1918* (Dublin: Gill & Macmillan, 1973), 9.

26. Póirtéir, *Famine Echoes*, 210.

27. Noel Kissane, *The Irish Famine: A Documentary History* (Syracuse, NY: Syracuse University Press, 1995), 171.

28. Kissane, *The Irish Famine*, 171.

29. Samuel Clark, "The Political Mobilization of Irish Farmers," *Canadian Review of Sociology/Revue Canadienne de Sociologie* 12, no. 4 (1975): 494.

30. Janet Nolan, *Ourselves Alone: Women's Emigration from Ireland, 1885–1920* (Lexington: University Press of Kentucky, 1986), 52.

31. John Hutchinson, *The Dynamics of Cultural Nationalism: The Gaelic Revival and the Creation of the Irish Nation State* (London: Allen & Unwin, 1987).

32. David George Boyce, *Nationalism in Ireland* (London: Routledge, 1995), 170.

33. Boyce, *Nationalism in Ireland*, 170.

34. Póirtéir, *Famine Echoes*, 218.

35. Cormac Ó Gráda, *Black '47 and Beyond: The Great Irish Famine in History, Economy, and Memory* (Princeton, NJ: Princeton University Press, 2000), 132.

36. Cormac Ó Gráda, *The Great Irish Famine* (Houndmills, UK: Macmillan, 1989), 66.

37. Póirtéir, *Famine Echoes*, 215.

38. Kinealy, *The Great Irish Famine*.

39. Póirtéir, *Famine Echoes*, 35.

40. Póirtéir, *Famine Echoes*, 39.

41. David W. Miller, "Irish Catholicism and the Great Famine," *Journal of Social History* 9, no. 1 (1975): 83.

42. Emmet Larkin, "The Devotional Revolution in Ireland, 1850–75," *American Historical Review* 77, no. 3 (1972): 625–652.

43. Miller, "Irish Catholicism and the Great Famine."

44. Larkin, "The Devotional Revolution in Ireland," 627.

45. Larkin, "The Devotional Revolution in Ireland," 632.

46. Philip W. Barker, *Religious Nationalism in Modern Europe: If God Be for Us* (London: Routledge, 2009), 46.

47. Larkin, "The Devotional Revolution in Ireland," 651.

48. Miller, "Irish Catholicism and the Great Famine," 93.

49. Larkin, "The Devotional Revolution in Ireland," 649.

50. Danièle Hervieu-Léger, *Religion as a Chain of Memory* (New Brunswick, NJ: Rutgers University Press, 2000).

51. Póirtéir, *Famine Echoes.*

52. Póirtéir, *Famine Echoes*, 70, 202.

53. Póirtéir, *Famine Echoes*, 145.

54. Póirtéir, *Famine Echoes*, 169.

55. Póirtéir, *Famine Echoes*, 167, 171.

56. Póirtéir, *Famine Echoes*, 177.

57. Fredrik Barth, "Introduction," in *Ethnic Groups and Boundaries: The Social Organization of Culture Difference* (Boston: Little, Brown, 1969); Anna Triandafyllidou, "National Identity and the 'Other,'" *Ethnic and Racial Studies* 21, no. 4 (July 1998): 593–612.

58. Sonia Roccas and Marilynn B. Brewer, "Social Identity Complexity," *Personality and Social Psychology Review* 6, no. 2 (2002): 88–106.

59. M. B. Brewer and K. P. Pierce, "Social Identity Complexity and Outgroup Tolerance," *Personality & Social Psychology Bulletin* 31, no. 3 (2005): 428–437.

60. Diarmuid Ó Giolláin, "The Fairy Belief and Official Religion in Ireland," in *The Good People: New Fairylore Essays*, edited by Peter Narváez (New York: Garland, 1991), 206.

61. John Eglinton, *Literary Ideals in Ireland* (New York: Lemma, 1973), 13.

62. Miller, "Irish Catholicism and the Great Famine."

63. Matthew Arnold, *The Works of Matthew Arnold . . . : On the Study of Celtic Literature and On Translating Homer*, edited by Thomas Burnett Smart, vol. 5 (New York: Macmillan and Company, 1903), 5.

64. Douglas Hyde, "The Necessity for De-Anglicising Ireland," in *The Revival of Irish Literature*, by George Sigerson, Charles Gavan Duffy, George Sigerson, and Douglas Hyde (New York: Lemma, 1973), 117–161.

65. Hyde, "The Necessity for De-Anglicising Ireland," 26.

66. Declan Kiberd and P. J. Mathews, *Handbook of the Irish Revival: An Anthology of Irish Cultural and Political Writings 1891–1922* (Notre Dame, IN: University of Notre Dame Press, 2016), 111.

67. Hutchinson, *The Dynamics of Cultural Nationalism*, 127.

68. Cited in Boyce, *Nationalism in Ireland*, 243.

69. Boyce, *Nationalism in Ireland*, 240.

70. Stopford Augustus Brooke, *The Need and Use of Getting Irish Literature into the English Tongue: An Address* (London: T. Fisher Unwin, 1893).

71. Kiberd and Mathews, *Handbook of the Irish Revival*, 144.

72. Gregory J. Goalwin, "The Curious Case of Cú Chulainn: Nationalism, Culture, and Meaning-Making in the Contested Symbols of Northern Ireland," *Studies in Ethnicity and Nationalism* 19, no. 3 (2019): 307–324.

73. Mary Colum, *Life and the Dream* (Garden City, NY: Doubleday, 1947), 114.

74. Kevin Collins, *Catholic Churchmen and the Celtic Revival in Ireland, 1848–1916* (Dublin: Four Courts Dublin, 2002), 161.

75. Kiberd and Mathews, *Handbook of the Irish Revival*, 149.

76. Máire Nic Shiubhlaigh and Edward Kenny, *The Splendid Years* (Dublin: J. Duffy, 1955).

77. Kiberd and Mathews, *Handbook of the Irish Revival*, 156.

78. Collins, *Catholic Churchmen and the Celtic Revival*, 163–164.

79. W. B. Yeats, Lady Gregory, and James Pethica, *Collaborative One-Act Plays, 1901–1903: Cathleen ni Houlihan, The Pot of Broth, The Country of the Young Heads or Harps: Manuscript Materials* (Ithaca, NY: Cornell University Press, 2006), 59.

80. Yeats, Gregory, and Pethica, *Collaborative One-Act Plays*, 95.

81. James Pethica, "'Our Kathleen': Yeats's Collaboration with Lady Gregory in the Writing of *Cathleen ni Houlihan*," in *Yeats Annual No. 6*, edited by Warwick Gould (Houndmills, UK: Macmillan, 1988), 3–31.

82. Francis X. Martin, "The 1916 Rising: A 'Coup d'État' or a 'Bloody Protest'?," *Studia Hibernica*, 8 (1968): 106–137.

83. Seán Farrell Moran, *Patrick Pearse and the Politics of Redemption: The Mind of the Easter Rising, 1916* (Washington, DC: Catholic University of America Press, 1994).

84. Desmond FitzGerald, *Memoirs of Desmond FitzGerald, 1913–1916* (London: Routledge/ Thoemms Press, 1968), 130.

85. FitzGerald, *Memoirs of Desmond FitzGerald*, 133.

86. Joseph Lee, *Ireland, 1912–1985: Politics and Society* (Cambridge: Cambridge University Press, 1989), 27–30.

87. "The Sinn Féin Leaders of 1916 with Fourteen Illustrations and Complete Lists of Deportees, Casualties" (Dublin: UCD Library, 1917), digital.ucd.ie/view/ivrla:30885.

88. "The 'Sinn Féin' Revolt Illustrated April 1916" (Dublin: UCD School of History and Archives, n.d.), digital.ucd.ie/view/ivrla:30653.

89. "Booklet Detailing the Dead 'Fianna Heroes of 1916'" (Dublin: UCD School of History and Archives, n.d.), digital.ucd.ie/view/ivrla:30626.

90. Kiberd and Mathews, *Handbook of the Irish Revival*, 444–446.

91. Collins, *Catholic Churchmen and the Celtic Revival*, 19.

92. John Newsinger, "'I Bring Not Peace but a Sword': The Religious Motif in the Irish War of Independence," *Journal of Contemporary History* 13, no. 3 (1978): 625–626.

93. Collins, *Catholic Churchmen and the Celtic Revival*, 161.

94. Bunreacht Na Héireann, "Constitution of Ireland" (Dublin: Stationery Office, 1937).

95. John Coakley, "Religion and Nationalism in the First World," in *Ethnonationalism in the Contemporary World: Walker Connor and the Study of Nationalism*, edited by Daniele Conversi (London: Routledge, 2002).

96. John Coakley, "Religion, National Identity and Political Change in Modern Ireland," *Irish Political Studies* 17, no. 1 (2002): 6.

97. Brian Girvin, "Social Change and Moral Politics: The Irish Constitutional Referendum 1983," *Political Studies* 34, no. 1 (1986): 61–81.

98. Christine P. James, "Céad Míle Fáilte: Ireland Welcomes Divorce: The 1995 Irish Divorce Referendum and the Family (Divorce) Act of 1996," *Duke Journal of Comparative & International Law* 8 (1997): 175.

99. Jo Murphy-Lawless and James McCarthy, "Social Policy and Fertility Change in Ireland: The Push to Legislate in Favour of Women's Agency," *European Journal of Women's Studies* 6, no. 1 (1999): 69–96.

100. Barker, *Religious Nationalism in Modern Europe*; Central Statistics Office, Government of Ireland, "2016 Irish Census," 2017, https://www.cso.ie/en/media/csoie/newsevents/documents /census2016summaryresultspart1/Census2016SummaryPart1.pdf.

101. Michael J. Carey, "Catholicism and Irish National Identity," *Religion and Politics in the Modern World*, 120 (1983): 105.

102. Thomas Burke, *Lectures on Faith and Fatherland* (London: Cameron and Ferguson, 1874), 117.

103. John Darby, *Conflict in Northern Ireland: The Development of a Polarised Community* (Dublin: Gill & Macmillan, 1976).

104. Sean Cronin, *Irish Nationalism: A History of Its Roots and Ideology* (London: Continuum, 1981), 177.

105. Dominic Murray, *Worlds Apart: Segregated Schools in Northern Ireland* (Belfast: Appletree Press, 1985).

106. Rod Thornton, "Getting It Wrong: The Crucial Mistakes Made in the Early Stages of the British Army's Deployment to Northern Ireland (August 1969 to March 1972)," *Journal of Strategic Studies* 30, no. 1 (2007): 73–107.

107. Raymond Murray, *State Violence in Northern Ireland, 1969–1997* (Cork: Mercier, 1998).

108. Desmond Hamill, *Pig in the Middle: The Army in Northern Ireland, 1969–1985* (London: Methuen, 1986), 62.

109. Liz Fawcett and Jo Campling, *Religion, Ethnicity, and Social Change* (Houndmills, UK: Macmillan, 2000).

110. Claire Mitchell, *Religion, Identity and Politics in Northern Ireland: Boundaries of Belonging and Belief* (Farnham, UK: Ashgate Publishing, 2013).

111. Ian McAllister, "The Devil, Miracles and the Afterlife: The Political Sociology of Religion in Northern Ireland," *British Journal of Sociology* 33, no. 3 (1982): 330–347.

112. Martin Dillon, *God and the Gun: The Church and Irish Terrorism* (New York: Routledge, 1998), 67.

113. Hervieu-Léger, *Religion as a Chain of Memory*.

114. Roccas and Brewer, "Social Identity Complexity."

115. Brewer and Pierce, "Social Identity Complexity and Outgroup Tolerance."

4. CONSTRUCTING THE NEW NATION

1. Erik Jan Zürcher, *The Young Turk Legacy and Nation Building: From the Ottoman Empire to Atatürk's Turkey* (London: I. B. Tauris, 2010), 13.

2. Zürcher, *The Young Turk Legacy*, 11.

3. Zürcher, *The Young Turk Legacy*.

4. Zürcher, *The Young Turk Legacy*, 41.

5. Carter V. Findley, *Turkey, Islam, Nationalism, and Modernity: A History, 1789–2007* (New Haven, CT: Yale University Press, 2010).

6. Feroz Ahmad, *The Making of Modern Turkey* (London: Routledge, 1993).

7. Zürcher, *The Young Turk Legacy*, 44.

8. Hugh Poulton, *Top Hat, Grey Wolf, and Crescent: Turkish Nationalism and the Turkish Republic* (London: C. Hurst & Co., 1997).

9. Tanil Bora, "Nationalist Discourses in Turkey," *South Atlantic Quarterly* 102, nos. 2/3 (2003): 433–451.

10. Ayşegül Aydingün and Ismail Aydingün, "The Role of Language in the Formation of Turkish National Identity and Turkishness," *Nationalism and Ethnic Politics* 10, no. 3 (2004): 415–432; Ilker Aytürk, "Turkish Linguists against the West: The Origins of Linguistic Nationalism in Atatürk's Turkey," *Middle Eastern Studies* 40, no. 6 (2004): 1–25.

11. Ryan Gingeras, *Sorrowful Shores: Violence, Ethnicity, and the End of the Ottoman Empire, 1912–1923* (Oxford: Oxford University Press, 2009); Umut Uzer, "The Genealogy of Turkish Nationalism: From Civic and Ethnic to Conservative Nationalism in Turkey," in *Symbiotic Antagonisms Competing Nationalisms in Turkey*, edited by Ayse Kadioglu and Emin Fuat Keyman (Salt Lake City: University of Utah Press, 2011).

12. Sener Aktürk, *Regimes of Ethnicity and Nationhood in Germany, Russia, and Turkey* (New York: Cambridge University Press, 2012); Ioannis N. Grigoriadis, *Instilling Religion in Greek and Turkish Nationalism: A "Sacred Synthesis"* (New York: Palgrave Macmillan, 2013).

13. Bernard Lewis, *The Emergence of Modern Turkey* (London: Oxford University Press, 1961), 321.

14. Mustafa Soykut, *Historical Image of the Turks in Europe: 15th Century to the Present: Political and Civilisational Aspects* (Istanbul: Isis Press, 2003).

15. Benjamin Braude and Bernard Lewis, *Christians and Jews in the Ottoman Empire: The Functioning of a Plural Society* (New York: Holmes and Meier Publishers, 1982).

16. Nicholas Doumanis, *Before the Nation: Muslim-Christian Coexistence and Its Destruction in Late Ottoman Anatolia* (Oxford: Oxford University Press, 2013).

17. Halil Inalcik, Donald Quataert, and Suraiya Faaroqhi, *An Economic and Social History of the Ottoman Empire* (Cambridge: Cambridge University Press, 1997).

18. Stanford Jay Shaw, *From Empire to Republic: The Turkish War of National Liberation, 1918–1923: A Documentary Study*, vol. 3, part 2: *From Turkish Resistance to the Turkish War of National Liberation, 1920–1922* (Ankara: Türk Tarih Kurumu Basimevi, 2000), 27.

19. Timur Kuran, "The Economic Ascent of the Middle East's Religious Minorities: The Role of Islamic Legal Pluralism," *Journal of Legal Studies* 33, no. 2 (2004): 475–515.

20. Max Weber, *Economy and Society: An Outline of Interpretive Sociology* (New York: Bedminster Press, 1968); Steve Bruce, *Religion and Modernization: Sociologists and Historians Debate the Secularization Thesis* (Oxford: Clarendon Press, 1992).

21. Kuran, "The Economic Ascent of the Middle East's Religious Minorities."

22. Lewis, *The Emergence of Modern Turkey*.

23. Erik Jan Zürcher, *Turkey: A Modern History* (London: I. B. Tauris, 1993).

24. Roderick Beaton and David Ricks, *The Making of Modern Greece: Nationalism, Romanticism, and the Uses of the Past (1797–1896)* (Farnham, UK: Ashgate, 2009).

25. C. Ernest Dawn, "The Origins of Arab Nationalism," in *The Origins of Arab Nationalism*, edited by Rashid Khalidi (New York: Columbia University Press, 1991).

26. Dawn, "The Origins of Arab Nationalism."

27. Harold William Vazeille Temperley, *England and the Near East* (London: Longmans, Green and Co., 1936).

28. Zürcher, *Turkey*, 62, 66.

29. Herbert J. Liebesny, *The Law of the Near and Middle East: Readings, Cases, and Materials* (Albany: State University of New York Press, 1975), 46–49.

30. Liebesny, *The Law of the Near and Middle East*, 49.

31. Liebesny, *The Law of the Near and Middle East*, 50.

32. Serif Mardin, *The Genesis of Young Ottoman Thought: A Study in the Modernization of Turkish Political Ideas* (Princeton, NJ: Princeton University Press, 1962).

33. Mardin, *The Genesis of Young Ottoman Thought*.

34. Caroline Finkel, *Osman's Dream: The Story of the Ottoman Empire, 1300–1923* (New York: Basic Books, 2006).

35. Stanford J. Shaw and Ezel Kural Shaw, *History of the Ottoman Empire and Modern Turkey* (Cambridge: Cambridge University Press, 1976).

36. Zürcher, *Turkey*, 77–78.

37. Mardin, *The Genesis of Young Ottoman Thought*, 80.

38. Mardin, *The Genesis of Young Ottoman Thought*, 4.

39. Zürcher, *The Young Turk Legacy and Nation Building*.

40. Zürcher, *The Young Turk Legacy and Nation Building*, 116.

41. Zürcher, *The Young Turk Legacy and Nation Building*, 17.

42. Zürcher, *The Young Turk Legacy and Nation Building*, 93.

43. M. Sükrü Hanioglu, *Preparation for a Revolution: The Young Turks, 1902–1908* (Oxford: Oxford University Press, 2001).

44. Taner Akçam, *The Young Turks' Crime against Humanity: The Armenian Genocide and Ethnic Cleansing in the Ottoman Empire* (Princeton, NJ: Princeton University Press, 2012).

45. Taner Akçam, *A Shameful Act: The Armenian Genocide and the Question of Turkish Responsibility* (New York: Metropolitan Books, 2006).

46. Lawrence Martin and John Reed, *The Treaties of Peace, 1919–1923*, vol. 2 (Clark, NJ: Lawbook Exchange, 2006).

47. Rogers Brubaker, "Aftermaths of Empire and the Unmixing of Peoples: Historical and Comparative Perspectives," *Ethnic and Racial Studies*, 18 (1995): 189–218.

48. Poulton, *Top Hat, Grey Wolf, and Crescent*, 93.

49. Great Britain, Foreign Office, *Lausanne Conference on Near Eastern Affairs 1922–1923: Records of Proceedings and Draft Terms of Peace* (London: H.M.S.O., 1923).

50. Indeed, in the Ottoman Empire the ethnic term "Turk" was often used derogatively to refer to nomads or rural and uncultured villagers, in contrast to the more civilized urban "Ottomans." See Lewis, *The Emergence of Modern Turkey*, 1.

51. Poulton, *Top Hat, Grey Wolf, and Crescent*, 94.

52. Poulton, *Top Hat, Grey Wolf, and Crescent*, 95.

53. Yusuf Akçura and Ismail Fehmi, "Yusuf Akçura's Uç Tarzi Siyaset" [Three Kinds of Policy], *Oriente Moderno* 61, no. 1/12 (1981): 7.

54. Poulton, *Top Hat, Grey Wolf, and Crescent*, 93.

55. Poulton, *Top Hat, Grey Wolf, and Crescent*, 100.

56. See, for example, the linguistic variants of Irish cultural nationalism discussed in chapter 3, or the Romantic forms of German nationalism espoused by Fichte and Herder, among others. Johann Gottlieb Fichte, *Addresses to the German Nation* (New York: Harper & Row, 1968); Johann Gottfried Herder, *Philosophical Writings*, translated by Michael N. Forster (Cambridge: Cambridge University Press, 2002).

57. Aysel Morin and Ronald Lee, "Constitutive Discourse of Turkish Nationalism: Atatürk's Nutuk and the Rhetorical Construction of the 'Turkish People,'" *Communication Studies* 61, no. 5 (2010): 485–506.

58. Poulton, *Top Hat, Grey Wolf, and Crescent*, 102.

59. Poulton, *Top Hat, Grey Wolf, and Crescent*, 113.

60. Once attributed to d'Azeglio's memoirs, the origin of this phrase is now in doubt. The sentiment, however, remains a powerful statement of the difficulties facing political nationalist movements that seek to impose national identity from above. Stephanie Malia Hom, "On the Origins of Making Italy: Massimo d'Azeglio and 'Fatta l'Italia, bisogna fare gli Italiani,'" *Italian Culture* 31, no. 1 (2013): 1–16.

61. Anthony D. Smith, *The Ethnic Origins of Nations* (Oxford: Blackwell, 1987).

62. Akçura and Fehmi, "Yusuf Akçura's Uç Tarzi Siyaset," 7.

63. Akçura and Fehmi, "Yusuf Akçura's Uç Tarzi Siyaset," 8.

64. Akçura and Fehmi, "Yusuf Akçura's Uç Tarzi Siyaset," 18.

65. Ziya Gökalp, *The Principles of Turkism*, translated by Robert Devereaux (Leiden: E. J. Brill, 1968), 13.

66. Gökalp, *The Principles of Turkism*, 15–16.

67. Akçam, *A Shameful Act*, 88.

68. Taha Parla, *The Social and Political Thought of Ziya Gökalp, 1876–1924* (Leiden: E. J. Brill, 1985), 7.

69. Muammer Kaylan, *The Kemalists: Islamic Revival and the Fate of Secular Turkey* (Amherst, NY: Prometheus Books, 2005), 75.

70. Sina Akşin, *Turkey from Empire to Revolutionary Republic: The Emergence of the Turkish Nation from 1789 to the Present* (New York: NYU Press, 2007), 75.

71. Jacob M. Landau, *Pan-Turkism: From Irredentism to Cooperation* (Bloomington: Indiana University Press, 1995), 133.

72. Poulton, *Top Hat, Grey Wolf, and Crescent*, 133.

73. Poulton, *Top Hat, Grey Wolf, and Crescent*.

74. Poulton, *Top Hat, Grey Wolf, and Crescent*, 153.

75. Şener Aktürk, "Persistence of the Islamic Millet as an Ottoman Legacy: Mono-Religious and Anti-Ethnic Definition of Turkish Nationhood," *Middle Eastern Studies* 45, no. 6 (2009): 893–909.

76. Kimberly Hart, *And Then We Work for God: Rural Sunni Islam in Western Turkey* (Stanford, CA: Stanford University Press, 2013).

77. Haldun Gülalp, "Using Islam as Political Ideology Turkey in Historical Perspective," *Cultural Dynamics* 14, no. 1 (2002): 21–39.

78. Akçura and Fehmi, "Yusuf Akçura's Uç Tarzi Siyaset," 15.

79. Akçura and Fehmi, "Yusuf Akçura's Uç Tarzi Siyaset," 16.

80. Akçura and Fehmi, "Yusuf Akçura's Uç Tarzi Siyaset," 18.

81. Akçam, *A Shameful Act*, 56.

82. Akçam, *The Young Turks' Crime against Humanity*.

83. Akçam, *A Shameful Act*, 122.

84. Bruce Clark, *Twice a Stranger: The Mass Expulsions That Forged Modern Greece and Turkey* (Cambridge, MA: Harvard University Press, 2006).

85. Evangelia Balta and Matthias Kappler, eds., *Cries and Whispers in Karamanlidika Books: Proceedings of the First International Conference on Karamanlidika Studies (Nicosia, 11th–13th September 2008)* (Wiesbaden: Harrassowitz, 2010).

86. Onur Yildirim, *Diplomacy and Displacement: Reconsidering the Turco-Greek Exchange of Populations, 1922–1934* (New York: Routledge, 2006), 59.

87. Onur Yildirim, "The 1923 Population Exchange: Refugees and National Historiographies in Greece and Turkey," *East European Quarterly* 40, no. 1 (2006): 45.

88. Soner Çağaptay, *Islam, Secularism, and Nationalism in Modern Turkey: Who Is a Turk?* (London: Routledge, 2006).

89. Çağaptay, *Islam, Secularism, and Nationalism*, 98.

90. Çağaptay, *Islam, Secularism, and Nationalism*, 85.

91. Çağaptay, *Islam, Secularism, and Nationalism*, 78.

92. Soner Çağaptay, "Citizenship Policies in Interwar Turkey," *Nations and Nationalism* 9, no. 4 (2003): 64.

93. Çağaptay, "Citizenship Policies in Interwar Turkey."

94. Çağaptay, "Citizenship Policies in Interwar Turkey."

95. Çağaptay, *Islam, Secularism, and Nationalism*, 70.

96. Sait Çetinoglu, "The Mechanisms for Terrorizing Minorities: The Capital Tax and Work Battalions in Turkey during the Second World War," *Mediterranean Quarterly* 23, no. 2 (2012): 14; Basak Ince, *Citizenship and Identity in Turkey: From Atatürk's Republic to the Present Day* (London: I. B. Tauris, 2012), 75.

97. Ali Tuna Kuyucu, "Ethno-Religious 'Unmixing' of Turkey: 6–7 September Riots as a Case in Turkish Nationalism," *Nations and Nationalism* 11, no. 3 (2005): 362.

98. Poulton, *Top Hat, Grey Wolf, and Crescent*, 98.

5. RELIGION AND NATION ARE ONE

1. Gavin D. Brockett, *How Happy to Call Oneself a Turk: Provincial Newspapers and the Negotiation of a Muslim National Identity* (Austin: University of Texas Press, 2011), 14.

2. Bernard Lewis, *The Emergence of Modern Turkey* (London: Oxford University Press, 1961).

3. Niyazi Berkeş, *The Development of Secularism in Turkey* (Montreal: McGill University Press, 1964).

4. Feroz Ahmad, *The Making of Modern Turkey* (London: Routledge, 1993).

5. Gavin D. Brockett, *Towards a Social History of Modern Turkey: Essays in Theory and Practice* (Istanbul: Libra Kitapçilik ve Yayincilik, 2011).

6. Brockett, *How Happy to Call Oneself a Turk.*

7. Nicholas Doumanis, *Before the Nation: Muslim-Christian Coexistence and Its Destruction in Late Ottoman Anatolia* (Oxford: Oxford University Press, 2013).

8. Lerna Ekmekçioğlu, *Recovering Armenia: The Limits of Belonging in Post-Genocide Turkey* (Stanford, CA: Stanford University Press, 2016).

9. Fatma Müge Göçek, *Denial of Violence: Ottoman Past, Turkish Present, and Collective Violence against the Armenians, 1789–2009* (Oxford: Oxford University Press, 2015).

10. Though there were certain notable exceptions. See, for example, those discussed in Ekmekçioğlu, *Recovering Armenia*, and the writings of Halide Edip: *Memoirs of Halide Edib* (New York: Century, 1926); *The Turkish Ordeal: Being the Further Memoirs of Halide Edib* (New York: Century, 1928).

11. Sonia Roccas and Marilynn B. Brewer, "Social Identity Complexity," *Personality and Social Psychology Review* 6, no. 2 (2002): 88–106.

12. K. Barkey and G. Gavrilis, "The Ottoman Millet System: Non-Territorial Autonomy and Its Contemporary Legacy," *Ethnopolitics* 15, no. 1 (2016): 24–42.

13. Ronald Grigor Suny, *"They Can Live in the Desert but Nowhere Else": A History of the Armenian Genocide* (Princeton, NJ: Princeton University Press, 2015), 46.

14. Benjamin Braude and Bernard Lewis, *Christians and Jews in the Ottoman Empire: The Functioning of a Plural Society* (New York: Holmes and Meier Publishers, 1982).

15. Kazim Nami Duru, *Ittihat ve Terakki Hatiralarim* (Istanbul: Sucuoglu Matbaasi, 1957), 76.

16. William Mitchell Ramsay, *Impressions of Turkey during Twelve Years' Wanderings* (London: G. P. Putnam's Sons, 1897), 31.

17. Doumanis, *Before the Nation*, 49.

18. Ayhan Aktar, "Homogenising the Nation, Turkifying the Economy: The Turkish Experience of Population Exchange Reconsidered," in *Crossing the Aegean: An Appraisal of the 1923 Compulsory Population Exchange between Greece and Turkey*, edited by Renee Hirschon (New York: Berghahn Books, 2008).

19. Doumanis, *Before the Nation*, 76.

20. Bernard Lewis, *The Jews of Islam* (Princeton, NJ: Princeton University Press, 1984).

21. Doumanis, *Before the Nation*, 48.

22. Doumanis, *Before the Nation*, 43.

23. Doumanis, *Before the Nation*, 16.

24. Suny, *"They Can Live in the Desert but Nowhere Else,"* 148.

25. Doumanis, *Before the Nation*, 36.

26. Charles A. Frazee, *The Orthodox Church and Independent Greece, 1821–1852* (London: Cambridge University Press, 1969), 18.

27. G. T. Mavrogordatos, "Orthodoxy and Nationalism in the Greek Case," *West European Politics* 26, no. 1 (January 2003): 117–136.

28. W. A. Morison, *The Revolt of the Serbs against the Turks (1804–1813)* (Cambridge: Cambridge University Press, 1942).

29. Rogers Brubaker, "Aftermaths of Empire and the Unmixing of Peoples: Historical and Comparative Perspectives," *Ethnic and Racial Studies* 18 (1995): 189–218.

30. Ahmet Akgündüz, "Migration to and from Turkey, 1783–1960: Types, Numbers and Ethnoreligious Dimensions," *Journal of Ethnic and Migration Studies* 24, no. 1 (1998): 100.

31. Hasan Kayali, *Arabs and Young Turks: Ottomanism, Arabism, and Islamism in the Ottoman Empire, 1908–1918* (Berkeley: University of California Press, 1997), 14.

32. Ahmed Hamdi Başar, *Ahmet Hamdi Başar'in Hatiralari*, edited by Murat Koraltürk (Istanbul: Istanbul Bilgi Universitesi, 2007), 75–77.

33. Göçek, *Denial of Violence*, 189.

34. Doumanis, *Before the Nation*, 140.

35. Doumanis, *Before the Nation*, 140.

36. Hasan Amça, *Doğmayan Hürriyet.* (Istanbul: Alfa Yayincilik, 1958), 118.

37. I. Hakki Sunata, *Gelibolu'dan Kafkaslar'a: Birinci Dünya Savaşi Hatiralirim* (Istanbul: Türkiye Iş Bankasi, 2003), 72–73.

38. Göçek, *Denial of Violence*, 1.

39. Taner Akçam, *A Shameful Act: The Armenian Genocide and the Question of Turkish Responsibility* (New York: Metropolitan Books, 2006); Taner Akçam, *The Young Turks' Crime against Humanity: The Armenian Genocide and Ethnic Cleansing in the Ottoman Empire* (Princeton, NJ: Princeton University Press, 2012); Suny, "They Can Live in the Desert but Nowhere Else"; Göçek, *Denial of Violence*.

40. Jennifer M. Dixon, *Dark Pasts: Changing the State's Story in Turkey and Japan* (Ithaca, NY: Cornell University Press, 2018).

41. Suny, "They Can Live in the Desert but Nowhere Else," 53.

42. Göçek, *Denial of Violence*, 118.

43. Suny, "They Can Live in the Desert but Nowhere Else," 180.

44. Şener Aktürk, "Religion and Nationalism: Contradictions of Islamic Origins and Secular Nation-Building in Turkey, Algeria, and Pakistan," *Social Science Quarterly* 96, no. 3 (2015): 789.

45. Göçek, *Denial of Violence*, 299.

46. Suny, "They Can Live in the Desert but Nowhere Else," 244.

47. Suny, "They Can Live in the Desert but Nowhere Else," 317.

48. Suny, "They Can Live in the Desert but Nowhere Else," 278.

49. Suny, "They Can Live in the Desert but Nowhere Else," 172.

50. Abraham H. Hartunian, *Neither to Laugh nor to Weep: A Memoir of the Armenian Genocide* (Boston: Beacon Press, 1968), 12.

51. Akçam, *A Shameful Act*, 97.

52. Göçek, *Denial of Violence*, 223.

53. Doumanis, *Before the Nation*, 151.

54. Çağri Erhan, *Greek Occupation of Izmir and Adjoining Territories: Report of the Inter-Allied Commission of Inquiry (May–September 1919)* (Ankara: Ministry of Foreign Affairs Center for Strategic Research, 1999), 7.

55. Doumanis, *Before the Nation*, 150.

56. Doumanis, *Before the Nation*, 153.

57. Erhan, *Greek Occupation of Izmir and Adjoining Territories*, 7.

58. Erhan, *Greek Occupation of Izmir and Adjoining Territories*, 8.

59. Ryan Gingeras, *Sorrowful Shores: Violence, Ethnicity, and the End of the Ottoman Empire, 1912–1923* (Oxford: Oxford University Press, 2009), 113.

60. Giles Milton, *Paradise Lost: Smyrna, 1922: The Destruction of a Christian City in the Islamic World* (New York: Basic Books, 2008).

61. Biray Kolluoğlu Kirli, "Forgetting the Smyrna Fire," *History Workshop Journal* 60, no. 1 (2005): 25–44.

62. Leyla Neyzi, "Remembering Smyrna/Izmir: Shared History, Shared Trauma," *History & Memory* 20, no. 2 (2008): 106–127.

63. Bruce Clark, *Twice a Stranger: The Mass Expulsions That Forged Modern Greece and Turkey* (Cambridge, MA: Harvard University Press, 2006), 35.

64. Andrew Mango, *Atatürk: The Biography of the Founder of Modern Turkey* (Woodstock, NY: Overlook Press, 2000), 217.

65. Clark, *Twice a Stranger*, 94.

66. Clark, *Twice a Stranger*, 39.

67. Clark, *Twice a Stranger*, 36.

68. Doumanis, *Before the Nation*, 142.

69. Clark, *Twice a Stranger*, 102.

70. Ahmad, *The Making of Modern Turkey*, 63.

71. Mustafa Kemal Atatürk, *Nutuk* (Ankara: Kültür Bakanligi, 1980), 1.

72. Atatürk, *Nutuk*, 513.

73. Great Britain, Foreign Office, *Lausanne Conference on Near Eastern Affairs 1922–1923: Records of Proceedings and Draft Terms of Peace* (London: H.M.S.O., 1923), 190–204.

74. Mango, *Atatürk*, 407.

75. Erik Jan Zürcher, *Turkey: A Modern History* (London: I. B. Tauris, 1993), 201.

76. Gavin D. Brockett, "Revisiting the Turkish Revolution, 1923–1938: Secular Reform and Religious Reaction1," *History Compass* 4, no. 6 (2006): 1067.

77. Ruth A. Miller, "The Ottoman and Islamic Substratum of Turkey's Swiss Civil Code," *Journal of Islamic Studies* 11, no. 3 (2000): 335–362.

78. Hale Yilmaz, *Becoming Turkish: Nationalist Reforms and Cultural Negotiations in Early Republican Turkey, 1923–1945* (Syracuse, NY: Syracuse University Press, 2013), 32.

79. Yilmaz, *Becoming Turkish*, 31.

80. Zürcher, *Turkey*, 194.

81. Yilmaz, *Becoming Turkish*, 35.

82. Yilmaz, *Becoming Turkish*, 33.

83. Yilmaz, *Becoming Turkish*, 35–36.

84. Yilmaz, *Becoming Turkish*, 38.

85. Mehmet Atif Iskilipli, *Frenk Mukallitliği ve Şapka* (Istanbul: Matbaa-i Kader, 1924).

86. Yilmaz, *Becoming Turkish*, 39.

87. Ahmet Emin Yalman, *Turkey in My Time.* (Norman: University of Oklahoma Press, 1956), 175.

88. Yilmaz, *Becoming Turkish*, 103.

89. Yilmaz, *Becoming Turkish*, 123.

90. Yilmaz, *Becoming Turkish*, 41–42.

91. James C. Scott, *Weapons of the Weak: Everyday Forms of Peasant Resistance* (New Haven, CT: Yale University Press, 1985).

92. Cem Emrence, "Politics of Discontent in the Midst of the Great Depression: The Free Republican Party of Turkey (1930)," *New Perspectives on Turkey* 23 (2000): 31–52.

93. Arnold Leder, "Party Competition in Rural Turkey: Agent of Change or Defender of Traditional Rule?," *Middle Eastern Studies* 22, no. 1 (1979): 77–94.

94. Brockett, *How Happy to Call Oneself a Turk*, 203.

95. Rifat N. Bali, *Revival of Islam in Turkey in the 1950's through the Reports of American Diplomats* (Istanbul: Libra, 2011); Bernard Lewis, "Islamic Revival in Turkey," *International Affairs* 28, no. 1 (1952): 38; Howard A. Reed, "Revival of Islam in Secular Turkey," *Middle East Journal* 8, no. 3 (1954): 267–282.

96. Benedict Anderson, *Imagined Communities: Reflections on the Origin and Spread of Nationalism* (London: Verso, 1983).

97. Brockett, *How Happy to Call Oneself a Turk*, 2.

98. Brockett, *How Happy to Call Oneself a Turk*, 127.

99. Brockett, *How Happy to Call Oneself a Turk*, 138.

100. Brockett, *How Happy to Call Oneself a Turk*, 125.

101. Alfred de Zayas, "The Istanbul Pogrom of 6–7 September 1955 in the Light of International Law," *Genocide Studies and Prevention* 2, no. 2 (2007): 137–154.

102. Ali Tuna Kuyucu, "Ethno-Religious 'Unmixing' of Turkey: 6–7 September Riots as a Case in Turkish Nationalism," *Nations and Nationalism* 11, no. 3 (2005): 376.

103. Kuyucu, "Ethno-Religious 'Unmixing' of Turkey," 375.

104. Kuyucu, "Ethno-Religious 'Unmixing' of Turkey," 363.

105. Savvas Tsilenis, *Η Μειονότητα Των Ορθόδοξων Χριστιανών Στις Επίσημες Στατιστικές Της Σύγχρονης Τουρκίας Και Στον Αστικό Χώρο* (Thessaly, Greece: Laboratory of Demographic and Social Analysis, University of Thessaly, n.d.).

106. George S. Harris, "The Causes of the 1960 Revolution in Turkey," *Middle East Journal* 24, no. 4 (1970): 438–454.

107. W. B. Sherwood, "The Rise of the Justice Party in Turkey," *World Politics* 20, no. 1 (1967): 59.

108. Jenny B. White, *Muslim Nationalism and the New Turks* (Princeton, NJ: Princeton University Press, 2013), 7.

109. Sebnem Gumuscu and Deniz Sert, "The Power of the Devout Bourgeoisie: The Case of the Justice and Development Party in Turkey," *Middle Eastern Studies* 45, no. 6 (2009): 953–968.

110. White, *Muslim Nationalism and the New Turks*, 8.

111. White, *Muslim Nationalism and the New Turks*, 8.

112. Burhanettin Duran, "The Justice and Development Party's 'New Politics': Steering toward Conservative Democracy, A Revised Islamic Agenda or Management of New Crises?," in *Secular and Islamic Politics in Turkey: The Making of the Justice and Development Party*, edited by Ümit Cizre (London: Routledge, 2008), 81.

113. Menderes Cinar, "Turkey's Transformation under the AKP Rule," *Muslim World* 96, no. 3 (2006): 470.

114. Ali Çarkoglu, "Turkey's 2011 General Elections: Towards a Dominant Party System?," *Insight Turkey* 13, no. 3 (2011).

115. Mustafa Gurbuz, "The Long Winter: Turkish Politics after the Corruption Scandal" (Washington, DC: Rethink Institute, 2014).

116. Ergun Özbudun, "Turkey's Judiciary and the Drift toward Competitive Authoritarianism," *International Spectator* 50, no. 2 (April 3, 2015): 42–55.

117. Amnesty International, *Gezi Park Protests: Brutal Denial of the Right to Peaceful Assembly in Turkey* (London: Author, 2013).

118. David Dolan and Gulsen Solaker, "Turkey Rounds Up Plot Suspects after Thwarting Coup Against Erdogan," *Reuters*, July 16, 2016, http://www.reuters.com/article/us-turkey-security-primeminister-idUSKCN0ZV2HK.

CONCLUSION

1. Andreas Wimmer, "The Making and Unmaking of Ethnic Boundaries: A Multilevel Process Theory," *American Journal of Sociology* 113, no. 4 (2008): 986.

2. Rogers Brubaker, *Ethnicity without Groups* (Cambridge, MA: Harvard University Press, 2004).

3. Frantz Fanon, *Black Skin, White Masks* (New York: Grove Press, 2008); for a thorough discussion, see Julian Go, *Postcolonial Thought and Social Theory* (New York: Oxford University Press, 2016).

4. Mark Juergensmeyer, *Global Rebellion: Religious Challenges to the Secular State, from Christian Militias to al Qaeda* (Berkeley: University of California Press, 2008).

5. Go, *Postcolonial Thought and Social Theory*.

6. Thomas Blom Hansen, *The Saffron Wave: Democracy and Hindu Nationalism in Modern India* (Princeton, NJ: Princeton University Press, 1999); John Zavos, *The Emergence of Hindu Nationalism in India* (New Delhi: Oxford University Press, 2000).

7. Andrew L Whitehead and Samuel L Perry, *Taking America Back for God: Christian Nationalism in the United States* (New York: Oxford University Press, 2020); Nathan Chapman Lean and John L. Esposito, *The Islamophobia Industry: How the Right Manufactures Fear of Muslims* (London: Pluto Press, 2012).

8. Nadav Gershon Shelef, *Evolving Nationalism: Homeland, Identity, and Religion in Israel, 1925–2005* (Ithaca, NY: Cornell University Press, 2010).

9. A. Triandafyllidou and R. Gropas, "Constructing Difference: The Mosque Debates in Greece," *Journal of Ethnic and Migration Studies* 35, no. 6 (2009): 957–975, https://doi.org/10.1080/13691830902957734; Daphne Halikiopoulou, *Patterns of Secularization: Church, State and Nation in Greece and the Republic of Ireland* (Farnham, UK: Ashgate, 2011).

BIBLIOGRAPHY

Abrecht, Ryan. "My Neighbor the Barbarian: Immigrant Neighborhoods in Classical Athens, Imperial Rome, and Tang Chang'an." Doctoral dissertation, University of California, Santa Barbara, 2014.

Adivar, Halide Edib. *Memoirs of Halide Edib.* New York: The Century Co., 1926.

Ahmad, Feroz. *The Making of Modern Turkey.* London: Routledge, 1993.

Akçam, Taner. *A Shameful Act: The Armenian Genocide and the Question of Turkish Responsibility.* New York: Metropolitan Books, 2006.

———. *The Turkish Ordeal: Being the Further Memoirs of Halide Edib.* New York: The Century Co., 1928.

———. *The Young Turks' Crime against Humanity: The Armenian Genocide and Ethnic Cleansing in the Ottoman Empire.* Princeton, NJ: Princeton University Press, 2012.

Akçura, Yusuf, and Ismail Fehmi. "Yusuf Akçura's Uç Tarzi Siyaset" [Three Kinds of Policy]. *Oriente Moderno* 61, no. 1/12 (1981): 1–20.

Akgündüz, Ahmet. "Migration to and from Turkey, 1783–1960: Types, Numbers and Ethnoreligious Dimensions." *Journal of Ethnic and Migration Studies* 24, no. 1 (1998): 97–120.

Akşin, Sina. *Turkey from Empire to Revolutionary Republic: The Emergence of the Turkish Nation from 1789 to the Present.* New York: NYU Press, 2007.

Aktar, Ayhan. "Homogenising the Nation, Turkifying the Economy: The Turkish Experience of Population Exchange Reconsidered." In *Crossing the Aegean: An Appraisal of the 1923 Compulsory Population Exchange between Greece and Turkey,* edited by Renee Hirschon. New York: Berghahn Books, 2008.

Aktürk, Şener. "Persistence of the Islamic Millet as an Ottoman Legacy: Mono-Religious and Anti-Ethnic Definition of Turkish Nationhood." *Middle Eastern Studies* 45, no. 6 (2009): 893–909.

———. *Regimes of Ethnicity and Nationhood in Germany, Russia, and Turkey.* New York: Cambridge University Press, 2012.

———. "Religion and Nationalism: Contradictions of Islamic Origins and Secular Nation-Building in Turkey, Algeria, and Pakistan." *Social Science Quarterly* 96, no. 3 (2015): 778–806.

Amça, Hasan. *Doğmayan Hürriyet.* Istanbul: Alfa Yayıncılık, 1958.

Ammerman, Nancy Tatom. *Everyday Religion: Observing Modern Religious Lives.* Oxford: Oxford University Press, 2007.

Amnesty International. *Gezi Park Protests: Brutal Denial of the Right to Peaceful Assembly in Turkey.* London: Author, 2013.

Anderson, Benedict. *Imagined Communities: Reflections on the Origin and Spread of Nationalism.* London: Verso, 1983.

Armstrong, John Alexander. *Nations before Nationalism.* Chapel Hill: University of North Carolina Press, 1982.

Armstrong, Karen. *Fields of Blood: Religion and the History of Violence.* New York: Anchor Books, 2014.

Arnold, Matthew. *The Works of Matthew Arnold...: On the Study of Celtic Literature and On Translating Homer.* Edited by Thomas Burnett Smart. Vol. 5. New York: Macmillan and Company, 1903.

Ashley, Maurice. *The Greatness of Oliver Cromwell*. New York: Macmillan, 1958.
Atatürk, Mustafa Kemal. *The Great Speech*. Ankara: Atatürk Research Center, 2005.
————. *Nutuk*. 2 vols. Ankara: Kültür Bakanligi, 1980.
Aydingün, Ayşegül, and Ismail Aydingün. "The Role of Language in the Formation of Turkish National Identity and Turkishness." *Nationalism and Ethnic Politics* 10, no. 3 (2004): 415–432.
Aytürk, Ilker. "Turkish Linguists against the West: The Origins of Linguistic Nationalism in Atatürk's Turkey." *Middle Eastern Studies* 40, no. 6 (2004): 1–25.
Bali, Rifat N. *Revival of Islam in Turkey in the 1950's through the Reports of American Diplomats*. Istanbul: Libra, 2011.
Balta, Evangelia, and Matthias Kappler, eds. *Cries and Whispers in Karamanlidika Books: Proceedings of the First International Conference on Karamanlidika Studies (Nicosia, 11th–13th September 2008)*. Wiesbaden: Harrassowitz, 2010.
Barker, Philip W. *Religious Nationalism in Modern Europe: If God Be for Us*. London: Routledge, 2009.
Barkey, K., and G. Gavrilis. "The Ottoman Millet System: Non-Territorial Autonomy and Its Contemporary Legacy." *Ethnopolitics* 15, no. 1 (2016): 24–42.
Barth, Fredrik. "Boundaries and Connections." In *Signifying Identities: Anthropological Perspectives on Boundaries and Contested Values*, edited by Anthony P. Cohen, 17–36. London: Routledge, 2000.
————. "Introduction." In *Ethnic Groups and Boundaries: The Social Organization of Culture Difference*. Boston: Little, Brown, 1969.
Bartlett, Thomas. *The Fall and Rise of the Irish Nation: The Catholic Question, 1690–1830*. Savage, MD: Barnes & Noble Books, 1992.
Başar, Ahmed Hamdi. *Ahmet Hamdi Başar'in Hatiralari*. Edited by Murat Koraltürk. Istanbul: Istanbul Bilgi Universitesi, 2007.
Beaton, Roderick, and David Ricks. *The Making of Modern Greece: Nationalism, Romanticism, and the Uses of the Past (1797–1896)*. Farnham, UK: Ashgate, 2009.
Bender, Courtney, Wendy Cadge, Peggy Levitt, and David Smilde, eds. *Religion on the Edge: De-Centering and Re-Centering the Sociology of Religion*. Oxford: Oxford University Press, 2012.
Berkeş, Niyazi. *The Development of Secularism in Turkey*. Montreal: McGill University Press, 1964.
"Booklet Detailing the Dead 'Fianna Heroes of 1916.'" Dublin: UCD School of History and Archives, n.d. digital.ucd.ie/view/ivrla:30626.
Bora, Tanil. "Nationalist Discourses in Turkey." *South Atlantic Quarterly* 102, no. 2/3 (2003): 433–451.
Bourdieu, Pierre. *Distinction: A Social Critique of the Judgement of Taste*. Cambridge, MA: Harvard University Press, 1984.
————. *Language and Symbolic Power*. Translated by John B. Thompson. Cambridge, MA: Harvard University Press, 1991.
Boyce, David George. *Nationalism in Ireland*. London: Routledge, 1995.
Braude, Benjamin, and Bernard Lewis. *Christians and Jews in the Ottoman Empire: The Functioning of a Plural Society*. New York: Holmes and Meier Publishers, 1982.
Brewer, M. B., and K. P. Pierce. "Social Identity Complexity and Outgroup Tolerance." *Personality & Social Psychology Bulletin* 31, no. 3 (2005): 428–437.
Brockett, Gavin D. *How Happy to Call Oneself a Turk: Provincial Newspapers and the Negotiation of a Muslim National Identity*. Austin: University of Texas Press, 2011.
————. "Revisiting the Turkish Revolution, 1923–1938: Secular Reform and Religious Reaction." *History Compass* 4, no. 6 (2006): 1060–1072.

———. *Towards a Social History of Modern Turkey: Essays in Theory and Practice.* Istanbul: Libra Kitapçilik ve Yayincilik, 2011.

Brooke, Stopford Augustus. *The Need and Use of Getting Irish Literature into the English Tongue: An Address.* London: T. Fisher Unwin, 1893.

Brubaker, Rogers. "Aftermaths of Empire and the Unmixing of Peoples: Historical and Comparative Perspectives." *Ethnic and Racial Studies* 18 (1995): 189–218.

———. "Categories of Analysis and Categories of Practice: A Note on the Study of Muslims in European Countries of Immigration." *Ethnic and Racial Studies* 36, no. 1 (2013): 1–8.

———. *Ethnicity without Groups.* Cambridge, MA: Harvard University Press, 2004.

———. *Nationalist Politics and Everyday Ethnicity in a Transylvanian Town.* Princeton, NJ: Princeton University Press, 2006.

———. "Religion and Nationalism: Four Approaches." *Nations and Nationalism* 18, no. 1 (2012): 2–20.

Bruce, Steve. *Religion and Modernization: Sociologists and Historians Debate the Secularization Thesis.* Oxford: Clarendon Press, 1992.

———. *Religion in the Modern World: From Cathedrals to Cults.* Oxford: Oxford University Press, 1996.

Burke, Thomas. *Lectures on Faith and Fatherland.* London: Cameron and Ferguson, 1874.

Burley, J., and F. Regan. "Divorce in Ireland: The Fear, the Floodgates and the Reality." *International Journal of Law, Policy and the Family* 16, no. 2 (2002): 202–222.

Busteed, M. A., Frank Neal, and Jonathan Tonge. *Irish Protestant Identities.* Manchester: Manchester University Press, 2008.

Byrne, F. J. *Irish Kings and High-Kings.* New York: St. Martin's Press, 1973.

Çağaptay, Soner. "Citizenship Policies in Interwar Turkey." *Nations and Nationalism* 9, no. 4 (2003): 601–619.

———. *Islam, Secularism, and Nationalism in Modern Turkey: Who Is a Turk?* London: Routledge, 2006.

Carey, Michael J. "Catholicism and Irish National Identity." *Religion and Politics in the Modern World* 120 (1983).

Çarkoglu, Ali. "Turkey's 2011 General Elections: Towards a Dominant Party System?" *Insight Turkey* 13, no. 3 (2011).

Central Statistics Office, Government of Ireland. "2016 Irish Census." 2017. https://www.cso.ie/en/media/csoie/newsevents/documents/census2016summaryresultspart1/Census2016SummaryPart1.pdf.

Çetinoglu, Sait. "The Mechanisms for Terrorizing Minorities: The Capital Tax and Work Battalions in Turkey during the Second World War." *Mediterranean Quarterly* 23, no. 2 (2012): 14–29.

Chakrabarty, Dipesh. *Provincializing Europe: Postcolonial Thought and Historical Difference.* Princeton, NJ: Princeton University Press, 2009.

Chandra, Kanchan. "What Is Ethnic Identity and Does It Matter?" *Annual Review of Political Science* 9 (2006): 397–424.

Cinar, Menderes. "Turkey's Transformation Under the AKP Rule." *Muslim World* 96, no. 3 (2006): 469–486.

Clark, Bruce. *Twice a Stranger: The Mass Expulsions That Forged Modern Greece and Turkey.* Cambridge, MA: Harvard University Press, 2006.

Clark, Samuel. "The Political Mobilization of Irish Farmers." *Canadian Review of Sociology/Revue Canadienne de Sociologie* 12, no. 4 (1975): 483–499.

Clarke, Aidan. *The Old English in Ireland, 1625–42.* Ithaca, NY: Cornell University Press, 1966.

Coakley, John. "Mobilizing the Past: Nationalist Images of History." *Nationalism & Ethnic Politics* 10 (2004): 531–560.

————. "Religion, National Identity and Political Change in Modern Ireland." *Irish Political Studies* 17, no. 1 (2002): 4–28.

————. "Religion and Nationalism in the First World." In *Ethnonationalism in the Contemporary World: Walker Connor and the Study of Nationalism*, edited by Daniele Conversi. London: Routledge, 2002.

Collins, Kevin. *Catholic Churchmen and the Celtic Revival in Ireland, 1848–1916*. Dublin: Four Courts Dublin, 2002.

Colum, Mary. *Life and the Dream*. Garden City, NY: Doubleday, 1947.

Connolly, S. J. *Contested Island: Ireland, 1460–1630*. Oxford: Oxford University Press, 2007.

Cronin, Maura. "'Of One Mind'? O'Connellite Crowds in the 1830s and 1840s." In *Crowds in Ireland, c. 1720–1920*, edited by Peter Jupp and Eoin Magennis. Houndmills, UK: Macmillan Press, 2000.

Cronin, Sean. *Irish Nationalism: A History of Its Roots and Ideology*. London: Continuum, 1981.

Curtis, Edmund, and R. B. McDowell, eds. *Irish Historical Documents: 1172–1922*. New York: Barnes & Noble, 1968.

Darby, John. *Conflict in Northern Ireland: The Development of a Polarised Community*. Dublin: Gill and Macmillan, 1976.

Davie, Grace. *Religion in Britain since 1945: Believing without Belonging*. Oxford: Blackwell, 1994.

Davis, Richard P. *The Young Ireland Movement*. Dublin: Gill & Macmillan, 1988.

Dawn, C. Ernest. "The Origins of Arab Nationalism." In *The Origins of Arab Nationalism*, edited by Rashid Khalidi. New York: Columbia University Press, 1991.

Demerath, N. Jay, III. "The Rise of 'Cultural Religion' in European Christianity: Learning from Poland, Northern Ireland, and Sweden." *Social Compass* 47, no. 1 (2000): 127–139.

Dillon, Martin. *God and the Gun: The Church and Irish Terrorism*. New York: Routledge, 1998.

Dixon, Jennifer M. *Dark Pasts: Changing the State's Story in Turkey and Japan*. Ithaca, NY: Cornell University Press, 2018.

Dolan, David, and Gulsen Solaker. "Turkey Rounds Up Plot Suspects after Thwarting Coup against Erdogan." *Reuters*, July 16, 2016. http://www.reuters.com/article/us-turkey-security-primeminister-idUSKCN0ZV2HK.

Doumanis, Nicholas. *Before the Nation: Muslim-Christian Coexistence and Its Destruction in Late Ottoman Anatolia*. Oxford: Oxford University Press, 2013.

Duffy, Charles Gavan. *Young Ireland: A Fragment of Irish History, 1840–1850*. London: Massell, Petter, Galphin, 1880.

Duran, Burhanettin. "The Justice and Development Party's 'New Politics': Steering toward Conservative Democracy, A Revised Islamic Agenda or Management of New Crises?" In *Secular and Islamic Politics in Turkey: The Making of the Justice and Development Party*, edited by Ümit Cizre. London: Routledge, 2008.

Duru, Kazim Nami. *Ittihat ve Terakki Hatiralarim*. Istanbul: Sucuoglu Matbaasi, 1957.

Earle, Edward Mead. "The New Constitution of Turkey." *Political Science Quarterly* 40, no. 1 (1925): 73–100.

"Editorial, Unsigned Article from *The Nation* (1842)." In *Ireland and England, 1798–1922: An Anthology of Sources*, edited by Dennis Dworkin. Indianapolis, IN: Hackett Publishing, 2012.

Eglinton, John. *Literary Ideals in Ireland*. New York: Lemma, 1973.

Eisenstadt, Shmuel Noah. *Tradition, Change, and Modernity*. New York: John Wiley & Sons, 1973.

Ekmekçioğlu, Lerna. *Recovering Armenia: The Limits of Belonging in Post-Genocide Turkey*. Stanford, CA: Stanford University Press, 2016.

Ellis, Peter Berresford. *Hell or Connaught! The Cromwellian Colonisation of Ireland, 1652–1660*. Belfast: Blackstaff, 1988.

Emrence, Cem. "Politics of Discontent in the Midst of the Great Depression: The Free Republican Party of Turkey (1930)." *New Perspectives on Turkey* 23 (2000): 31–52.

Erhan, Çağri. *Greek Occupation of Izmir and Adjoining Territories: Report of the Inter-Allied Commission of Inquiry (May–September 1919).* Ankara: Ministry of Foreign Affairs Center for Strategic Research, 1999.

Fanon, Frantz. *Black Skin, White Masks.* New York: Grove Press, 2008.

Fawcett, Liz, and Jo Campling. *Religion, Ethnicity, and Social Change.* Houndmills, UK: Macmillan, 2000.

Ferriter, Diarmaid. *Judging Dev: A Reassessment of the Life and Legacy of Eamon de Valera.* Dublin: Royal Irish Academy, 2007.

———. *The Transformation of Ireland.* Woodstock, NY: Overlook Press, 2005.

Fichte, Johann Gottlieb. *Addresses to the German Nation.* New York: Harper & Row, 1968.

Findley, Carter V. *Turkey, Islam, Nationalism, and Modernity: A History, 1789–2007.* New Haven, CT: Yale University Press, 2010.

Finkel, Caroline. *Osman's Dream: The Story of the Ottoman Empire, 1300–1923.* New York: Basic Books, 2006.

FitzGerald, Desmond. *Memoirs of Desmond FitzGerald, 1913–1916.* London: Routledge/Thoemms Press, 1968.

Forker, Martin, and Jonathan McCormick. "Walls of History: The Use of Mythomoteurs in Northern Ireland Murals." *Irish Studies Review* 17, no. 4 (2009): 423–465.

Foy, Michael, and Brian Barton. *The Easter Rising.* Stroud, UK: Sutton, 1999.

Frazee, Charles A. *The Orthodox Church and Independent Greece, 1821–1852.* London: Cambridge University Press, 1969.

Friedland, Roger. "Religious Nationalism and the Problem of Collective Representation." *Annual Review of Sociology* 27, no. 1 (2001): 125–152.

———. "When God Walks in History: The Institutional Politics of Religious Nationalism." *International Sociology* 14, no. 3 (1999): 301–319.

Gellner, Ernest. *Nations and Nationalism.* Ithaca, NY: Cornell University Press, 1983.

Gilbert, John Thomas. *History of the Irish Confederation and the War in Ireland, 1641–1649.* 7 vols. New York: AMS Press, 1973.

Gilmore, Huston. "'The Shouts of Vanished Crowds': Literacy, Orality, and Popular Politics in the Campaign to Repeal the Act of Union in Ireland, 1840–48." *Interdisciplinary Studies in the Long Nineteenth Century* 19 (2014).

Gingeras, Ryan. *Sorrowful Shores: Violence, Ethnicity, and the End of the Ottoman Empire, 1912–1923.* Oxford: Oxford University Press, 2009.

Girvin, Brian. "Social Change and Moral Politics: The Irish Constitutional Referendum 1983." *Political Studies* 34, no. 1 (1986): 61–81.

Go, Julian. *Postcolonial Thought and Social Theory.* New York: Oxford University Press, 2016.

Goalwin, Gregory J. "The Art of War: Instability, Insecurity, and Ideological Imagery in Northern Ireland's Political Murals, 1979–1998." *International Journal of Politics, Culture, and Society* 26, no. 3 (2013): 189–215.

———. "Bandits, Militants, and Martyrs: Sub-state Violence as Claim to Authority in Late Antique North Africa." *Journal of Historical Sociology* 34, no. 3 (2021): 452–465.

———. "The Curious Case of Cú Chulainn: Nationalism, Culture, and Meaning-Making in the Contested Symbols of Northern Ireland." *Studies in Ethnicity and Nationalism* 19, no. 3 (2019): 307–324.

Göçek, Fatma Müge. *Denial of Violence: Ottoman Past, Turkish Present, and Collective Violence against the Armenians, 1789–2009.* Oxford: Oxford University Press, 2015.

Gökalp, Ziya. *The Principles of Turkism.* Translated by Robert Devereaux. Leiden: E. J. Brill, 1968.

Gorski, Philip. *American Covenant: A History of Civil Religion from the Puritans to the Present.* Princeton, NJ: Princeton University Press, 2019.

Gorski, Philip S., and Ateş Altınordu. "After Secularization?" *Annual Review of Sociology* 34 (2008): 55–85.

Gorski, Philip S., and Gülay Türkmen-Dervişoğlu. "Religion, Nationalism, and Violence: An Integrated Approach." *Annual Review of Sociology* 39 (2013): 193–210.

Grattan, Henry. *Memoirs of the Life and Times of Henry Grattan*, vol. 1. London: Henry Colburn, 1839.

———. *The Speeches of Henry Grattan, in the Irish, and in the Imperial Parliament.* London: Longman, Hurst, Rees, Orme, and Brown, 1822.

Great Britain, Foreign Office. *Lausanne Conference on Near Eastern Affairs 1922–1923: Records of Proceedings and Draft Terms of Peace.* London: H.M.S.O., 1923.

Grigoriadis, Ioannis N. *Instilling Religion in Greek and Turkish Nationalism: A "Sacred Synthesis."* New York: Palgrave Macmillan, 2013.

Gülalp, Haldun. "Using Islam as Political Ideology Turkey in Historical Perspective." *Cultural Dynamics* 14, no. 1 (2002): 21–39.

Gumuscu, Sebnem, and Deniz Sert. "The Power of the Devout Bourgeoisie: The Case of the Justice and Development Party in Turkey." *Middle Eastern Studies* 45, no. 6 (2009): 953–968.

Gurbuz, Mustafa. "The Long Winter: Turkish Politics after the Corruption Scandal." Washington, DC: Rethink Institute, 2014.

Halikiopoulou, Daphne. *Patterns of Secularization: Church, State and Nation in Greece and the Republic of Ireland.* Farnham, UK: Ashgate, 2011.

Hämäläinen, Pekka, and Samuel Truett. "On Borderlands." *Journal of American History* 98, no. 2 (2011): 338–361.

Hamill, Desmond. *Pig in the Middle: The Army in Northern Ireland, 1969–1985.* London: Methuen, 1986.

Hanioglu, M. Sükrü. *Preparation for a Revolution: The Young Turks, 1902–1908.* Oxford: Oxford University Press, 2001.

Hansen, Thomas Blom. *The Saffron Wave: Democracy and Hindu Nationalism in Modern India.* Princeton, NJ: Princeton University Press, 1999.

Harris, George S. "The Causes of the 1960 Revolution in Turkey." *Middle East Journal* 24, no. 4 (1970): 438–454.

Hart, Kimberly. *And Then We Work for God: Rural Sunni Islam in Western Turkey.* Stanford, CA: Stanford University Press, 2013.

Heaphy, Brian. *Late Modernity and Social Change: Reconstructing Social and Personal Life.* London: Routledge, 2007.

Héireann, Bunreacht Na. "Constitution of Ireland." Dublin: Stationery Office, 1937.

Herder, Johann Gottfried. *Philosophical Writings.* Translated by Michael N. Forster. Cambridge: Cambridge University Press, 2002.

Hervieu-Léger, Danièle. *Religion as a Chain of Memory.* New Brunswick, NJ: Rutgers University Press, 2000.

Higgins, Roisín. "The Nation Reading Rooms." In *The Oxford History of the Irish Book*, vol. 4, 262–273. Oxford: Oxford University Press, 2011.

Hobsbawm, E. J. *Nations and Nationalism since 1780: Programme, Myth, Reality.* Cambridge: Cambridge University Press, 1990.

Hobsbawm, E. J., and T. O. Ranger. *The Invention of Tradition.* Cambridge: Cambridge University Press, 1983.

Hollis, Daniel Webster. *The History of Ireland.* Westport, CT: Greenwood Press, 2001.

Hom, Stephanie Malia. "On the Origins of Making Italy: Massimo d'Azeglio and 'Fatta l'Italia, bisogna fare gli Italiani.'" *Italian Culture* 31, no. 1 (2013): 1–16.

Hug, Chrystel, and Jo Campling. *The Politics of Sexual Morality in Ireland.* New York: St. Martin's Press, 1999.

Huntington, Samuel P. *The Clash of Civilizations and the Remaking of World Order.* New York: Simon & Schuster, 1996.

Hutchinson, John. "Archaeology and the Irish Rediscovery of the Celtic Past." *Nations and Nationalism* 7, no. 4 (2001): 505–519.

———. *The Dynamics of Cultural Nationalism: The Gaelic Revival and the Creation of the Irish Nation State.* London: Allen & Unwin, 1987.

Hyde, Douglas. "The Necessity for De-Anglicising Ireland." In *The Revival of Irish Literature,* by Charles Gavan Duffy, George Sigerson, and Douglas Hyde, 117–161. New York: Lemma, 1973.

Inalcik, Halil, Donald Quataert, and Suraiya Faaroqhi. *An Economic and Social History of the Ottoman Empire.* Cambridge: Cambridge University Press, 1997.

Ince, Basak. *Citizenship and Identity in Turkey: From Atatürk's Republic to the Present Day.* London: I. B. Tauris, 2012.

Inglis, Tom. "Individualisation and Secularisation in Catholic Ireland." In *Contemporary Ireland: A Sociological Map,* edited by Sara O'Sullivan. Dublin: University College Dublin Press, 2007.

Iskilipli, Mehmet Atif. *Frenk Mukallitliği ve Şapka.* Istanbul: Matbaa-i Kader, 1924.

James, Christine P. "Céad Míle Fáilte: Ireland Welcomes Divorce: The 1995 Irish Divorce Referendum and the Family (Divorce) Act of 1996." *Duke Journal of Comparative & International Law* 8 (1997): 175–228.

Juergensmeyer, Mark. *Global Rebellion: Religious Challenges to the Secular State, from Christian Militias to al Qaeda.* Berkeley: University of California Press, 2008.

Kayali, Hasan. *Arabs and Young Turks: Ottomanism, Arabism, and Islamism in the Ottoman Empire, 1908–1918.* Berkeley: University of California Press, 1997.

Kaylan, Muammer. *The Kemalists: Islamic Revival and the Fate of Secular Turkey.* Amherst, NY: Prometheus Books, 2005.

Kee, Robert. *The Green Flag: A History of Irish Nationalism.* London: Weidenfeld and Nicolson, 1972.

Kelly, James. *Henry Flood: Patriots and Politics in Eighteenth-Century Ireland.* Notre Dame, IN: University of Notre Dame Press, 1998.

Kiberd, Declan, and P. J. Mathews, eds. *Handbook of the Irish Revival: An Anthology of Irish Cultural and Political Writings 1891–1922.* Notre Dame, IN: University of Notre Dame Press, 2016.

Kimmerling, Baruch. "Religion, Nationalism, and Democracy in Israel." *Constellations* 6, no. 3 (1999): 339–363.

Kinealy, Christine. *The Great Irish Famine: Impact, Ideology, and Rebellion.* Houndmills, UK: New York: Palgrave, 2002.

Kissane, Noel. *The Irish Famine: A Documentary History.* Syracuse, NY: Syracuse University Press, 1995.

Kohn, Hans. *The Idea of Nationalism: A Study in Its Origins and Background.* New York: Macmillan Co., 1944.

Kolluoğlu Kirli, Biray. "Forgetting the Smyrna Fire." *History Workshop Journal* 60, no. 1 (2005): 25–44.

Kuran, Timur. "The Economic Ascent of the Middle East's Religious Minorities: The Role of Islamic Legal Pluralism." *Journal of Legal Studies* 33, no. 2 (2004): 475–515.

Kuyucu, Ali Tuna. "Ethno-Religious 'Unmixing' of Turkey: 6–7 September Riots as a Case in Turkish Nationalism." *Nations and Nationalism* 11, no. 3 (2005): 361–380.

Laffan, Michael. *The Resurrection of Ireland: The Sinn Féin Party, 1916–1923.* Cambridge: Cambridge University Press, 1999.

Landau, Jacob M. *Pan-Turkism: From Irredentism to Cooperation.* Bloomington: Indiana University Press, 1995.

Larkin, Emmet. "The Devotional Revolution in Ireland, 1850–75." *American Historical Review* 77, no. 3 (1972): 625–652.

Lean, Nathan Chapman, and John L. Esposito. *The Islamophobia Industry: How the Right Manufactures Fear of Muslims.* London: Pluto Press, 2012.

Leder, Arnold. "Party Competition in Rural Turkey: Agent of Change or Defender of Traditional Rule?" *Middle Eastern Studies* 22, no. 1 (1979): 77–94.

Lee, Joseph. *Ireland, 1912–1985: Politics and Society.* Cambridge: Cambridge University Press, 1989.

———. *The Modernisation of Irish Society, 1848–1918.* Dublin: Gill & Macmillan, 1973.

Lewis, Bernard. *The Emergence of Modern Turkey.* London: Oxford University Press, 1961.

———. "Islamic Revival in Turkey." *International Affairs* 28, no. 1 (1952): 38–48.

———. *The Jews of Islam.* Princeton, NJ: Princeton University Press, 1984.

Lichterman, Paul. "Religion in Public Action: From Actors to Settings." *Sociological Theory* 30, no. 1 (2012): 83–104.

Liebesny, Herbert J. *The Law of the Near & Middle East: Readings, Cases, and Materials.* Albany: State University of New York Press, 1975.

Loughlin, James. "The Irish Protestant Home Rule Association and Nationalist Politics, 1886–93." *Irish Historical Studies* 24, no. 95 (1985): 341–360.

MacNevin, Thomas. "Custom House Ward: Repeal Reading Rooms." *The Nation,* February 8, 1845.

Mango, Andrew. *Atatürk: The Biography of the Founder of Modern Turkey.* Woodstock, NY: Overlook Press, 2000.

Mardin, Serif. *The Genesis of Young Ottoman Thought: A Study in the Modernization of Turkish Political Ideas.* Princeton, NJ: Princeton University Press, 1962.

Martin, Francis X. "The 1916 Rising: A 'Coup d'Etat' or a 'Bloody Protest'?" *Studia Hibernica* 8 (1968): 106–137.

Martin, Lawrence, and John Reed. *The Treaties of Peace, 1919–1923,* vol. 2. Clark, NJ: Lawbook Exchange, 2006.

Marx, Anthony W. *Faith in Nation: Exclusionary Origins of Nationalism.* New York: Oxford University Press, 2003.

Mavrogordatos, G. T. "Orthodoxy and Nationalism in the Greek Case." *West European Politics* 26, no. 1 (2003): 117–136.

McAllister, Ian. "The Devil, Miracles and the Afterlife: The Political Sociology of Religion in Northern Ireland." *British Journal of Sociology* 33, no. 3 (1982): 330–347.

McGarry, John, and Brendan O'Leary. *Explaining Northern Ireland: Broken Images.* Oxford: Blackwell, 2000.

McGrath, Charles Ivar. "Securing the Protestant Interest: The Origins and Purpose of the Penal Laws of 1695." *Irish Historical Studies* 30, no. 117 (1996): 25–46.

McKay, Susan. *Northern Protestants: An Unsettled People.* Belfast: Blackstaff Press, 2000.

Miller, David W. "Irish Catholicism and the Great Famine." *Journal of Social History* 9, no. 1 (1975): 81–98.

Miller, Ruth A. "The Ottoman and Islamic Substratum of Turkey's Swiss Civil Code." *Journal of Islamic Studies* 11, no. 3 (2000): 335–362.

Milton, Giles. *Paradise Lost: Smyrna, 1922: The Destruction of a Christian City in the Islamic World.* New York: Basic Books, 2008.

Mitchell, Claire. *Religion, Identity and Politics in Northern Ireland: Boundaries of Belonging and Belief*. Farnham, UK: Ashgate Publishing, 2013.

Molyneux, William. *The Case of Ireland Stated*. Dublin: Cadenus Press, 1977.

Moore, Seán. "Our Irish Copper-Farthen Dean: Swift's *Drapier's Letters*, the Forging of a Modernist Anglo-Irish Literature, and the Atlantic World of Paper Credit." *Atlantic Studies* 2, no. 1 (2005): 65–92.

Moran, Seán Farrell. *Patrick Pearse and the Politics of Redemption: The Mind of the Easter Rising, 1916*. Washington, DC: Catholic University of America Press, 1994.

Morin, Aysel, and Ronald Lee. "Constitutive Discourse of Turkish Nationalism: Atatürk's Nutuk and the Rhetorical Construction of the 'Turkish People.'" *Communication Studies* 61, no. 5 (2010): 485–506.

Morison, W. A. *The Revolt of the Serbs against the Turks (1804–1813)*. Cambridge: Cambridge University Press, 1942.

Muldoon, James. *Identity on the Medieval Irish Frontier: Degenerate Englishmen, Wild Irishmen, Middle Nations*. Gainesville: University Press of Florida, 2003.

Murphy, Andrew. "Bringing the Nation to the Book: Literacy and Irish Nationalism." Lecture, Trinity College Dublin, May 18, 2015. https://www.tcd.ie/trinitylongroomhub/events/details/2015/2015-05-18bringing_the_nation.php.

Murphy-Lawless, Jo, and James McCarthy. "Social Policy and Fertility Change in Ireland: The Push to Legislate in Favour of Women's Agency." *European Journal of Women's Studies* 6, no. 1 (1999): 69–96.

Murray, Dominic. *Worlds Apart: Segregated Schools in Northern Ireland*. Belfast: Appletree Press, 1985.

Murray, Raymond. *State Violence in Northern Ireland, 1969–1997*. Cork: Mercier, 1998.

Newsinger, John. "'I Bring Not Peace but a Sword': The Religious Motif in the Irish War of Independence." *Journal of Contemporary History* 13, no. 3 (1978): 609–628.

Neyzi, Leyla. "Remembering Smyrna/Izmir: Shared History, Shared Trauma." *History & Memory* 20, no. 2 (2008): 106–127.

Nolan, Janet. *Ourselves Alone: Women's Emigration from Ireland, 1885–1920*. Lexington: University Press of Kentucky, 1986.

Nowlan, Kevin B. *The Politics of Repeal: A Study in the Relations between Great Britain and Ireland, 1841–50*. London: Routledge & Kegan Paul, 1965.

O'Brien, Conor Cruise. *Ancestral Voices: Religion and Nationalism in Ireland*. Chicago: University of Chicago Press, 1995.

Ó Ciardha, Éamonn, and Micheál Ó Siochrú. *The Plantation of Ulster: Ideology and Practice*. Manchester: Manchester University Press, 2012.

Ó Giolláin, Diarmuid. "The Fairy Belief and Official Religion in Ireland." In *The Good People: New Fairylore Essays*, edited by Peter Narváez, 199–214. New York: Garland, 1991.

Ó Gráda, Cormac. *Black '47 and Beyond: The Great Irish Famine in History, Economy, and Memory*. Princeton, NJ: Princeton University Press, 2000.

———. *The Great Irish Famine*. Houndmills, UK: Macmillan, 1989.

Ó Gráda, Cormac, and Andrés Eiríksson. *Ireland's Great Famine: Interdisciplinary Perspectives*. Dublin: University College Dublin Press, 2006.

Ó Siochrú, Micheál. *God's Executioner: Oliver Cromwell and the Conquest of Ireland*. London: Faber & Faber, 2008.

Owens, Gary. "Nationalism without Words: Symbolism and Ritual Behaviour in the Repeal 'Monster Meetings' of 1843–5." In *Irish Popular Culture 1650–1850*, edited by James S. Donnelly Jr. and Kerby A. Miller, 242–269. Dublin: Irish Academic Press, 1998.

Özbudun, Ergun. "Turkey's Judiciary and the Drift toward Competitive Authoritarianism." *International Spectator* 50, no. 2 (2015): 42–55.

Parla, Taha. *The Social and Political Thought of Ziya Gökalp, 1876–1924*. Leiden: E. J. Brill, 1985.

Pearse, Padraic. *Political Writings and Speeches*. Dublin: Talbot Press, 1952.

Perry, Samuel L., and Andrew L. Whitehead. "Christian Nationalism and White Racial Boundaries: Examining Whites' Opposition to Interracial Marriage." *Ethnic and Racial Studies* 1 (2015): 1–19.

Pethica, James. "'Our Kathleen': Yeats's Collaboration with Lady Gregory in the Writing of *Cathleen ni Houlihan*." In *Yeats Annual No. 6*, edited by Warwick Gould, 3–31. Houndmills, UK: Macmillan, 1988.

Póirtéir, Cathal. *Famine Echoes*. Dublin: Gill & Macmillan, 1995.

Poulton, Hugh. *Top Hat, Grey Wolf, and Crescent: Turkish Nationalism and the Turkish Republic*. London: C. Hurst & Co., 1997.

Ramsay, William Mitchell. *Impressions of Turkey during Twelve Years' Wanderings*. London: G. P. Putnam's Sons, 1897.

Ray, Thomas. "First Quarterly Report upon Repeal Reading Rooms." In *Reports of the Parliamentary Committee of the Loyal National Repeal Association of Ireland*, vol. 2, 329–336. Dublin: Browne, 1845.

Reed, Howard A. "Revival of Islam in Secular Turkey." *Middle East Journal* 8, no. 3 (1954): 267–282.

Reed, Isaac Ariail. "Between Structural Breakdown and Crisis Action: Interpretation in the Whiskey Rebellion and the Salem Witch Trials." *Critical Historical Studies* 3, no. 1 (2016): 27–64.

"Repeal Education." *The Nation*, May 10, 1845.

Reyes, Victoria. *Global Borderlands: Fantasy, Violence, and Empire in Subic Bay, Philippines*. Stanford, CA: Stanford University Press, 2019.

Rieffer, Barbara-Ann J. "Religion and Nationalism: Understanding the Consequences of a Complex Relationship." *Ethnicities* 3, no. 2 (2003): 215–242.

Rifkin, Jeremy. *Beyond Beef: The Rise and Fall of the Cattle Culture*. New York: Dutton, 1992.

Roccas, Sonia, and Marilynn B. Brewer. "Social Identity Complexity." *Personality and Social Psychology Review* 6, no. 2 (2002): 88–106.

Ruane, Joseph, and Jennifer Todd. "Ethnicity and Religion: Redefining the Research Agenda." *Ethnopolitics* 9, no. 1 (2010): 1–8.

Rubin, Aviad. "The Status of Religion in Emergent Political Regimes: Lessons from Turkey and Israel." *Nations and Nationalism* 19, no. 3 (2013): 493–512.

Ruether, Rosemary Radford, and Herman J. Ruether. *The Wrath of Jonah: The Crisis of Religious Nationalism in the Israeli-Palestinian Conflict*. Minneapolis: Fortress Press, 2002.

Schaffer, Patricia M. "Laws in Ireland for the Suppression of Popery Commonly Known as the Penal Laws." 2000. http://library.law.umn.edu/irishlaw/intro.html.

Schielke, Samuli. "Second Thoughts about the Anthropology of Islam, or How to Make Sense of Grand Schemes in Everyday Life." *Zentrum Moderner Orient Working Papers* 2 (2010).

Schmid, K., M. Hewstone, N. Tausch, E. Cairns, and J. Hughes. "Antecedents and Consequences of Social Identity Complexity: Intergroup Contact, Distinctiveness Threat, and Outgroup Attitudes." *Personality & Social Psychology Bulletin* 35, no. 8 (2009): 1085–1098.

Scott, James C. *Weapons of the Weak: Everyday Forms of Peasant Resistance*. New Haven, CT: Yale University Press, 1985.

Sewell, William H., Jr. *Logics of History: Social Theory and Social Transformation*. Chicago: University of Chicago Press, 2005.

Shaw, Stanford Jay. *From Empire to Republic: The Turkish War of National Liberation, 1918–1923: A Documentary Study*, vol. 3, part 2: *From Turkish Resistance to the Turkish War of National Liberation, 1920–1922*. Ankara: Türk Tarih Kurumu Basimevi, 2000.

Shaw, Stanford J., and Ezel Kural Shaw. *History of the Ottoman Empire and Modern Turkey*. Cambridge: Cambridge University Press, 1976.

Shelef, Nadav Gershon. *Evolving Nationalism: Homeland, Identity, and Religion in Israel, 1925–2005*. Ithaca, NY: Cornell University Press, 2010.

Sherwood, W. B. "The Rise of the Justice Party in Turkey." *World Politics* 20, no. 1 (1967): 54–65.

Shiubhlaigh, Máire Nic, and Edward Kenny. *The Splendid Years*. Dublin: J. Duffy, 1955.

"The Sinn Féin Leaders of 1916 with Fourteen Illustrations and Complete Lists of Deportees, Casualties." Dublin: UCD Library, 1917. digital.ucd.ie/view/ivrla:30885.

"The 'Sinn Féin' Revolt Illustrated April 1916." Dublin: UCD School of History and Archives, n.d. digital.ucd.ie/view/ivrla:30653.

Smith, Anthony D. *Chosen Peoples: Sacred Sources of National Identity*. Oxford: Oxford University Press, 2003.

———. *The Ethnic Origins of Nations*. Oxford: Blackwell, 1987.

———. *Myths and Memories of the Nation*. Oxford: Oxford University Press, 1999.

Soper, J. Christopher, and Joel S. Fetzer. *Religion and Nationalism in Global Perspective*. Cambridge: Cambridge University Press, 2018.

Soykut, Mustafa. *Historical Image of the Turks in Europe: 15th Century to the Present: Political and Civilisational Aspects*. Istanbul: Isis Press, 2003.

Spickard, James V. *Alternative Sociologies of Religion: Through Non-Western Eyes*. New York: NYU Press, 2017.

Stanbridge, Karen. "Nationalism, International Factors and the Irish Question in the Era of the First World War." *Nations and Nationalism* 11, no. 1 (2005): 21–42.

Sunata, I. Hakki. *Gelibolu'dan Kafkaslar'a: Birinci Dünya Savaşi Hatiralirim*. Istanbul: Türkiye Iş Bankasi, 2003.

Suny, Ronald Grigor. *"They Can Live in the Desert but Nowhere Else": A History of the Armenian Genocide*. Princeton, NJ: Princeton University Press, 2015.

Swatos, William H., and Kevin J. Christiano. "Secularization Theory: The Course of a Concept." *Sociology of Religion* 60, no. 3 (1999): 209–228.

Swift, Jonathan. *A Modest Proposal and Other Satires*. Amherst, NY: Prometheus Books, 1995.

Temperley, Harold William Vazeille. *England and the Near East*. London: Longmans, Green and Co., 1936.

Thornton, Rod. "Getting It Wrong: The Crucial Mistakes Made in the Early Stages of the British Army's Deployment to Northern Ireland (August 1969 to March 1972)." *Journal of Strategic Studies* 30, no. 1 (2007): 73–107.

Triandafyllidou, Anna. "National Identity and the 'Other.'" *Ethnic and Racial Studies* 21, no. 4 (1998): 593–612.

Triandafyllidou, A., and R. Gropas. "Constructing Difference: The Mosque Debates in Greece." *Journal of Ethnic and Migration Studies* 35, no. 6 (2009): 957–975. https://doi.org/10.1080/13691830902957734.

Tsilenis, Savvas. *Η Μειονότητα Των Ορθόδοξων Χριστιανών Στις Επίσημες Στατιστικές Της Σύγχρονης Τουρκίας Και Στον Αστικό Χώρο*. Thessaly, Greece: Laboratory of Demographic and Social Analysis, University of Thessaly, n.d.

Uzer, Umut. "The Genealogy of Turkish Nationalism: From Civic and Ethnic to Conservative Nationalism in Turkey." In *Symbiotic Antagonisms Competing Nationalisms in Turkey*, edited by Ayse Kadioglu and Emin Fuat Keyman. Salt Lake City: University of Utah Press, 2011.

van der Veer, Peter. *Religious Nationalism: Hindus and Muslims in India*. Berkeley: University of California Press, 1994.

Wall, Maureen. "The Rise of a Catholic Middle Class in Eighteenth-Century Ireland." *Irish Historical Studies* 11, no. 42 (1958): 91–115.

Weber, Eugen. *Peasants into Frenchmen: The Modernization of Rural France, 1870–1914*. Stanford, CA: Stanford University Press, 1976.

Weber, Max. *Economy and Society: An Outline of Interpretive Sociology*. New York: Bedminster Press, 1968.

White, Jenny B. *Muslim Nationalism and the New Turks*. Princeton, NJ: Princeton University Press, 2013.

Whitehead, Andrew L., and Samuel L. Perry. *Taking America Back for God: Christian Nationalism in the United States*. New York: Oxford University Press, 2020.

Wimmer, Andreas. "Elementary Strategies of Ethnic Boundary Making." *Ethnic and Racial Studies* 31, no. 6 (2008): 1025–1055.

——. *Ethnic Boundary Making: Institutions, Power, Networks*. New York: Oxford University Press, 2013.

——. "The Making and Unmaking of Ethnic Boundaries: A Multilevel Process Theory." *American Journal of Sociology* 113, no. 4 (2008): 970–1022.

Wyse, Thomas. *Historical Sketch of the Late Catholic Association of Ireland*. London: H. Colburn, 1829.

Yalman, Ahmet Emin. *Turkey in My Time*. Norman: University of Oklahoma Press, 1956.

Yeats, W. B., Lady Gregory, and James Pethica. *Collaborative One-Act Plays, 1901–1903: Cathleen ni Houlihan, The Pot of Broth, The Country of the Young Heads or Harps: Manuscript Materials*. Ithaca, NY: Cornell University Press, 2006.

Yildirim, Onur. "The 1923 Population Exchange: Refugees and National Historiographies in Greece and Turkey." *East European Quarterly* 40, no. 1 (2006): 45–70.

——. *Diplomacy and Displacement: Reconsidering the Turco-Greek Exchange of Populations, 1922–1934*. New York: Routledge, 2006.

Yilmaz, Hale. *Becoming Turkish: Nationalist Reforms and Cultural Negotiations in Early Republican Turkey, 1923–1945*. Syracuse, NY: Syracuse University Press, 2013.

Zavos, John. *The Emergence of Hindu Nationalism in India*. New Delhi: Oxford University Press, 2000.

Zavos, John, and Thomas Blom Hansen. *Hindu Nationalism and Indian Politics*. New Delhi: Oxford University Press, 2004.

Zayas, Alfred de. "The Istanbul Pogrom of 6–7 September 1955 in the Light of International Law." *Genocide Studies and Prevention* 2, no. 2 (2007): 137–154.

Zubrzycki, Geneviève. *The Crosses of Auschwitz: Nationalism and Religion in Post-Communist Poland*. Chicago: University of Chicago Press, 2009.

Zürcher, Erik Jan. *Turkey: A Modern History*. London: I. B. Tauris, 1993.

——. *The Young Turk Legacy and Nation Building: From the Ottoman Empire to Atatürk's Turkey*. London: I. B. Tauris, 2010.

INDEX